California
Its Government and Politics

Third Edition

California
Its Government and Politics

Third Edition

Michael J. Ross
*San Diego State University
and
Grossmont College*

Brooks/Cole Publishing Company
Pacific Grove, California

For my mother

Brooks/Cole Publishing Company
A Division of Wadsworth, Inc.

Printed in the United States of America

10 9 8 7 6 5 4 3

Library of Congress Cataloging-in-Publication Data

Ross, Michael J. [date]
    California, its government and politics.

    Includes bibliographical references and index
    1. California—Politics and government—1951-
I. Title.
JK8716.R67   1987   320.9794   87-21834
ISBN 0-534-08436-2

Sponsoring Editor: *Cynthia C. Stormer*
Editorial Assistant: *Linda Loba*
Production Editor: *Penelope Sky*
Production Assistant: *Dorothy Bell*
Permissions Editor: *Carline Haga*
Interior Design: *Vernon T. Boes*
Cover Design: *Roy R. Neuhaus*
Cover Illustration: *Erin Mauterer, Bluewater A. & D.*
Art Coordinator: *Lisa Torri*
Interior Illustration: *Accurate Art*
Photo Researcher: *Marquita Flemming*
Typesetting: *TypeLink, Inc., San Diego, California*
Cover Printing: *The Lehigh Press Company, Pennsauken, New Jersey*
Printing and Binding: *R. R. Donnelley & Sons Company, Crawfordsville, Indiana*

Preface

California: Its Government and Politics is intended to serve three purposes: (1) Its brevity and readability make it suitable as a supplement in lower-division courses on California or United States government. (2) It contains the information necessary for the California section of upper-division courses on American state and local government. (3) It is directed to any reader who is trying to make some sense out of what may appear to be buzzing confusion in Sacramento or in city hall. I have tried to describe California government in a manner that is clear, concise, and lively.

For this edition I have completely rewritten Chapter 1 to include the public policy issues that Californians must confront in the 1990s. I have emphasized toxic waste issues and recent landmark state legislation in the areas of education, welfare, and medical care for poor people. I have substantially revised Chapters 2, 3, 9, and 10, on federalism, politics, courts, and finance, stressing new federal immigration and tax laws, the state supreme court after the defeat of Chief Justice Rose Bird, and the Gann Spending Limit. In all the chapters I emphasize not only the institutional features of state and local government, but also the power struggles, ideological controversies, and engaging personalities that currently mold this state. The glossary includes the more than 100 key terms that are set in boldface type when they first appear in the text.

I wish to thank the numerous people who helped me write this book. Many instructors used the first and second editions; their support has been very gratifying. The following reviewers were capable and discerning: George Blair, Claremont Graduate School; Edward Erler, California State University, San Bernardino; Ken Kennedy, College of San Mateo; Ronald Loveridge, University of California at Riverside; Barbara McFadyen, College of the Desert; Robert Pritchard, Los Angeles Valley College; and Thomas Watts, California State University, Bakersfield. Sponsoring Editor Cindy Stormer and Production Editor Penelope Sky eased the book through various writings and rewritings. In both the last edition and this one, Penelope's skill and judgment have been invaluable at critical junctures. Monica Wagner typed and retyped the manuscript with accuracy and good cheer.

The men and women who first came to California long ago came with courage and hope in their hearts. May we live the same way.

Michael J. Ross

Contents

PART 3
Major Institutions   118

PART 4
Local Government and State
and Local Government Finance 176

California
Its Government and Politics

Third Edition

P A R T

1

Political issues touch nearly every aspect of our lives in California. We can't get away from questions of public policy. How can we create more jobs in California? What is being done about air pollution? Do we need urban mass transit? How is education to be financed? Are the needs of the state's poor and elderly being met? Does the state have an adequate energy supply? Will California be able to meet its future water needs? Are taxes too high?

In Chapter 1 we consider these and other issues. We also note that California state and local governments have attempted to resolve these issues and have been reasonably successful, even in the wake of the belt tightening necessitated by the Jarvis property-tax amendment. In Chapter 2, we point out that California need not grapple alone with these problems. The federal government and other state governments (through interstate compacts) can lend assistance. We also point out that almost every major contemporary policy issue involves all levels of government: federal, state, and local. The primary reason for multilevel governmental involvement in most issues is that the federal government transfers substantial amounts of money to the state government, counties, cities, and school districts.

Setting of California Government and Politics

Decision makers address issues such as energy, transportation, and education in a series of overlapping stages that might be termed a policy process. At all levels of government, decision makers follow roughly five steps as they deal with policy issues. One step may begin before another is actually completed.

1. *Problem identification:* Public decision makers are presented with demands for action to resolve a problem.
2. *Policy formulation:* A course of action is chosen after various alternatives for dealing with a problem have been considered.
3. *Adoption:* A legitimate source of authority—for example, the state legislature or a city mayor—gives approval and often appropriates money for the course of action chosen.
4. *Implementation:* The policy, or plan of action, is carried out.
5. *Evaluation:* Decision makers determine whether the plan of action is accomplishing its objectives and whether adjustments need to be made in the policy.

This process of determination-implementation-evaluation is not static, but dynamic. It is appropriate that a dynamic process should be utilized by a state that usually seems to be in motion—California.

1

Policy Issues

Over the years, California has meant many different things to different people. To millions of Americans, it has represented (and still represents) hope—a hope for something better than they have had—and that hope is why they came here. To other Americans, California has stood for diversity, opportunity, and the chance to break out of the restrictive patterns of the past. This state has also stood for creativity and innovation. (For example, political scientists rate California state government as one of the most innovative in the nation.) Carey McWilliams writes that restless California is the "giant adolescent [who] has been outgrowing its governmental clothes, now, for a hundred years. . . . Other states have gone through this phase too, but California has never emerged from it."[1]

Indisputably, California has meant growth. And until recently, Californians have welcomed growth as a blessing. A state of considerable size geographically (see Figure 1.1), it is first in population (with over 28 million people) and therefore has the largest number of members in the U.S. House of Representatives (45) and of electoral votes (47). Although California's population continues to increase, the *rate* of increase is slower than in the past. The California growth rate, which was once twice the national rate, is projected to be fairly close to the national average for the current decade. The state is growing in some unexpected locations: The sparsely populated rural areas of the Sierra Nevada foothills are showing large percentage increases. People fleeing urban congestion and smog may head for El Dorado County or Placer County. Among more urban counties, Riverside and San Bernardino are experiencing rapid increases, but San Francisco is losing population. In a reversal of past trends, northern California is growing faster than southern California (the eight counties south of the Tehachapi Mountains). Slightly over one-half of the statewide increase has resulted from births exceeding deaths (natural increase), and the rest from immigration. California's foreign-born population has more than doubled in the last decade: recent immigrants have come from the Americas and from Asia, rather than from Europe. The state's availability of jobs, convenient location, and history of non-European migration have spurred this immigration, which has settled overwhelmingly in the larger metropolitan areas.

Other changes have affected, and will continue to affect, the state's population. According to one prediction, the next two decades will see California's

5

FIGURE 1.1   Giant California superimposed on East Coast. Reprinted by permission from the *Los Angeles Times,* December 17, 1978, pt. I, p. 3.

school-age population shrink, its working-age population stabilize, and its retirement-age population grow.[2] As the labor force matures because there are fewer very young and very old workers, this more experienced labor force should be more productive and earn higher wages. A greater number of working wives also increases family earning power, which in turn fuels consumer demand for goods and services. As more women enter the work force and as the state's retirement-age population increases, day care for children and medical care for the elderly become important governmental issues.

Rapid population increase has fostered rapid social change in other respects as well. California has been on the cutting edge of new trends, new beliefs, and new lifestyles. People often say that if you want to see the future, look at California. Whether you consider the results good or bad, the Golden State has often led the way in everything from tax revolts to Eastern mystical cults. One writer notes that "this state leads the nation in pornography, . . . suicide, home burglary, mind-meddling cults, and skateboard accidents. At the same time, perhaps for the same reasons, it leads the nation in microelectronics, solar energy, accredited law schools, Nobel Prize winners, women mayors, Olympic medalists, library use, salad lettuce, dates, figs, and nectarines."[3] The U.S. Census Bureau, which has the responsibility for gathering information on

TABLE 1.1   California Rankings[a]

Item	Rank
Total population	1st
Land area (in sq. mi.)	3rd
Population per square mile	14th
Metropolitan population	1st
Median age (in years)	20th
Population 65 years old and over	34th
Latino population	3rd
Black population	21st
Asian and Pacific Islander population	2nd
American Indian, Eskimo, and Aleut population	15th
Marriage rate (per 1,000 resident population)	35th
Divorce rate (per 1,000 resident population)	18th
Homeownership rate	48th
Median value of owner-occupied housing units	2nd
Crime rate per 100,000 resident population in 1981	4th
Federal and state prisoners per 100,000 population in 1981	27th
Percent high school graduates (persons 25 years old and over)	11th
Undergraduate enrollment in institutions of higher education (1979)	1st
Motor vehicles per 1,000 population	22nd
Percent of workers commuting to work using car, truck, or van	29th
Percent of workers commuting in carpools	47th
Motor vehicle traffic fatalities per 100,000 licensed drivers	31st
Energy consumption per capita	42nd

[a]All rankings are for 1980 unless otherwise specified.
SOURCE: U.S. Department of Commerce Bureau of the Census, "Significant Rankings Among Fifty States: California" (Washington, D.C.: Bureau of the Census, 1984).

an amazing variety of topics, lists California's rankings on a number of key indicators. Please see Table 1.1.

California is also characterized by highly **advanced industrialism.** The state relies on high-technology industry based on scientific expertise for the sustained application of theoretical knowledge for practical ends.[4] The best example of such "knowledge-intensive" manufacturing is electronics. Furthermore, 30 percent of all U.S. aeronautical engineers are located in California. Sophisticated technology depends upon research and development ("R & D," as it is called), in which the state excels: California is a national leader in education and in the creation of knowledge. Both the government and private industry make vast sums of money available to the state's universities and research institutes for R & D purposes. The key role of universities in generating the new knowledge and technology necessary to support advanced industries can be seen from the fact that Santa Clara's Silicon Valley grew up around Stanford University; other important high-tech centers are in Los Angeles, Orange, and San Diego counties. Industrialization has affected other areas of California's economy as well. Because of the high degree of automation in the state's farms and factories, fewer people are needed to work in these sectors, and more people can work in service jobs, which are increasing in number. Seven out of ten Californians work in service industries such as education, medicine, law, communications, banking, real estate, transportation, and government rather than in the manufacturing of heavy durable goods. More generally, as we will see, life in a highly advanced industrial state such as California is becoming highly complex, its development characterized by rapid change and innovation. This is illustrated in the next section, where we consider the numerous policy issues facing the Golden State.

THE STATE'S ECONOMY

If California were a nation, its **gross national product (GNP)** would rank seventh in the world. In the 1980 census, California's per capita personal income was the fourth highest in the United States, and its median family income was the twelfth highest. However, the state is dropping on the latter measure: it was fifth in the 1960 census and ninth in the 1970 census. Fortunately, the percentage of families below the U.S. Census Bureau's officially defined poverty level is 1 percent less in California than for the nation as a whole.

If it is to continue to flourish economically, California must retain its lead in the aerospace, semiconductor, computer, biotechnology, and other high-technology industries. These industries provide jobs, and they pay significant amounts of taxes. States such as Texas, Illinois, Maryland, North Carolina, Florida, Kentucky, and Tennessee are trying to lure these employers away. California is aided by its climatic and cultural advantages, the size and quality of its markets, its access to investment capital, the availability of many state-supported services, its location as gateway to the Pacific Basin, and especially its huge highway system. However, firms deciding to locate to or remain in this state sometimes claim that it has liabilities: occupational safety and health regulations which surpass federal standards, delays and inconsistencies in the regulatory and permit process regarding construction and energy, high labor costs, the declining quality of the state's high schools, crowding and congestion, excessive worker's compensation premiums, steep unemployment insurance taxes, and high corporate taxes. (Actually, tax considerations may not be paramount in an industry's choice of location.) Two key factors are the high costs of housing for employees, and the availability and expense of land for employers to use for their facilities. Other key concerns are the California inflation rate, which is usually higher than the nation's, and the state's heavy dependence on military contracts and space projects. (The latter will be discussed in the next chapter.) Although California's advanced industrial economy is quite complex and high powered, it is also somewhat fragile and vulnerable to changes in federal procurement priorities, to energy shortages, and even to drought.

Despite these disadvantages, of course, thousands of firms do flourish here. The following list of California's leading companies includes many oil or energy firms.

California's Top Twenty Companies
1. Standard Oil of California
2. Atlantic Richfield
3. Safeway Stores
4. Occidental Petroleum
5. Bank of America
6. Union Oil of California
7. Lockheed
8. Lucky Stores
9. Pacific Telesis Group
10. Pacific Gas & Electric
11. Transamerica
12. Hewlett–Packard
13. Security Pacific Bank
14. Southern California Edison
15. Pacific Lighting
16. Northrop
17. McKesson
18. Litton Industries
19. First Interstate Bank
20. Fluor Corporation

SOURCE: "The California 500," *California Business* (May 1986): 26.

California is an important international exporter of computer equipment, office machinery, aerospace and telecommunications equipment, medical instruments, cotton, fruits, nuts, and crude oil. Its most important trading partners for both exports and imports are Australia, Singapore, Taiwan, Hong Kong, the Republic of Korea, and Japan; in fact, we export more to Japan than to all of Europe. Although the state government spends much more on export promotion than does any other state, California only recently established overseas offices in Tokyo and London; many other states have had these offices for a long time. As a result of all of this activity, California has more foreign investment than any other state.

Governor George Deukmejian has made attracting new employers and jobs a central feature of his administration. The creation of new jobs is of critical importance because young people, people from racial and ethnic minorities, and women are trying to break into the labor market. Jobs must be created to accommodate them. If unemployment increases, so will unemployment compensation and welfare payments, social problems, and disillusionment. As one measure, both tourism and motion pictures are important sources of income for this state; therefore, Deukmejian became the first governor in state history to budget money to attract tourists through television commercials, billboards, and magazine ads. Before this campaign got underway, tourism had been seriously declining. Also sliding was the number of films made in California, a very significant source of wealth for this state. To sum up, the California economy is highly complex and diverse. Some of its salient characteristics are presented here.

California Economic Capsule
- California has a high percentage of the work force in service industries, and so it is less vulnerable than other states to economic downturns.
- California is located on the edge of the Pacific Basin and Latin America, which afford good export markets for its products.
- One-fifth of all American aircraft manufacturing jobs and three-fifths of its space and missile equipment production are in California.
- Tourism supports jobs for more than 515,000 Californians.
- The multi-billion-dollar entertainment industry has an important "multiplier" or ripple economic effect.
- California is the nation's fourth largest producer of oil, is second in amount of forested land (covering 40 percent of the state), and is richer in certain minerals, such as asbestos, boron, and tungsten, than any other state.
- California is the nation's foremost agricultural state, leading all states in the production of forty-nine different crops and livestock products.

SOURCE: Libby Lane, "Economic Climate Forecast," *California Journal* (September 1981): 323–325.

Some of these areas of the economy, such as agriculture, will be dealt with in greater detail below.

ENVIRONMENT

As the creation of new jobs continues, economic progress must not come at the expense of environmental quality. The California Environmental Quality Act (CEQA) of 1970, which is intended to curb unplanned land use and haphazard growth, is crucial in this respect. The act requires that the environmental effects of all proposed public and private construction be evaluated. Those who want to build must submit environmental impact reports for reviewing agencies. The passage in 1972 of Proposition 20, the Coastal Zone Conservation Act, further exemplified Californians' concern for the environment. The act mandates strict control of commercial and industrial development along California's scenic coastline.

Air pollution has been with Californians for more than forty years. Shortly after World War II, people in Los Angeles began to notice that the sky was more gray than blue, especially on hot days. Headaches, respiratory diseases such as emphysema and bronchitis, deterioration of rubber products, and crop losses soon followed. In 1947, the first air pollution control district (APCD) was formed. California is making considerable progress in reducing smog, in part because of the aggressive efforts of the state Air Resources Board (ARB), described in Chapter 6. In the counties of Los Angeles, Orange, San Bernardino, and Riverside, second-stage smog alerts have been reduced by 80 percent since 1978. During a second-stage smog alert, large companies must require carpools for employees and must curtail industrial emissions. Vigorous outdoor activity on the part of the public is discouraged. Third-stage alerts are the most serious kind, requiring people to remain indoors. So far, they are rare—the last one was in 1974. The ARB attempts to reduce carbon monoxide (from motor vehicles), hydrocarbons (from motor vehicles and storage tanks at gas stations), sulfur dioxide (from power plants and industry), nitrogen oxides (from the above sources), and ozone. Various parts of northern and southern California are also plagued by acid rain, formed when cars and factories discharge sulfur and nitrous oxides, which are converted into sulfuric and nitric acid. Acid rain kills fish and damages crops and trees. The Air Resources Board has announced that as a result of new research more controls are being placed on emissions of oxides of nitrogen (NOx) in order to reduce acid rain and acid fog, although these requirements will cost electrical utilities a great deal of money. In addition, the ARB has established auto emission standards that will reduce nitrogen oxides by 15 percent per year. The ARB has also required new diesel cars to meet strict emission standards because they emit more than thirty times as much soot and ten times as much sulfur oxides as gasoline-powered cars, and it has also required new trucks and buses to be virtually smoke free by 1994.

Since automobiles are the source of over half of the hydrocarbons and nitrogen oxides and almost all of the carbon monoxide, the state legislature has required that cars in more urbanized counties be checked every two years, at a garage or service station approved by the state, to see if they meet emission standards. Inspection costs between $15 and $25, and the cost of tune-ups cannot exceed $50. The program is in force in the counties of Los Angeles, San Diego, Santa Barbara, Ventura, San Francisco, Sacramento, and Fresno. In other areas of the state, cars are inspected and repaired only when first registered in California or when ownership changes. Biennial inspection decreased vehicle emissions from inspected cars by 14 percent in the first two years of the program. The legislature had long been reluctant to require inspections, fearing that inconvenienced Californians would retaliate at the polls. However, the federal Environmental Protection Agency (EPA) imposed a moratorium on the construction or expansion of factories which would increase air pollution, and also cut off federal aid for construction of highways and sewage treatment plants. This action forced the state legislature, which had hesitated for years, into formulating a decisive plan for pollution abatement.

Noise abatement is uppermost in the minds of many of the state's residents, especially those who live near airports. The level of noise in a typical city can be very dangerous, as prolonged exposure to nearby noise of about 80 decibels leads to permanent hearing loss. Examples of 90-decibel noise are a jackhammer, a chain saw, a jet plane, a motorcycle, a garbage disposal, and a rock band. However, according to the Environmental Protection Agency, the threshold for serious hearing damage may actually be 70 decibels. Depending on distance, we receive that level from a pickup truck engine, a freight train closer than 50 feet away, a vacuum cleaner, an electric razor, and a nearby freeway. Noise, which we encounter as a normal part of California living, can have psychological as well as physical effects, such as reduced sociability and reduced sensitivity to the needs of other people.

Hazardous wastes and dangerous chemicals generated by various industries also present a serious environmental problem. These toxic substances, which usually take the form of acids, caustics, corrosives, or solvents, may be flammable and explosive as well as poisonous. Perhaps most dangerous is their long duration in the environment. Toxic substances can be spilled in a highway accident on the way to a dump site or, at the site, can contaminate underground water supplies. In fact, toxic contaminants have been found in 18 percent of the state's wells, especially in industrial counties such as Los Angeles, San Bernardino, Riverside, and Santa Clara, and in agricultural counties in the San Joaquin Valley. The State Water Resources Control Board has estimated that there are 30,000 underground gasoline storage tanks leaking benzene, which causes cancer. Cleanup may take 15 years to complete, at a cost of $5 billion. Toxic substances leaking into the water supply can cause birth defects, sterility, and cancer. More than 10 million tons of toxic waste are produced per year in California, or about one pickup truckload per Californian. Of the 70,000 industrial chemicals now in use, there are toxicity data on only 25 percent of them showing their effects on human beings and the environment. California has attempted to regulate the handling, processing, and disposal of those materials since 1972. Wastes are classified according to their danger, and disposal sites are graded in terms of geological security and their separation from water supplies. However, disposal sites are becoming scarce, and many companies such as Occidental Petroleum dump their chemical wastes at the site where they were produced. In fact, more than half of all wastes are disposed of in this manner. In an attempt to prevent clandestine "midnight dumpers" who discard their cargoes in remote areas, the state registers haulers and issues them permits. Drivers must carry a manifest of the toxic chemicals they are transporting and must have information on first-aid antidotes in case of an accidental spill. Unfortunately, this cradle-to-grave monitoring has not been vigorously maintained by the state.

Environmentalists' concerns that current laws to protect the environment are not strong enough prompted these activists to sponsor a successful 1986 ballot proposition prohibiting release into a source of drinking water of any chemical in an amount known to cause cancer. Also forbidden is the release of an amount that exceeds 1/1,000 of the amount necessary for an observable effect on "reproductive toxicity" (however, the proposition did not define this term). The governor must issue a list of substances causing cancer or reproductive toxicity, and industries or farmers must warn the public before exposing people to chemicals causing these dangers. The measure also provided for civil penalties and increased fines for toxic discharges, and allowed private individuals to sue violators and collect 25 percent of the penalties assessed. The prospect of a law with such far-reaching effects prompted considerable political conflict. Arrayed on one side in favor were most Democratic Party candidates, environmentalists, actress Jane Fonda, and many other Hollywood personalities. On the other side were most Republican Party candidates, agricultural interests, the high-technology industry, and Chevron Oil. Proponents rejected the idea that environmental and health risks should be weighed on a scale against the economic benefits of toxics use. They further argued that the burden of proof in toxics use should be changed: rather than requiring the government to prove that a chemical causes cancer before forbidding it, users of the chemical should prove that it does *not* cause cancer, a much more difficult task. Proponents also claimed that current fines do little to discourage violators. Opponents such as the *Sacramento Bee* argued that "for some economic activity, the price between a very small risk and no risk—a price either in dollars or in health risks—can be astronomical."[5] The *Los Angeles Times* editorialized that the measure "deals with amounts of substances that are so minute they now can be detected in terms of parts per trillion. Unfortunately, the science of determining the health risk from these chemicals, or lack of a risk, is not as advanced as our ability to measure them." Opponents also claimed that the award of 25 percent of assessed penalties going to victorious litigants amounted to "frontier justice for bounty hunters." Amidst these vigorous claims and counterclaims, the measure passed. It is now left to the state legislature and the courts to define the measure's key terms, such as what level of chemical discharge causes a "significant risk" and which required exposure warnings are "clear and reasonable."

Hazardous wastes are both an urban and a rural problem, as was demonstrated by the 1985 controversy regarding Kesterson Reservoir and National Wildlife Refuge in western Merced County. Kesterson is on the receiving end of the San Luis Drain, a federal project collecting runoff agricultural water from the west side of the San Joaquin Valley. The reservoir began receiving toxic waters containing dangerous pesticides and selenium, which causes death to waterfowl or birth defects. For example, some birds were born with multiple beaks. Moreover, since the reservoir was unlined, this toxic water was seeping into the groundwater. The State Water Resources Control Board, relying on the Toxic Pits Cleanup Act (described later in this chapter), ordered the U.S. Bureau of Reclamation to close Kesterson or clean it up. If the Kesterson reservoir were closed, there would be nowhere for agricultural wastewater to drain, which would result in 42,000 acres of farmland taken out of production. Crops valued at $45 million per year and 1,450 jobs were at stake. The Bureau of Reclamation decided that it must close Kesterson in order to comply with the Migratory Bird Treaty Act; under criminal penalty, this requires the Bureau to prevent conditions leading to the death of waterfowl migrating through the United States to or from other countries. Finally, the U.S. Department of the Interior gave farmers a one-year reprieve before closing Kesterson, after which it will close it and clean it up, which will take three to five years to complete.

The state legislature has passed numerous recent laws dealing with toxic wastes, only a few of which can be discussed here. As noted above, on-site dumping is a very serious issue; this process is known as surface impoundment, or more commonly, pits, ponds, and lagoons. More than half of all toxic wastes generated in California are handled on-site, where they leak into groundwater basins, overflow into streams and lakes, or evaporate into the air. Recent notorious contaminations are the Stringfellow acid pits near Chino and the Aerojet-General Corporation plant near Sacramento, which was one of the worst groundwater pollution problems in the United States. The legislature passed the Toxic Pits Cleanup Act, which requires that hazardous liquid waste pools and ponds which are one-half mile from drinking water supplies must be closed. All others must be double-lined and equipped with leak detection and groundwater monitoring equipment. Another law designed to protect the subterranean aquifers which supply so much of our drinking water requires the State Water Resources Control Board (which is described in Chapter 6) to set rules for underground tanks storing motor vehicle fuels. These tanks must be monitored facility-wide (but not inspected tank-by-tank) for leaks and corrosion. Liability for safety is borne by the oil and chemical companies that own the tanks. Yet another recent law is intended to prepare for toxic chemical fires. Prior to the passage of the act, companies were not required by state law to supply emergency-response officials with current information on hazardous materials they were storing. (However, some cities and counties required this information to be on file.) Some companies store pesticides such as malathion, paraquat, or diazinon, which are deadly substances derived from World War II nerve gases designed to attack the central nervous system. These substances are fatal if absorbed in sufficient quantity, and they pose a serious danger to firefighters who respond to a call but do not know what kind of danger they face. Moreover, a wide variety of companies—for example, pool chemical companies, paint manufacturers, and high-tech research firms—store dangerous materials. The legislature has now required companies to disclose their inventory of hazardous materials and prepare community-response plans in case of emergencies. Chemical manufacturing companies argue that if they are required to reveal all the ingredients of their products, this requirement will violate a federal law protecting trade secrets.[6]

The federal government has adopted many of California's procedures as part of its Superfund program. For example, industries must report the kinds and amounts of hazardous substances found on their premises and must report any releases into the environment of dangerous chemicals which cause or are suspected of causing cancer, birth defects, or any chronic health problem. The Superfund program provides $9 billion to clean up abandoned dumps and allows citizens to sue the federal Environmental Protection Agency or private parties if the citizens believe a particular cleanup job is unsatisfactory or for any violation of the Superfund law. The program is funded by a tax on imported and domestically produced petroleum, a broad-based tax on large corporations, and general revenues. The program has played an important role in cleaning up the groundwater basin which provides drinking water for one-half million people in the Los Angeles area. California also has its own Superfund to clean up abandoned dumps, to respond to emergency spills, and to compensate victims for medical expenses. The fund is financed by assessments on the chemical, mining, and petroleum companies that generate the waste. There are 93 sites on the California priority list, and 19 of these are also on the federal government's Superfund list. Average cleanup costs are more than $7.5 million, but some may run as high as $40 million. The only major cleanup completed by the California Superfund is the Capri Pumping Services site in east Los Angeles, which took in 2.4 million gallons of hazardous chemical wastes in the 1970s. Although city inspectors knew about Capri, it still took them two years to persuade city officials to close it down, and an additional two and one-half years to get the cleanup started. In a more encouraging vein, promising methods for eliminating these dangerous materials include baking them into hard blocks or incinerating them in cement kilns. These processes also incidentally produce energy.

As we have seen, the problems of the Kesterson Reservoir and toxic fires are related to the use of pesticides, herbicides, and fungicides. More than 300 million pounds of these chemicals are used each year by California agriculture. Although pesticides are helpful in controlling pest-destroying crops, environmentalists argue that these chemicals are poisoning food eaten by the public. In addition, many farmworkers, pilots who fly cropdusters, and rural residents are harmed every year by pesticides that may cause cancer, nerve damage, sterility, birth defects, and other health hazards. Incidences of injury to farmworkers are underreported because many of these people are in the country illegally and they do not want to draw attention to themselves. Considerable effort will be needed to solve these problems; as one measure, the legislature has passed the Birth Defect Prevention Act. This requires pesticide manufacturers to provide the California Department of Food and Agriculture with a complete list of all tests for health hazards that have been conducted of the active ingredients of pesticides previously registered in California and of any to be registered in the future.

Solid waste management, especially the disposal of garbage, is also a nagging problem. Californians have deposited garbage in landfills, covered it with soil, and forgotten about it. But this is not always easy to do, since, for example, rotting trash at the massive Monterey Park landfill produces 36,000 gallons a day of a black, oily juice that smells terrible and is hazardous. This dump, which has more than 20,000 people within one mile of it, emits methane gas that can explode and also carcinogenic vinyl chloride. It is unknown how many other landfills may do the same thing in the future. Whatever their faults, California's dumps are filling up rapidly. Californians annually dispose of 1.5 tons of solid waste for each person in the state. Unless new landfills are opened, the state will run out of disposal ground around 1998. Hence, there is great interest in trash-to-energy incinerators which not only reduce the total volume of garbage but also generate electricity. Facilities are planned or completed in Commerce, Long Beach, and San Marcos. Although these plants are an excellent idea, they pose air pollution problems and may even emit dioxin, a carcinogen.

For too long, California has tolerated throwaway consumer items, such as containers. Between 1965 and 1986, fourteen bills to require deposits on all beer and soft-drink containers were defeated in the legislature. Opponents of the bills claimed that mandatory deposits would cause severe unemployment in the bottle and can industries, increase retail prices of beverages, and not significantly reduce the amount of total litter and trash (which also includes cigarette butts, newspapers, paper cups, and paper bags). Grocers argued that storing dirty cans is unsanitary. Proponents of returnable containers said that California is being inundated with discarded cans and bottles (63 percent of the soft drinks sold in California are in disposable containers—the national average is 38 percent). They also argued that broken bottles are a safety hazard, and that besides reducing litter, returnable containers can be recycled, thereby saving energy in the manufacturing process. Moreover, recycling containers will save space in landfills. An initiative statute to require mandatory deposits appeared on the ballot in 1982, but it was defeated after being heavily outspent by the bottling and beverage industries. Finally, in 1986 the legislature ended this two-decade struggle by passing a mandatory deposit bill covering aluminum, glass, and plastic containers. The bill requires beverage distributors to pay $.01 per container into a recycling fund, and they may pass this cost on to consumers as part of the price of their product. People returning containers then receive $.02 per can and $.15 per glass bottle (the increased payment results from the scrap value of the containers and from uncollected deposits). Retailers do not have to accept returned containers, which prompted them to end their opposition to mandatory deposits, because the law provides for a statewide network of thousands of recycling centers. Twelve billion beverage containers are sold in this state each year, and the new bill will go a long way toward a cleaner California. One possible drawback is that the $.02 per container reward does not provide the incentive given by $.05 per container bounties found in nine other states with bottle-bill laws and in Yosemite.

Since the mid-1960s, California has sought to preserve open-space and agricultural lands, particularly those around cities. The Williamson Land Conservation Act provides that cities and counties can enter into ten-year contracts with local farmers that provide that the farmer's land shall be assessed at a lower agricultural rate if it is not sold for development as houses, shopping centers, or factories. The intent of this 1965 law is to encourage landowners to preserve their land from development. The state government reimburses cities and counties for property tax revenue lost as a result of the program. About

Yosemite Shows Worth of Bottle Bill

Californians who are uncertain about a bottle law in this state should look to their own Yosemite National Park.

It has had a 5-cent deposit on aluminum beverage cans and beer bottles for nine years, and the anti-litter program runs like clockwork.

Before the park required deposits, the Yosemite recycling center took in one ton of aluminum cans a year. Since the program was implemented, the center recycles a ton each week.

Any can left as litter is picked up quickly by volunteers who seek the 5-cent deposit. And panhandling has ceased to be a nuisance. Former panhandlers are out after stray cans instead of soliciting visitors for spare change.

The anti-litter effort was launched by The Yosemite Park and Curry Company—the concessionaire that con-

tracts to provide such guest services as hotels and food markets in Yosemite Park. It has been so successful that the Environmental Protection Agency is encouraging all national parks to start a deposit program.

The Yosemite Park and Curry Company says it gains about $6,000 in unredeemed deposits each year because visitors carry some of their beverage purchases out of the park. The surplus is used to finance park cleanup programs and nature projects.

The Yosemite experiment proves a bottle-deposit system works wonders in handling the unsightly litter that can be seen beside our state highways . . . .

SOURCE: "Yosemite Shows Worth of Bottle Bill" (editorial), *San Diego Tribune*, August 24, 1985, p. C3.

one-third of the privately owned land in the state is covered by the law. Because only 3 percent of the acreage affected by the Williamson Act is farmland near cities, some critics argue that landowners are receiving a tax break on land that is really not threatened by development. They point out that the other 70 percent is forest land, grazing land, wildlife habitats, wetlands, salt ponds, submerged lands, and recreational areas. At the urging of developers, the legislature allowed a five-month period in 1982 during which local governments could cancel Williamson Act contracts. This action weakened the law, as did a later amendment to the law which allowed leapfrog development. Moreover, the passage of Proposition 13 (described in Chapter 10) has reduced the tax incentives under the Williamson Act by about 20 percent.

ENERGY

Coupled with the desire for a clean environment is the search for less-polluting or nonpolluting sources of energy. California needs less-polluting energy sources because if it were a country, it would rank ninth in the world in terms of total energy consumed. However, Californians use considerably less energy per capita for residential, commercial, and industrial purposes than do other Americans: we rank forty-second. Despite this state's "car culture," energy devoted to transportation per capita does not greatly exceed the national average. Petroleum provides 61 percent of the state's energy requirements; natural gas provides 30 percent; coal 3 percent; and hydropower, geothermal power, and nuclear power 6 percent. In terms of end use, transportation receives 47 percent of the energy (virtually all of it from petroleum), industrial and commercial uses receive 39 percent (mostly from natural gas and petroleum), and residential uses receive 14 percent (especially from natural gas). Dependence on coal, solar energy, biomass, cogeneration, wind power, and geothermal power is expected to increase in the future.

No source of energy is without drawbacks. Oil is expensive, the supply is uncertain, and dependence on it subjects the country to foreign control. This is a crucial issue: "California uses more gasoline than every country in the world except the United States and the Soviet Union. . . . California's continued overdependence on oil remains the state's fundamental energy problem."[7] Although today's cars are nearly twice as efficient as those built in the mid-1970s, we have not significantly reduced our dependence on oil. Half of the oil consumed in California is produced here, 8 percent comes from other countries, and 42 percent is from Alaska and the outer continental shelf. Methanol is a promising substitute for gasoline: it is cleaner burning; it can be produced from oil, coal, natural gas, or even biomass (described later); and it could be economically competitive if sold to a mass market. However, methanol is a victim of the "chicken–egg" dilemma. Auto makers will not build methanol cars because gas stations do not have methanol pumps; on the other hand, station owners will not install a methanol pump because there are few methanol cars. Coal is heavily polluting: burning it releases sulfur dioxide and nitrogen dioxide. Furthermore, mining coal leads to black-lung disease in miners, or is accomplished by ugly strip mining that devours the landscape.

The price of natural gas is expected to increase, and hydroelectric power involves damming scenic rivers.

Nuclear-fission power has inspired a storm of protest. In 1981, a two-week demonstration at the Diablo Canyon nuclear power plant near San Luis Obispo resulted in the arrest of nearly two thousand people, and $3 million in law enforcement expenses. Opponents of nuclear power seek to ban all nuclear power plants in California, fearing a reactor-core meltdown that would release dangerous radioactive materials as happened at Chernobyl in the Soviet Union. In addition, atomic wastes (like spent fuel rods) are toxic for centuries, and no safe disposal process has been developed. Opponents of nuclear power also warn that terrorists might steal sufficient atomic materials to construct a bomb. In contrast, proponents claim that risk factors have been overstated.

The development of nuclear power in California was seriously curtailed in 1983. The U.S. Supreme Court upheld a state law requiring that no new nuclear plants be built in California until the state Energy Resources Conservation and Development Commission (described in Chapter 6) certifies that a demonstrated technology to dispose of high-level nuclear waste has been developed (*Pacific Gas and Electric Company v. Energy Resources Conservation and Development Commission*, 463 U.S. 1230 [1983]). Further clouding the future of nuclear power is the declining demand for electricity.

The "least worst" calculations associated with all these energy sources have led environmentalists to trumpet various alternatives to meet a larger share of the state's energy needs. Interest in solar energy is keen, and California, with one-fourth of all American solar installations, is the national leader. Solar collectors are used principally for home water heating and swimming pool heating. A well-designed system can provide 80 percent of a home's water heating and can cost 92 percent less than gas heaters in swimming pool heating. By means of passive solar building design, a home or office with large windows facing south, a slab concrete floor, and insulation can efficiently collect and store heat. The cities of Ukiah, Palo Alto, Bakersfield, San Dimas, Santa Monica, and Oceanside have established municipal solar utility districts which install collector panels and lease them to the property owner, with the city providing maintenance. The advantages of solar energy are that it is safe and nonpolluting, and that it can supplant some of the state's natural gas use. Although installation costs are high, most systems pay for themselves after about 15 years. As perhaps an indication of things to come, a large 43-megawatt solar facility has been built on the desert at Daggett (near Barstow). At Solar One, acres of mirrored reflectors focus the sun's rays on a pipe at the center to create steam which turns a turbine to generate electricity.

Another alternative energy source is wind-generated electric power. If California can utilize the benefits of the sun, it can take advantage of the wind as well. The state's utilities have built some giant windmills and wind turbine generators in San Gorgonio Pass near Palm Springs and in Altamont Pass east of San Francisco, and they are considering building more in windy areas of the state such as the Tehachapi Mountain passes. When these "wind farms" are supplying electricity, the utilities can scale back their use of oil-fired power plants. Wind power, too, has its drawbacks though: since these generators take

Electricity-producing windmills stretch into the distance at Alameda County's Altamont Pass; 2200 are in operation here.   SOURCE: Los Angeles Times Photo

the form of either giant propeller blades or huge inverted eggbeaters, they could become colossal eyesores comparable to the offshore oil derricks near Santa Barbara. Although loss of state and federal tax credits for buyers and investors has hurt the wind industry, California still has the largest installed capacity of wind turbines in the world.

Energy can also be produced by burning organic waste material from orchards, logging operations and sawmills, feed and grain mills, packing houses, canneries, and other sources. This so-called **biomass conversion** also includes the burning of such otherwise useless materials as kelp, walnut shells, apricot pits, corn stalks, wood chips, and even cow chips to generate heat or electricity. These materials can be used most efficiently on the sites where they are produced, because otherwise they must be collected, chopped or densified, and then transported for storage or burning; these operations are expensive and energy consuming. For a biomass operation to be economically feasible, it must have a continuous source of waste material from fields and forests. Such a source could be the five to six million tons of crop and forest residues that are burned in open fields each year. Yet another process using energy that otherwise would be wasted is **cogeneration.** Through this process, factories produce electricity and steam at the same site and thereby derive approximately twice as much energy from the same oil, coal, or gas. Without cogeneration, "about half of the energy used by industry is consumed just to produce steam. Cogeneration simply interposes an electric generator between the boiler that produces this steam and the point where the factory uses it. High-pressure steam runs an electricity-generating turbine, which in turn emits lower-pressure steam adequate for most industrial and commercial requirements."[8] Cogeneration was once in extensive use in this country, and it currently supplies 20 percent of the energy in England. California users of cogeneration include oil refiners, paper manufacturing and food processing companies, hospitals, hotels, schools, and many others.

Geothermal power is also in limited use. This process taps hot steam in the earth to drive turbines that generate electricity; it is used at The Geysers plant in the Napa–Sonoma area. Moving into a more speculative vein, we should also mention atomic *fusion* (as opposed to *fission*) as a potential energy source. In the *fusion* process, energy is released when relatively light, nonradioactive atoms are joined together. In the *fission* process, atoms of heavy radioactive material are split to release energy. Radioactive hazards associated with fusion reactors are much less than those associated with fission reactors: "The threat of a runaway process or explosion does not exist, and the inherent temptation for theft or sabotage would be smaller."[9] Another long-range possibility is ocean thermal power, deriving electricity from differences in temperature between the upper layers of the ocean and deeper, colder layers.

The final energy resource that we will consider is conservation. By conserving energy, California can avoid having to build expensive new power plants. Devices such as storm windows, insulation, weatherstripping, caulking, water heater insulation blankets, and low-flow shower heads can save a great deal of energy. The state's utilities also provide energy audits and interest-free loans to install such devices under the zero-interest-plan (ZIP). The California Energy Commission establishes minimum residential appliance efficiency standards for appliances to be sold in this state, for example, standards for refrigerators. Refrigerators use 27 percent of the electrical energy consumed in the average California household; the conservation potential of the Energy Commission's standards for refrigerators alone will save the state's consumers the cost of building a major (1,000-megawatt) nuclear or coal plant costing more than $3 billion.[10] In order to encourage conservation, the California residential rate structure provides that as consumption goes up, cost per unit of natural gas also goes up. (However, lower-income people are protected by "lifeline" rates that are low for the lowest levels of consumption.) Two other ways of lessening the need for new power plants are load management and time-of-use rates. Both of these attempt to decrease electricity demand at peak periods of use by transferring it to off-peak periods. This is facilitated by charging higher rates during peak periods than in off-peak periods.

TRANSPORTATION

California has attempted to lessen its previous heavy reliance on cars and freeways to transport people. The recent approach is multimodal: it mixes mass transit, car pools, van pools, group taxis, and jitneys, and includes preferential driving lanes and metered on-ramps. The boxed newspaper article describes an ambitious transit system in the San Francisco area.

After Shaky Start, BART Is Now Purring, Growing

SAN FRANCISCO—It began in June, 1964, when President Lyndon B. Johnson attended the official start of its construction. The Bay Area Rapid Transit system was heralded as a speedy, stylish model for mass transportation of the future.

But it was not until September, 1972, that BART, as it came to be known, began operating in Oakland and vicinity. It was September, 1973, before San Francisco was connected through a tunnel beneath the bay.

BART was four years late and cost $500 million more than anticipated. And its troubles were just beginning. Plagued by breakdowns, rush-hour crowding and a bewildering array of technical problems, the system was assailed by critics. Through the years, headlines like "BART—a White Elephant" and "$1.6-Billion Mistake" were common in local newspapers as authorities, commentators and the public alike lambasted the system.

Now . . . there are signs that for all its problems, the system may be starting to live up to its promise. BART ridership [is up].

BART's general manager, Keith Bernard, believes that the sharp growth reflects "a new era of public confidence" in the system. And some transit authorities, including past critics, seem inclined to agree.

"BART's reliability has improved quite a lot," said Melvin M. Webber, director of the Institute of Urban and Regional Development at the University of California, Berkeley.

"People don't have to wait on the platforms as long. In the past, a lot of people had just got fed up waiting and quit using BART . . . If BART can keep going without a lot of breakdowns, people will ride it. They ought to—it's the biggest bargain now in transportation."

Webber, in a two-year study of the system published in 1976, had been highly critical of BART.

Bernard and other transit officials attribute the system's ridership gains to several factors—the most prominent being the spiraling cost of operating an automobile. BART's improved reliability (95% of the time it is within five minutes of schedule) and a better public awareness of its service and convenience also are cited as contributors to increased patronage.

The system's ridership, lagging behind in the past, is now matching a statewide increase in the use of public transit, according to the state Department of Transportation. . . .

BART officials say the new riders are coming from automobiles, not buses or other forms of mass transit.

"That's the market we're shooting for and we think we're getting it," said BART spokesman Sy Mouber. "These new riders are leaving their cars at home."

BART's lines stretch through Contra Costa and Alameda counties in the East Bay and over to San Francisco and Daly City on the west side of the bay.

For those who can reach a BART line comfortably (and, if driving, find a place to park) a trip on BART is an inviting one—clean, secure and usually fast.

It is also a bargain. The average ride on BART costs $1. A 30-mile trip from Concord to San Francisco costs $1.65 one way.

SOURCE: "After Shaky Start, BART Is Now Purring, Growing," by P. Hager, *Los Angeles Times*, February 16, 1982, pt. I, p. 1. Copyright 1982, Los Angeles Times. Reprinted by permission.

Rush-hour freeways in many parts of the state have reached the point of saturation. Unless the vehicle occupancy rate can be increased through car pools or some other means, major freeways will simply become giant parking lots at critical times. According to one writer,

> technological and economic evidence points to rail transit as the only reasonable way to move persons in and out of the central city at rush hours. Automobiles on expressways can move about two thousand people per lane per hour, buses can move between six thousand and nine thousand, but rail systems can carry up to sixty thousand persons per hour. In other words, one rail line is estimated to be equal to that of twenty or thirty expressway lanes of automobiles in terms of its ability to move people.[11]

A successful example of light-rail transportation is San Diego's Tijuana Trolley.

If people are to be enticed out of single-passenger cars and if the reign of one-person, one-car travel is to be ended, the alternative must have some of the appealing features of the private automobile. Such a system should take people exactly where they want to go, leave at a time when they are ready to leave, and afford privacy. Hence, there is renewed interest in private jitneys (sometimes called "Gypsy cabs") running on fixed short routes at peak rush periods. Ridesharing, including van pools and car pools, is promoted by many employers and local governments.

Inflation and fuel-efficient cars have hurt the state highway fund by decreasing the demand for gasoline. If the state gas tax were a percentage of the price per gallon, rather than a flat $.09 per gallon, revenues would rise as the price of gas increased. Presently, gas tax revenues are shared with cities and counties, are split 60–40 between southern and northern regions, and can only be spent on highways and mass transit guideways. Weight fees on commercial vehicles should be increased greatly: according to CalTrans (California Department of Transportation), 99 percent of the damage to pavement is caused by vehicles heavier than automobiles (vehicles over 6,000 pounds). An 80,000-pound truck causes 10,000 times more damage to a highway than does a car.[12] However, such a weight fee raise is very unlikely: truckers are a powerful interest group. Types of strategies that truckers and other interest groups use are described in detail in Chapter 4.

WATER

Water has always been a very sensitive issue in California politics, and recent conflicts over the Peripheral Canal, the protection of scenic wild rivers, and groundwater overdrafting are some of the latest skirmishes in a struggle that has been continuing for more than a century. The source of the problem is that 66 percent of the state's rain and snow occur in the northern third of the state, but 80 percent of the need for water is in the southern two-thirds. The potential for political conflict is obvious.

Runoffs from snowpacks in the High Sierras provide 70 percent of the state's water. The snowpack "generally begins in November and increases steadily through the winter months, reaching a maximum depth and water content about 1 April."[13] If the water is not where the people are, massive aqueducts and dams and pumps are needed. The State Water Project and the federal government's Central Valley Project comprise the world's largest water project. They are so huge that "the astronauts who landed on the moon reported they could see the California project, the only manmade item they could identify from that distance."[14]

The 1959 Burns–Porter Act authorized the State Water Project, and in 1960 voters approved a $1.75 billion bond issue to help finance the project. It consists of a 600-mile-long series of dams, reservoirs, pumping plants, canals, and pipelines intended to move water from the Sierras as far south as the thirsty southern California desert. One has to be amazed at both the engineering acumen and the political determination needed to undertake such an endeavor. The keystone is Oroville Dam in Butte County (the largest of eighteen state dams), which moves 1.6 million acre-feet of water per year (an acre-foot is 326,000 gallons, or the amount of water that will cover one acre of ground with one foot of water). After passing through the Sacramento–San Joaquin delta and down the Gov. Edmund G. Brown California Aqueduct, the water must be pumped 2,000 feet up the north slope of the Tehachapi Mountains to reach the Metropolitan Water District of Southern California. Along the way, the North Bay Aqueduct supplies Napa and Solano counties, and the South Bay Aqueduct supplies Alameda and Santa Clara counties. San Francisco has its own Hetch Hetchy water project.

As a result of the big drought in the late 1920s and early 1930s, the federal government (the U.S. Bureau of Reclamation) built the Central Valley Project (CVP). It consists of about thirty dams, the most important of which is Shasta Dam: "The northern portion of the CVP includes Shasta, Trinity, Folsom, Whiskeytown, and San Luis dams. . . . The southern system of the CVP includes Friant Dam, Millerton Lake, and the Friant–Kern and Madera Canals."[15] The Bureau of Reclamation supplies one-third of the state's total water needs; most of its customers are farmers located in the Sacramento and San Joaquin valleys, for example, the Westlands Water District in Fresno.

The federal government also affects state water policy through its sale of low-cost water from federal reclamation projects. By means of the Newlands Reclamation Act of 1902, Congress tried to foster small farms in the arid west by selling federally subsidized water from its dams and canals. The 1902 act provided that a landowner could buy only enough water to irrigate 160 acres (320 acres in the case of a married couple). The act was never strictly enforced, but in the late 1970s, agrarian reformers persuaded the federal courts that the provisions of the act should be carried out. Congress responded in 1982 by rewriting the law and raised the amount of subsidized water which can be purchased to an amount sufficient to irrigate 960 acres. Water over this amount may be purchased at a higher price.

The Sacramento–San Joaquin Delta figures prominently in California water policy. This 740,000-acre area, where the Sacramento and San Joaquin rivers meet, discharges over 40 percent of the state's natural runoff; hence it is a key link in the transportation of water from northern California to southern California. The Delta is an important fish spawning area and bird habitat. Its rich agricultural lands and wildlife habitats, such as the Suisun Marsh, must receive fresh water to repel the intrusion of salt water from San Francisco Bay. Delta farmers fear that in a future drought too much water will be shipped to southern California; environmentalists and recreationists fear that Delta water quality thus would be lowered. All of these concerns came to a head in the emotional 1982 struggle over the Peripheral Canal. Southern California water interests argued that a 43-mile canal should be built around the periphery of the Delta to transport water south. They claimed that the canal would capture useful water that was not needed to protect Delta water quality; canal opponents rejected this argument. Opponents further argued that southern California does not need the water that the canal would deliver and that the canal would cost much more money than the state could afford. The interests on either side of the issue amounted to a roster of the state's major powers. For the canal were Getty Oil and Union Oil, the Metropolitan Water District of Southern California, the California Chamber of Commerce, the Association of California Water Agencies, the Irvine Company, and the *Los Angeles Times*. Opposed were the California Farm Bureau Federation, the California Cattlemen's Association, J.G. Boswell Co. and Salyer Land Co., the Environmental Defense Fund, the Sierra Club, and the *Sacramento Bee*. The Peripheral Canal was soundly defeated by a margin of 62 percent to 38 percent.

In addition to the allocation of water, other key concerns are water quality, groundwater overdraft, conservation, and the "watermarket" issue (see pp. 26–27). We noted recent attempts to prevent toxics in the water supply in our discussion of the environment, but California has long had water treatment programs whose purpose is to remove suspended material and to kill harmful organisms. Water is filtered, treated chemically, and sterilized by chlorination of by exposure to ultraviolet light.[16] Sewage must also be treated to remove organic material and other materials which lower the oxygen content of water. The three levels of sewage treatment are primary (to remove solids such as trash or oils), secondary (to remove biological and chemical impurities), and tertiary (to remove nutrients). To conserve water, California must also increase its reclamation of wastewater. Such reused water can supply industry, irrigate crops and recreational areas, and recharge groundwater.

About 40 percent of the water used in California is groundwater that has been pumped from below the surface. If farmers find that it is cheaper to draw water out of the ground than to purchase it from the federal or state government, serious overdrafting occurs, especially since there are few governmental restrictions on this practice. Current overdrafts in the San Joaquin Valley amount to more than 1.5 million acre-feet per year. Although overdrafting lowers the water table and increases the costs of pumping, individual farmers continue to do it because they believe that if they do not pump heavily, other farmers will do so and will use the available water. Moreover, we noted earlier that toxic contaminants have been found in 18 percent of the state's wells.

State water policy should be guided by the principle that water is a limited resource. Conservation must increase, especially on the part of agriculture, the chief water user, and by water suppliers. For example, the Imperial Irrigation District in El Centro allows excessive seepage from unlined canals and also allows too much water to flow into the Salton Sea. The supply of California's water is fixed by nature, yet the state's population is increasing. In fact, the state's supply of water can actually be considered to be decreasing because California will lose 1.6 million acre-feet of water per year by 1992 from the Colorado River when Arizona completes its Central Arizona project. Unless wild and scenic north coast rivers like the Eel, American, Klamath, Trinity, and Smith are tapped, as farmers hope and environmentalists fear, conservation must be pursued. A law passed by the legislature in 1982 will encourage such conservation: farmers or water districts can temporarily sell surplus water accumulated through conservation without losing their legal right to the water. It is estimated that this measure will save 172,000 acre-feet of water per year. It is sometimes claimed that California has no shortage of water, only a shortage of *cheap* water. Since water is frequently underpriced by the Central Valley Project and the State Water Project, it is not used efficiently. If its price were to rise, water would be put to its most efficient use.

A bill recently passed by Congress may prove very valuable in the event of future droughts. Congress has provided for coordinated operation of the federal Central Valley Project and the State Water Project so that the former may use the latter's conveyance system of aqueducts, canals, pumps, and other facilities. In times of water shortage, more water can now be shipped to southern California without lowering water quality in the Sacramento–San Joaquin Delta. The CVP is now required to meet minimum water quality standards for the Delta that are set by the state Water Resources Control Board and that are intended to prevent saltwater intrusion from San Francisco Bay. The possibility of future droughts should not be taken lightly, and the drought of the mid-1970s was surely not the last one of this century. As we noted earlier, the state's economic system is complex and interdependent—and the thread of interconnection is water. Any shortage of water vastly complicates other problems such as unemployment, pollution, and energy.

AGRICULTURE

Agriculture uses more than 85 percent of the state's water. California is the nation's foremost agricultural state, leading all states in the production of forty-nine different crops and livestock products. Three crops are produced only in California, 90 percent of nine others is produced here, and more than half of twelve others is grown in this state. The leading agricultural counties in terms of value of production are Fresno, Tulare, and Kern, and the most important farm products by value are milk and cream, cattle and calves, cotton, grapes, and hay. An accurate picture of California agriculture should not omit marijuana. Although precise data cannot be secured, seasoned observers note that grower earnings of more than $1 billion would not be on the high side. Such an accounting would place marijuana between grapes and hay in cash value.

California's success in agriculture can be attributed to many factors, including mild climate, plentiful water supply, and research and development. Just as research has helped to make this state a leader in advanced industrialism, it has also contributed to our extraordinarily high value of crops per acre.

Although the amount of land being farmed has fallen slightly in recent years, the number of farms has risen, especially the number of small farms under 10 acres. California's acreage per farm is eighteenth in the United States and is below the national average.

Some of the central issues of California farm policy have already been noted: the safe use of pesticides and ensuring an adequate water supply. Other pressing matters are the buildup of salt in the soil of the San Joaquin Valley, the financial condition of the state's farmers, and fair treatment for farm laborers. The fertile San Joaquin, one of the richest agricultural areas in the entire world, has seen the salinity of its water tables increase with each gallon of imported water. Water tables contaminated by salt that are close to the topsoil sterilize the soil and make it useless except for very salt-tolerant crops. In addition to on-farm salt purification systems, drainage canals need to be built that can

A Water Market

Each year, municipalities and some individuals in a number of Southern California ground-water basins buy and sell the rights to use more than 14 billion gallons of water. Similar systems of water markets for both surface and ground water exist in other Western states, such as Colorado and Utah. Yet the idea of a statewide water market seems like nothing less than heresy to many Californians, including most of those who make or try to influence statewide water policy.

Nevertheless, by the early 21st Century some form of a statewide water market will likely exist in California for the same compelling reasons that brought them into being elsewhere. Economically, strong pressures exist to find low-cost ways to allocate California's scarce water. Politically, our system requires consensus to solve policy problems. Of the available options, only a water market can do both.

A water market involves *voluntary* transactions in which water users decide individually whether to use their water or sell it to others who value it more highly. In California, the cost of using water varies enormously, from as little as $2 an acre-foot for many farmers in "water-rich" areas to $200 or more per acre-foot in the "water-poor" areas of Southern California. These large disparities create an enormous

potential for moving water to where its economic benefits are greater.

Further, the voluntary exchange of a market generates strong pressures for stretching available water supplies. Those with access to cheap water will find ways to conserve it and sell their rights to those with greater water requirements. For instance, farmers might switch from water-intensive crops.

Despite the potential desirability of water markets, questions and misconceptions abound:

• Won't a water market stop necessary construction of water projects? No. Markets affect the conservation/ construction balance, but they are not intended to supplant all new water development. For example, a delta transfer facility, like the Peripheral Canal, may still be necessary. But we would expect *fewer* projects to be built as water-poor areas discover that statewide conservation is much cheaper than construction of new dams.

• Wouldn't markets impose large losses on some groups? Not necessarily. Depending upon how it is designed, a market can stem financial losses and assure that all Californians share in the wealth created by a better water policy. More than any other policy option, a market has the potential to achieve consensus of farmers, urban dwellers

effectively carry away subsurface salt—possibly the San Luis Drain can be extended to the Sacramento Delta or a massive pipeline built to the Pacific Ocean. In any case, such plans would be very expensive.

It was once thought that the special advantages of California farmers insulated them from the boom-and-bust cycles faced by farmers elsewhere in the country. Favorable weather and soil conditions allow this state's farmers to plant throughout the year. They can also diversify, hence cover their bets by planting anything from avocados to zucchini—they are not dependent on a single crop as in the Midwest. But in the 1980s, farm exports decreased, especially for cotton, wheat, and rice. This development was crucial because one-third of all acres planted in California are for export. Moreover, farmers had bought a great deal of land in the 1970s and had gone heavily into debt to do so. Overproduction, lower commodity prices, and shrunken markets make

and environmentalists, in both water-poor and water-rich areas.

By moving water, doesn't a market threaten significant environmental damage to some areas? No. Many environmentalists favor markets because they rely more on conservation and not just on construction. However, under *any* future water policy, water will move among basins. Transfers under a market should be monitored by a public agency to ensure environmental safeguards.

• Because a market increases the cost of using water, won't it drive farmers out of business? No. In areas, such as the southern San Joaquin Valley, a market will increase supplies of affordable water. In others, farmers will find profit in selling both water and crops. Some support industries built around specific crops could suffer (while others gain), but mechanisms to mitigate large losses could and should be developed.

• Wouldn't a water market be difficult to implement? Yes. But so will any solutions to our complex water problems. In the case of water markets, much of the groundwork already exists. Some legal barriers to water sales have already been overcome. To achieve the benefits of a market, we must convert, wherever feasible, ill-defined water rights into *explicit* own-

ership rights that would be transferable through either permanent sales or temporary leases, subject to environmental and other safeguards.

None of this will happen, of course, unless the Legislature takes a new policy direction. To allay current fears and demonstrate the practicality of water markets, the Legislature should promote studies that quantify a market's benefits, drawbacks and costs, and educate Californians about water-policy choices. Finally, we should develop management systems to protect ground-water users in export areas and improve existing management in import areas.

Change in California's water policy is inevitable. Today, we still have an opportunity to shape our water destiny. The alternative is planning by crisis, which almost always leads to dire environmental, social and economic disruption. Traditional approaches that emphasize construction, such as the governor's recent water plan, continue to fail. To secure an economically and politically sensible future, we had better get used to "newfangled" ideas such as a water market.

SOURCE: "If Water-Rich Californians Could Sell, We'd All Profit," by N. Y. Moore and T. H. Quinn, *Los Angeles Times*, September, 17, 1984, pt. II, p. 6. Copyright 1984, Los Angeles Times. Reprinted by permission.

it difficult for California farmers to make payments. Foreclosures and bank-ruptcies are up, and land values are down.[17] In addition, the Reagan Admin-istration cut farm price supports, a good example of how decisions made in Washington, D.C., affect California. (Federalism is the topic of the next chapter.)

Recent studies by the University of California, the California Employment Development Department, and the *Sacramento Bee* have shed considerable light on the situation of California's farm laborers.[18] About three-fourths of these workers were born and raised in Mexico, and they move around California following the harvest in a generally south to north pattern, usually working for a particular employer for only two to six weeks. They are employed for about half of the year and are paid hourly or piece-rate, with the latter paying more. Farmworkers live in poverty, are ill-fed and poorly housed; proper sanitation and nutrition are serious problems; many suffer illness from pesticides or work-related accidents. Medical care is inadequate, especially for pregnant women and new babies. Dental care and eye care are usually not available. Many farm laborers are illiterate, even in their first language, and the children of migrant workers often must work in the fields themselves, thus furthering the illiteracy problem. Those children who do go to school must frequently move from school to school, receiving only a sporadic education—they even-tually drop out of school entirely. As growers must compete with low-cost foreign competition, they turn to mechanization rather than hand labor, espe-cially in the tomato, carrot, and cotton harvests, but also in orchards and vineyards.

Farm laborers have been organized for over two decades under the United Farm Workers (UFW), led by César Chavez. This union is very active politi-cally; for example, in 1982 Chavez contributed $660,000 to political candidates, which is more money than that given by any of the following groups: the California Medical Association, United for California (various large corpora-tions), the realtors, and the growers. The UFW and growers have clashed repeatedly over the Agricultural Labor Relations Board (ALRB), which was originally created in 1975 to bring peace to California's fields. The initial members of the board were appointed by Gov. Jerry Brown and were biased in favor of the UFW. Recent members have been chosen by Gov. George Deukme-jian and are equally pro-grower. In addition, Deukmejian appointed a very controversial general counsel for the board whose job it is to decide which complaints from growers and farmworkers shall be dismissed, which shall be settled administratively, and which must be brought to the board for final decision.

EDUCATION

Education is an important and expensive state activity: approximately 33 percent of the state budget is spent on elementary and secondary education, and an additional 13 percent is spent on higher education. Proposition 13 of June 1978 (the Jarvis–Gann Initiative) substantially reduced local property tax revenues and forced school districts to rely heavily on state aid. The state pays approximately 80 percent of local school costs, about three-fourths of which are for salaries and benefits. Teachers' unions urge the state legislature to increase state aid, pointing out that class sizes are the largest in the nation and that prior to the establishment of the state lottery, California ranked in the bottom tenth of the states in elementary and secondary educational expenditures expressed as a percent of personal income. However, spending expressed as a percent of income is a misleading statistic because this is a wealthy state, and a low spending percentage still amounts to a great deal of money. Moreover, we spend less because we also rank very low in terms of the percentage of our population who are age 5 to 17. In addition, California spends much less per pupil on school administration and transportation than do other states.

State funding of elementary and secondary education is supposed to be guided by the state supreme court's ruling in the case of *Serrano v. Priest.* In that case, the court declared unconstitutional the manner in which the property tax was used to finance public schools. The court decided that because certain school districts had a higher tax *base* (in terms of industrial, commercial, or residential real estate), they were able to set a lower tax *rate* and still generate *higher* revenue for schools. The state supreme court ruled that this method of financing schools violated the equal protection clause of the California Constitution. (Since the U.S. Supreme Court has ruled that this method of school funding does not violate the equal protection clause of the U.S. Constitution, the *Serrano* decision is an example of the "independent state grounds" doctrine described in Chapter 8. The California Supreme Court may use the state constitution as grounds for a more expansive, but not more restrictive, interpretation of constitutional rights than is allowed by the U.S. Constitution.) The reasoning of the state's highest court was that the property tax, as then administered, made the quality of a student's education (expressed in terms of the amount of money spent per pupil) dependent on the presence of nearby industry or high-priced homes. The California Supreme Court ordered the governor and the state legislature to devise an acceptable plan to pay for the education of more than 4.4 million elementary and secondary school students. Whether the court's requirements have been met is a matter of legal controversy.

Public opinion polls indicate that however schools may be financed, taxpayers feel that they are not getting their money's worth. Many parents and employers, to say nothing of elementary and secondary students themselves, are concerned that many young people are graduating from the state's high schools without mastering basic skills in reading, writing, and mathematics. In 1976, the legislature passed the Pupil Proficiency Law, which mandates testing of students in grades three, six, eight, ten, and twelve. Standards of proficiency are determined by local school districts, and those students who fail can be denied high school diplomas.

If the minimum competency of students can be tested, why not test the competency of faculty as well? California now requires beginning elementary and secondary school teachers to pass a basic skills test in reading, writing, and computation. Two authorities on education have written that the declining quality of the state's elementary and secondary teachers is the public schools' toughest problem.[19] They cite the following evidence of deterioration: scores on the Scholastic Aptitude Test (SAT) for prospective teachers have fallen precipitously in recent years; surveys of college students show that potential teachers are weak in English and mathematics; only two-thirds of those taking the California Basic Educational Skills Test mentioned earlier can pass it; those people who leave teaching are generally the youngest and the most competent. Various explanations have been offered for the decline in teacher quality, but probably the most persuasive is that the 1980s offer many career possibilities for capable young women. Whereas once they were steered into teaching, nursing, or librarianship, women now can pursue a wide range of fields including business management, medicine, and law. In addition, elementary and secondary teaching is perceived by many talented people as lacking in prestige, as stressful, and sometimes as violent. Moreover, beginning salaries are lower than in almost every other profession requiring a college degree.

In 1983, the state legislature responded to public dissatisfaction with the general quality of education by passing landmark legislation known as the Hart–Hughes Act. More than 490 pages long and contained in two volumes, this comprehensive act is outlined here:

The Hart–Hughes Education Reform Act of 1983 (SB 813)

Statewide Graduation Requirements
- three years of English and social science, two years of mathematics and science, one year of fine arts or foreign language (not since 1969 has California had statewide rather than just local requirements)

Curricula, New Programs, Instructional Time
- money provided for summer school classes
- increased money for textbooks in grades K–12 (money had never been previously provided for textbooks in grades 9–12)
- expanded academic and career counseling
- **fiscal** incentives to encourage year-round use of schools
- both school day and school year lengthened (a very expensive change)

Student Discipline
- mandatory suspension or expulsion for weapons possession, robbery, and drug sales

Teachers and Administrators
- beginning teacher salaries increased to attract more competent people
- mentor teacher program established in which outstanding teachers receive an additional $4,000 to assist other instructors and to develop curriculum
- lifetime teaching credential eliminated (teachers must complete continuing education courses to maintain their credential)
- rules changed to make it easier to discipline or dismiss incompetent teachers and administrators
- new program initiated for selecting, training, and evaluating school principals

Fiscal Aspects
- state aid increased by approximately 8 percent per district
- financed by amending the property tax laws to increase revenues and by increasing income taxes

The Hart–Hughes Act is intended to deal with issues such as students taking too few demanding courses, too short a school day and school year, poorly qualified teachers, and the watering down of academic standards. It is frequently said that "there's many a slip betwixt cup and lip"; therefore, it may take quite a few years to see if the legislature's good intentions and the public's increased spending will produce measurable results. Clearly the number of mathematics and science courses being taught has increased, despite critical teacher shortages in these subject areas. The number of vocational courses taught has decreased, which has led some critics to claim the Hart–Hughes Act favors college-bound students.

The decline in the number of vocational courses taught has exacerbated the already serious problem of school dropouts, as more young people considering quitting school find fewer courses for them to take. More than 30 percent of all California students drop out before completing high school, a dramatic increase from the 1972 dropout rate of 20 percent. The rate for blacks and Latinos is 43 percent and is especially serious in the Los Angeles Unified School District, where Latinos constitute a majority of the students. The human dimension of the dropout statistic is that dropouts find it much more difficult to secure steady employment later in life, and they may end up on welfare or may turn to crime.

Another vexing problem is the state's shortage of classrooms. There is presently serious overcrowding in California schools, but the problem will even intensify because the current enrollment of 4.4 million students is expected to increase to 5 million by 1994. Unless the classroom shortage is corrected, it may undermine any beneficial effects of the Hart–Hughes Act. In 1986, the legislature developed a massive 5-year, $5 billion school construction program. The plan relies on bond issues appearing on the 1986 and 1988 ballots, state tidelands oil revenue, and school district fees levied upon real estate developers. The program also includes financial incentives for local districts to adopt year-round schools as a way of making the most of current space.

In the field of higher education, California is guided by the Master Plan for Highway Education, which specifies the functions of the University of California, the California State University System, and the community colleges. (The governing boards of California higher education will be discussed in Chapter 6.) The University of California provides higher education in the fields of liberal arts and the sciences, and in professional fields such as law and medicine. It awards the bachelor's, master's and Ph.D. degrees and conducts a substantial amount of basic research. Those seeking undergraduate admission must be in the top eighth of the state's graduating high school classes. The California State University System also provides higher education in the liberal arts and sciences and trains many of the state's elementary and secondary school teachers.

The CSU System awards the bachelor's and master's degrees and, jointly with private universities and the University of California, the Ph.D. degree. Entering undergraduates must have graduated in the top third of the year's high school classes. The California community college system, the nation's largest two-year system, offers postsecondary instruction leading to the A.A. (Associate of Arts) degree. More than three-fourths of all community college students attend part-time; approximately 3 percent transfer to four-year institutions to finish their education. The community colleges are open to all high school graduates or to persons eighteen years of age or older who can profit from the instruction offered.

The California community college system is a truly massive operation: it consists of 70 districts with 106 colleges. Total full-time and part-time enrollment is *twice* the combined total of UC and CSU system enrollments and is one-fifth of all community college enrollment in the nation. The community colleges used to receive about half of their revenue from property taxes and were hit hard by Proposition 13. They now receive a higher percentage of their revenue from the state government than do elementary and secondary schools. Given these circumstances, can the community colleges maintain their tradition of local autonomy? Funding from the state is becoming increasingly restricted as the state government seeks to force local districts to establish priorities among programs. For example, the state does not want to pay for personal improvement or recreational courses, and it has established fees of $50 per semester for students taking six or more units. In 1986, a state commission created to review the Master Plan for Higher Education urged that the community colleges maintain their policy of open access, but limit the number of remedial courses each student can take. The commission also suggested that the community colleges require the testing, assessment, and counseling of all students and that enrollment in particular classes be restricted to those who are qualified to do the course work. Other observers would like to change the way the community colleges receive state aid. The present system based on number of students enrolled might be changed to a formula reflecting not only the number of hours students spend in class, but also fixed costs such as physical plant and libraries.

As noted earlier, universities are necessary to support California's advanced industrialism. The state has many excellent private institutions; in addition the University of California has 9 campuses serving approximately 145,000 students and the California State University System has 19 campuses with 320,000 students, which makes the latter the largest system of its kind in the nation. Despite these impressive figures, California still has a lower percentage of people attending colleges and universities awarding the baccalaureate and higher degrees than the national average. Current issues facing public higher education include the CSU system's proposal to grant its own Ph.D. degree, which touched off a nasty turf war with the University of California, and inadequate financial support from the state government despite the receipt of lottery revenues. Leaders of faculty unions point out that salaries lag behind those in other states and that valuable faculty members are being lured away by other states or private industry. Other issues include research for military and defense purposes, and agricultural research at the University of California. With regard to UC agricultural research, which has greatly contributed to farm productivity, have grants from private farm interests induced public university employees to perform what is really private research? Has such research favored large farmers over small farmers?

WELFARE, HEALTH, AND HOUSING

After education, the next most important component of the state budget is welfare and health, which constitutes about 30 percent of the budget. The major welfare programs are Aid to Families with Dependent Children (AFDC), Supplemental Security Income (SSI/SSP), general relief, food stamps, and Social Services (Title XX of the Social Security Act). Aid to Families with Dependent Children is the largest assistance program and it provides grants to poor families in which one parent is missing or involuntarily unemployed. Most AFDC families are headed by a woman. Half of the program is financed by the federal government, with the state paying most of the rest, and the counties paying a smaller portion. Standards of eligibililty and the level of benefits are set by the state government, and AFDC recipients also use many of the other programs, especially Medi-Cal (described later). Supplemental Security Income (SSI/SSP) benefits aged, blind, and disabled persons with low incomes and few assets; because of the characteristics of SSI/SSP recipients, this program does not prompt bitter political disputes in the state legislature as does AFDC. Many recipients of the latter program are minority-group members, many are unwed mothers, many are illegitimate children, and some are able-bodied men. General relief is financed entirely by the counties and provides income for people who cannot qualify for either of the previous programs, for example, male transients or alcoholics. County governments determine eligibility rules and frequently impose work requirements—payments vary widely from county to county. Food stamps are a federal program in which the state and counties pay half of the administrative costs: low-income individuals are given coupons which serve as money at grocery stores. The Social Services Program is intended to promote social goals such as keeping families intact and preventing child abuse, promoting family planning, and allowing elderly or disabled persons to live in their own homes rather than in institutions. For example, the program furnishes day care for children and homemaker support services for senior citizens. In sum, California provides a wide range of social welfare services. Moreover, benefit levels are high: California is second in AFDC and food-stamp benefits among mainland states (excluding Alaska and Hawaii). Not only is this a wealthy state with the resources to pay for programs, but AFDC and SSI/SSP grants go up automatically without a politically dangerous vote required by the state legislature because these grants are indexed to the California Necessities Index.

In 1985, Republican Governor George Deukmejian and the state legislature, controlled heavily by Democrats, reached a historic compromise on the controversial issue of workfare. Conservatives had long favored the idea of requiring welfare recipients to perform public service work as a requirement for receiving their grant, and liberals had previously regarded such a plan as punitive "slave labor." Liberals agreed to the compromise because they received in return a "latchkey children" program in which government-run childcare centers would provide services for children left unattended while their parents are at work. (Because such children must carry a key to let themselves into an empty home when they return from school, they are referred to as latchkey children.) In addition, research indicated that welfare dependency was clearly increasing; for example, families were staying on welfare longer than they were a decade earlier and were receiving no earnings from work. The new program is the "biggest single attack on the cycle of welfare dependency in the country."[20] Moreover, the plan is essentially the same as a successful pilot program in San Diego County in which participants overwhelmingly said that the program's mandatory job-seeking requirements and work requirements were fair to them. Finally, labor unions, which had blocked similar proposals in the past, withdrew their opposition after getting provisions into the law prohibiting workfare people from taking the jobs of regular employees.

The workfare law, known as GAIN (Greater Avenues to Independence), concentrates on the one-third of the adults on welfare who are able-bodied mothers with school-age children. Other welfare recipients, for example mothers of preschool children, may participate voluntarily. Participants are then screened: non-English speakers receive English language instruction; those who have worked in the last two years are enrolled in a three-month "job club" emphasizing skills that will lead to an interview with a prospective employer. If the job club does not lead to employment, the next step is either two years of on-the-job training, subsidized private employment, or vocationally oriented community college. Early experience with the program indicates that more than half of the participants need remedial education in reading and basic arithmetic. Participants must negotiate a contract binding upon both the recipient and the welfare bureaucracy. Those who have not worked in the last two years are immediately enrolled in a suitable training program. All persons unemployed after completing a training program must work for public or nonprofit agencies for one year in what is really the work-for-welfare component of the program. These jobs are valued at the average hourly rate of starting positions in California and are intended to be preparation for permanent employment, not make-work positions. If a permanent position has not been secured during this year of government work, the recipient returns to the training cycle. Participants who do not follow the program's rules, for example, by not showing up at their workfare job, lose a fraction of the welfare checks.

The workfare law is a significant piece of legislation—only time (and follow-up studies) will tell if it meets its objectives of moving people off the welfare rolls and onto the work rolls. Two other welfare-related areas needing attention are collection of child-support payments and excessive administrative errors in the welfare program. California is not particularly forceful in its child-support laws—other states are much more likely to send delinquent parents who do not pay to jail. About 350,000 children in California are receiving welfare because their parents do not pay court-ordered child support. In a recent fiscal year, this state ranked thirty-fifth in percentage of AFDC payments recovered through child-support collections. Furthermore, California had to pay the federal government $35 million in penalties in 1985 based on its excessive 1981 error rate in welfare administration. Twenty-six states had to pay $81 million in penalties, but California's total was far higher than the second-ranking state, which paid $6.8 million. The error rate is defined as payments to ineligible persons or overpayments to qualified recipients.

The most costly element in California's welfare and health benefits system is the Medi-Cal program, which is financed half by the federal government and half by the state. Minimum levels of services are established by the federal government, which California supplements, as well as optional categories of coverage whose cost the national government will share with California. Thirty-two services fall into the latter category; California provides thirty of these services, with the national average among states being eighteen optional services provided.[21] Federal law requires that all people receiving AFDC or SSI/SSP also receive Medi-Cal.

Because of rapidly rising costs, the state legislature in 1982 instituted sweeping changes in the Medi-Cal program by turning to competition among health care providers as the means to drive down costs. Prior to that time, the poor person chose a doctor or hospital to visit, and then the state (and the federal government) paid the bill. This is known as the fee-for-service system, in which the doctor or hospital sets the fees—the potential for steep cost increases is obvious. In 1982, the legislature created a Medi-Cal hospital negotiator (known informally as the "Medi-Cal Czar") to procure the most economical hospital care for the state's poor. A seven-member commission, appointed by the governor and legislative leaders, oversees the negotiator who bargains with providers and signs contracts only with those who offer maximum services for minimum cost at specified rates. (It is important to note that California did not solve the problem of escalating public health care costs by regulating rates as was done by some other states.) The leverage which the negotiator uses is the nearly 3 million Medi-Cal patients who will visit only those health care providers who sign the contracts and thus become Preferred Provider Organizations (PPOs). Wisely, the legislature also gave the same bargaining power to insurance companies such as Blue Cross and Blue Shield to seek lower rates for their insurees. This was done so that health care providers could not shift the lower costs for Medi-Cal recipients on to other patients. Critics of the law claim that hospitals are not giving Medi-Cal patients all of the services that these people need. One unfortunate aspect of the 1982 Medi-Cal reforms is that the state transferred the working poor (classified as "medically indigent adults") to county care, but gave the counties only 70 percent of the money formerly spent on their health care. (Chapter 9 will show that the state government regularly unloads responsibilities on local governments without providing sufficient funding.)

In 1984 the state legislature phased out the certificate-of-need requirement which had forced hospitals to justify their equipment purchases or new construction in terms of their service area's need for new services or facilities. The hospitals argued that cost disciplines resulting from the earlier 1982 reforms made certificates of need no longer necessary because competition dictates construction decisions.

Because California has an extraordinarily high concentration of older people, and because the median age in this state is going up, private health care costs and Medi-Cal costs will become an even larger responsibility in the future. In the mid-1980s, reports by the state's "Little Hoover" commission (see Chapter 6) shocked Californians with descriptions of conditions in the state's 22,000 private board-and-care facilities for the elderly, mentally ill, and retarded. The commission found instances of a woman strapped into a bed lying in her own excrement, and of elderly people covered with ants. There were widespread examples of overcrowding, lack of food, poor toilet facilities, and inadequate fire escapes. Board-and-care facilities provide only custodial care, but conditions were not significantly better in the state's 1,200 nursing homes which additionally provide medical care. The legislature responded by passing bills to increase the penalties for neglect or abuse of patients and to improve the training of inspectors employed by the state.

The field of health care is replete with tragic and heartrending situations, but perhaps none is more so than care of the mentally ill. California has long sought humane treatment in this field, going back to the Short–Doyle Act of 1957 (which provides state financial assistance to counties for mental health treatment in local facilities). Counties may either run their own programs or contract with private providers, but in any event are governed by state standards and regulations. The Lanterman–Petris–Short Act of 1967 sought to end the practice of warehousing senile persons and chronic alcoholics in mental hospitals:

> To assure that the state hospitals were not arbitrarily incarcerating the mentally ill, LPS placed restrictions on the power of the courts to commit people to mental hospitals. A disordered person may be involuntarily detained for evaluation and treatment for 72 hours if he shows signs of being a danger to himself or others, or is unable to provide for his personal needs. After medical certification, this period may be followed by 14 days of intense treatment. If the person shows signs of being dangerous during this period, he may be incarcerated for up to 90 days in a treatment facility. For those persons who meet the standard of being "gravely disabled," the court is authorized to appoint a conservator, who may place the mentally ill person in a hospital for a period of one year. The conservatorship automatically expires after one year, but the court may renew it if the person is certified as needing continued treatment by medical personnel. LPS also assures certain civil rights to conservatees in state hospitals. They have the right to confidential correspondence and phone calls, and may refuse shock treatment and lobotomy operations.[22]

The Lanterman–Petris–Short Act sought to reserve state mental hospitals only for those who are a danger to themselves or to others, or who suffer severe psychological disabilities, with senile people and alcoholics being directed to less harsh local facilities. The act was certainly well intentioned at its time of enactment, but it has made it more difficult to meet the needs of today's homeless people (described below).

The theory that has governed California's mental health policy for three decades is **deinstitutionalization.** This has meant getting mentally ill people out of large, isolated, restrictive institutions with their staffing problems into smaller community care facilities closer to their homes that are believed to be more economical, effective, and humane in treatment. Hence the number of patients in state mental hospitals has dropped from 37,500 in 1959 to 5,000 today. But critics of deinstitutionalization now argue that community programs are inadequate to meet the need because counties are unable or unwilling to establish comprehensive mental health treatment programs and that community programs are actually more expensive than state hospitals. They claim that because of economies of scale, hospitals can have sufficient staff, pay less per patient for the physical plant, and have a higher occupancy rate. Opponents of deinstitutionalization say that it has seriously contributed to the large numbers of people "in the skid rows of cities, where former mental patients are numerous among the homeless and semi-homeless who wander the streets, dine in soup kitchens, sleep when they can afford it in fleabag hotels."[23] According to a mental-health professional who helped draft LPS:

> In our zeal to move people out of very restrictive, very inhumane places, we forgot that there were a whole variety of supports that were provided [by institutions]. . . . We had a simplistic notion that basically what you could do is take people out of institutions, move them into the community and provide outpatient mental health care. But what we forgot is that institutions provide people with shelter, food, health care, and a whole variety of other basic human needs.[24]

Psychiatrists in the 1950s supported deinstitutionalization because they had great faith in tranquilizers and other drugs as a way of helping people live outside of institutions. Now, it is not at all certain how well the drugs work or even whether they help or harm the patient. Drugs may be used merely to make troublesome patients more manageable or to get people through the bureaucratic system as quickly as possible without really doing anything for them.

Yet another vexing public policy issue is supplying affordable housing for middle-income people or those of modest means. Sunday editions of major California newspapers regularly publish an "affordability index" showing how much income is necessary to purchase a local home—most Californians are priced out of the market, especially first-time home buyers. Residents of this state have to spend 48 percent more of their income on housing than do residents of other states, but their salaries are only 8 percent higher than the national average. Hence it is not surprising that California is ranked forty-eighth in homeownership rate. Will California's economic growth be throttled by high housing prices? Various companies have indicated that they do not want to stay in California, or relocate here, because housing costs force them to pay their employees more here than elsewhere. The slow-growth policies of many California cities (see Chapter 9) restrict the number of housing units that can be built. Simple supply and demand bids up per-unit costs, and it thus eliminates moderately priced housing. Developers fees (also Chapter 9) have the same effect. Stringent environmental regulations and building codes cause delay, string out the permit approval process, and ultimately increase housing costs. In any event, quick solutions are nowhere to be found. Providing affordable housing may be one of those issues that state policymakers, or government policymakers at any level, are unable to solve at reasonable cost.

One solution that has been attempted at the local level, with mixed success, is rent control. In fact, about half of California's population lives in communities with rent control. Proponents point out that it saves money for renters by preventing rent-gouging by landlords. Opponents claim that rent control aids renters in the short run but seriously harms them in the long run because it reduces the supply of rental housing. Investors would rather spend their money on more profitable office buildings or invest in cities without rent control. (However, all rent control ordinances enacted in California so far exempt new rental housing.) Finally, opponents argue that under rent control, landlords will not perform needed maintenance and will let units deteriorate; they will also spend less for heating and lighting. These claims and counterclaims were carefully examined by a commission appointed by Los Angeles Mayor Tom Bradley to study that city's rent control law. The commission's findings surprised both sides and pleased neither side.[25] Not only did the law have little effect on the rate of increase in rents compared to nearby cities with no rent control, but it also reduced only slightly landlord profits compared to those of landlords in adjacent cities. Rent control neither saved tenants much money (only $7 per household per month), nor had much effect on owners' incentives to maintain apartment buildings.

PUBLIC SAFETY

Public concern over crime, particularly violent crime, was one of the leading issues of the 1980s. The list of "California Rankings" on page 7 indicates that this state does indeed have one of the nation's highest crime rates. Elected officials, especially the state legislature, responded with "get-tough" oratory, defined more acts as criminal, and increased prison terms for present offenses. However, increasing the *penalty* for getting caught, without increasing the currently very low *chances* of being caught, is misguided. A stiff prison term unlikely to be served does not deter crime.

Paul Gann, coauthor of the 1978 tax-cutting Proposition 13, in 1982 persuaded voters to pass a ballot initiative known as the Victim's Bill of Rights. Provisions of this far-reaching measure address the use of seized evidence, the diminished-capacity defense, bail, plea bargaining, restitution for victims, and the right to safe schools.

The Gann crime initiative allows the use in a criminal trial of evidence seized by police through eavesdropping, wiretapping, and searches of persons and property. Approximately fifty state supreme court rulings that required stricter rules of evidence for California trials than are required by the U.S. Supreme Court were negated. The state legislature is allowed to exclude by a two-thirds vote certain evidence from trials. Persons who had previously been convicted of a serious felony now receive an extra five years of sentence if they are convicted of another serious felony. This provision may be the most important part of the law because it results in more guilty pleas by defendants who are

SOURCE: Wallmeyer Cartoons

afraid to risk going on trial, being convicted, and then having their prior conviction give them a longer term for the current offense. In fact, sentences enhanced by a prior conviction must be served one after another.

Another provision completely abolishes the defense of diminished capacity in the guilt phase of a criminal hearing and establishes a new definition of legal insanity. Pretrial bail is no longer guaranteed and is now to be granted only if the accused person is not a threat to public safety. When a judge grants or denies bail, he or she must state why in the court record. Critics charge that this section of the initiative reverses the presumption that a person is innocent until proven guilty. Also on the same ballot as the Gann crime initiative was a constitutional amendment proposed by the legislature to limit bail. (This amendment is Proposition 4 in Figure 5.1, and the Gann initiative is Proposition 8.) The legislature's amendment was approved, and since it is more carefully drawn than Gann's, it probably will not be struck down by the courts.

The Gann initiative restricts plea bargaining in cases involving twenty-five different crimes. **Plea bargaining** is the practice of pleading guilty to a reduced charge or sentence rather than standing trial on a more serious offense. Plea bargaining is often described as unjust because a guilty person can escape paying the full penalty for his or her crime. District attorneys , on the other hand, point out that plea bargaining relieves congested court calendars. If all cases were to go to trial, some cases would have to be dismissed because they could not receive the speedy trial required by law. In addition, "in many instances, by the time a criminal case comes to trial, evidence for some of the charges may be difficult if not impossible to obtain. Unexpected developments can arise, turning the pursuit of a conviction into a hopeless venture."[26] In short, a total ban on plea bargaining leads to unfortunate rigidity. Because of some peculiar wording in the initiative, most plea bargaining now takes place in Municipal Court rather than in Superior Court.

Another section of the initiative requires criminals to pay restitution to their victims. California has long had a somewhat similar program; in fact, this was the first state to compensate the victims of violent crime. Victims must be informed that they have a right to file a claim for losses not covered by insurance. Such losses are medical expenses (California is one of the few states to also include psychological counseling expenses), funeral expenses, loss of income, job rehabilitation, and lawyers' fees. There are dollar limits on the amount that may be claimed. In addition, the Gann initiative gives victims or their surviving next of kin the right to attend all sentencing and parole hearings and to make a statement. Probation officers are required to notify them of the date of the hearing. Finally, the initiative places in the constitution an "inalienable right to attend campuses which are safe, secure, and peaceful" for all public elementary and secondary school students and staff members. However, the broad terms *safe, secure,* and *peaceful* are not defined. Teachers' unions fear that scarce school funds will have to be spent on additional school guards. Can students refuse to attend schools which they consider unsafe?

There can be no doubt that the Gann crime initiative is a comprehensive measure. Cases are now working their way through the court system challenging a number of its provisions, and it may take some years before the courts give specific meanings for its terms.

California is seriously short of prison cells. As the legislature and the judiciary responded to the public's concern about crime, more people were sent to prison and for longer terms: between 1981 and 1986, the prison population doubled. But prisons to house those sentenced were not built, and the state's prisons have far more inmates than the structures were intended to hold. Prison construction is expensive, and few people want a new prison built in their community. California prisons are dangerously overcrowded, a condition which leads to a constant threat of violence against both guards and inmates. Putting two prisoners in a cell built for one (double-celling) is very common. Toilet facilities are poor, cells are dirty, lighting is inadequate, and prisoners feel that there is not enough exercise time. The State Department of Health Services has refused to license three of the four prison hospitals, and the state fire marshal will not give these three a fire safety clearance. To make matters worse, today's prisoners are younger and more violent. In contrast with inmates of earlier years, they are more likely to have been sentenced for a violent crime than for a property crime. Many have makeshift weapons, and racially oriented gangs are commonplace. Although guards are predominantly white, racial minorities constitute more than 60 percent of the prisoners. As recently as 1970, racial minorities were only 30 percent of the prison population. The potential for a serious prison uprising is clearly present.

As public fear of crime has increased, so have handgun sales. Gun deaths have risen as well; in fact, the incidence of homicide by guns per 100,000 people is more than *fifty* times higher in America than in England, West Germany,

Norway, Greece, or Japan.[27] Seventy percent of the homicides involve disputes between family members or friends, or are "lovers'" quarrels. These murders are acts of passion, not premeditation. In an attempt to limit such killings, an initiative statute was placed on the ballot in 1982. That measure provided that all handguns must be registered with the attorney general or would become illegal. Further, anyone carrying an unregistered handgun outside of home or business would receive a mandatory sentence of at least six months in jail. In addition, only registered handguns could be sold, thus putting a cap on the state's number of handguns. The prison sentence for illegal gun sales would be one year. The initiative placed no restrictions on rifles, and it prohibited the legislature from making any restrictions on rifles or banning the ownership of handguns. Despite the initiative's limited effect, it was bitterly opposed by the National Rifle Association (NRA) and the Gun Owners of California, two politically potent groups. Pro-gun groups stressed that the measure would infringe on a constitutionally protected right and that it would make criminals more likely than law-abiding people to have guns. The proposition was defeated by a margin of 63 percent to 37 percent.

OTHER ISSUES

According to historian James S. Holliday, Emeritus Director of the California Historical Society, it has always been the case that California's most important export is images: the streets are paved with gold, anything is possible, this state does not require you to conform. Note that California's founding fathers were the gold-seeking 49ers, and consider how this contrasts with having the Mayflower Pilgrims as founders. Holliday contends that two key viewpoints have contested for preeminence since the time of statehood. On the one hand is the miner's psychology that people can do whatever they want with the natural endowments of California; on the other is the psychology of naturalist John Muir that he would always side with nature against man.[28] In any event, Californians have always had a tendency to experiment: recent policymaking in the areas of education reform, workfare, and Medi-Cal finance, to say nothing of the plethora of ballot propositions described in Chapter 5, confirms this. Carey McWilliams places great faith in "the factor of newness, that is, the willingness to experiment simply because the weight of tradition is less" here than elsewhere.[29]

At the beginning of this chapter we indicated that one of the key characteristics of California is diversity. Consider the variety of climate, terrain, and natural features exhibited by this state's mountains, deserts, and coastal areas. Mt. Whitney, at 14,494 feet, is the highest point in the United States outside Alaska, but only 60 miles away is Death Valley at 282 feet below sea level, which is the lowest point in the Western Hemisphere. However, the diversity is not merely in the land; it is in the people as well. One sympathetic observer of the California scene has written

Half the people living here have arrived from somewhere else. If California has a working history, it really consists of this intersection of pasts from every direction, from Arkansas and Sonora and Vietnam and Bengal and Armenia and Canada and

Italy. That is what California is, an intersection, a world crossroads of extraordinary and sometimes maddening diversity. There is enormous interchange and energy and vitality and motion and flux.[30]

One out of every five residents of the state is a Latino, and 7.5 percent of the state's people are black. Another 7 percent are Filipinos, Chinese, Japanese, Vietnamese, Native Americans, and many more people of other ethnic or racial backgrounds. Will these various people reach an amicable understanding with the white majority and with each other? Many minority group members are poor, and therefore are intensive users of social services such as education, welfare, and Medi-Cal. Decisions made in the public policy arena have a direct and immediate effect on their well-being.

One emerging public policy issue that will surely test California's innovativeness is the "comparable worth" issue, which has arisen because women working for California state government earn only 80 percent of what men earn. Female-dominated jobs such as nurses or office secretaries pay 20 percent less than male-dominated jobs. The importance of the issue was underscored by a 1984 report of the United States Department of Labor that announced that for the first time, more women over the age of twenty were working in paying jobs than those without paying jobs. (In 1948, only 30 percent of American women had paying jobs.) A federal district court judge ordered the state of Washington to award $800 million in back pay to female workers because he found a 20 percent pay differential in jobs having the same intrinsic value. (A federal court of appeal later reversed this decision. The legal issues involved in comparable worth will ultimately be decided by the United States Supreme Court).[31] Opponents of the comparable worth concept argue that there is no truly objective way to establish the worth of quite dissimilar jobs—they prefer to allow the interplay of supply and demand to set salaries. Proponents believe that the following factors can be evaluated to determine the value of a job: knowledge, mental demands, problem-solving aspects, skill level, responsibility, accountability, effort, and working conditions. Opponents attribute pay differentials to the fact that women must sometimes take time off from their jobs because of pregnancy, women may be more recent entrants into the job market, and women may have fewer years of seniority. Opponents further argue that comparable worth will price women out of some jobs, and that it will result in taxpayers or consumers footing a tremendous bill. If the comparable worth concept were to be fully implemented in California, it would take a giant bureaucracy to reset all state and local wages (and ultimately private-sector salaries as well). In the resetting process, some male-dominated jobs would have to be downgraded, because if all female-dominated jobs were upgraded, massive inflation would result. Deciding which male-dominated jobs to downgrade involves immense political dangers. At the present time, the comparable worth issue is being handled as a negotiable item in the collective bargaining process between state management and public employee unions.

What can we conclude about bustling, restless California? Some observers note that the symbol of the State of California is the mighty California grizzly bear—but the grizzly has been extinct since 1911. Nevertheless, life in California has a way of encouraging pessimists and sobering optimists. In a recent statewide poll, nearly four out of five Californians rated this state as one of the best places to live; only one in fifty say that it is a poor place to live.[32] Men and women of goodwill might take note of the state flower, the golden poppy, that is said to be found blooming somewhere in California throughout the year.

It was the lure of high Sierra gold that triggered the rush to California in 1849. In those days the American economy was based on dollars redeemable in gold. Today the economy and its currency are based on the natural riches of the land and the productivity of the people. The rush to California continues.

The Golden State possesses vast natural resources—water and trees, wind and sun, geysers and gas. It also possesses the intellectual and spiritual energies of people who still are pathfinders and pioneers, dreamers and builders.[33]

SUMMARY

In this introductory chapter, we have considered the many vexing policy issues on the state's political agenda. Economic prosperity, environmental protection, wise growth management, energy sources, transportation problems, an adequate supply of water, educational policy, public safety, and other issues are matters of vital concern. Although these problems are serious, close attention to them can prevent their getting out of hand. With a vigilant citizenry, dedicated public officials, and perhaps a little bit of luck, we can fulfill the expectations of those first hearty souls who came to California looking for a better life.

DISCUSSION QUESTIONS

1. What characteristics make California a highly advanced industrial society?
2. Name some of the environmental dangers threatening Californians and indicate what is being done about these conditions.
3. What are California's sources of energy? Which sources are we likely to rely upon more heavily in the future?
4. The private automobile is the chief means of transporting Californians. Name other modes of transportation now used or proposed for the future.
5. Why is water policy such an explosive issue in California politics?
6. California, which is a heavily urbanized advanced industrial society, is also the nation's number one agricultural state. Explain this seeming contradiction.
7. In addition to a lack of money, what are some of the issues facing public elementary, secondary, and higher education?
8. What are the major welfare programs in California? How is workfare intended to solve the problem of welfare dependency?
9. Medi-Cal is the most costly element in California's system of welfare and health benefits. How has the state legislature sought to rein in spiraling costs?
10. How has California recently tried to deal with the problem of crime?

NOTES

1. Carey McWilliams, *California: The Great Exception* (New York: A.A. Wyn, 1949), p. 17.
2. Kevin McCarthy and R.B. Valdez, "California's Demographic Future," in *California Policy Choices*, Vol. 2, ed. John Kirlin and Donald Winkler (Sacramento: Sacramento Public Affairs Center, 1985), chap. 3.
3. James D. Houston, *Californians: Searching for the Golden State* (New York: Knopf, 1982), p. 4.
4. Ted K. Bradshaw, "New Issues for California, the World's Most Advanced Industrial Society," *Public Affairs Report*, University of California at Berkeley, 17 (August 1976): 1–3; Bradshaw, "Trying out the Future," *The Wilson Quarterly* (Summer 1980): 71–73; Everett Ladd, *The American Polity*, 2nd ed. (New York: Norton, 1987), chap. 2; John Naisbitt, *Megatrends* (New York: Warner Books, 1982), chap. 1.
5. "The Risks of Proposition 65" (editorial), *Sacramento Bee*, October 16, 1986, p. B10. All other quotations are from "No on Toxics Initiative" (editorial), *Los Angeles Times*, October 29, 1986, pt. II, p. 6.
6. Kim Murphy, "Toxic Fires: Peril Can Be Anywhere," *Los Angeles Times*, July 3, 1985, pt. I, p. 1; see also Zenia Cleigh, " 'Monstrous' Tidal Wave Poised to Engulf State," *San Diego Tribune*, January 27, 1986, p. A1; Mark Stein, "Capri Controversy Marks State Superfund's Debut," *Los Angeles Times*, April 3, 1985, pt. I, p. 1.
7. California Energy Commission, *Fifth Biennial Report* (Sacramento: CEC, 1985), p. 32. See also pp. 4, 14, 34–36.
8. "Cogeneration," *Los Angeles Times*, September 23, 1979, pt. IV, p. 1.
9. Herman Kahn, William Brown, and Leon Martel, *The Next 200 Years* (New York: Morrow, 1976), p. 77. A great deal of fusion research is conducted at the Lawrence Livermore Laboratory near San Francisco.
10. California Energy Commission, *Fourth Biennial Report* (Sacramento: CEC, 1983), p. 132. See also "Refrigerators as Villains" (editorial), *Los Angeles Times*, December 28, 1984, pt. II, p. 8.
11. Thomas Dye, *Politics in States and Communities*, 5th ed. (Englewood Cliffs, NJ: Prentice-Hall, 1985), p. 454. When it comes to carrying freight, trains are four times as energy-efficient as are trucks.
12. Assembly Transportation Committee, *California Transportation Today* (Sacramento: California Assembly, 1979), p. 38.
13. California Department of Water Resources, *The California Drought—1977, An Update* (Sacramento, 1977), p. 43.
14. Susan Sward, "California's Water Project—Largest One in the World," *Santa Barbara News-Press*, March 6, 1977, p. A4.
15. *California Drought*, pp. 46, 58. See also p. 10.
16. William L. Kahrl, *The California Water Atlas* (Los Altos, CA: William Kaufmann, 1979), pp. 99–100, 110.
17. Bob Shallit, "California's Hungry Farmers," *Golden State Report* (March 1986): 7–22; Bill Stall, "California: To Grow On?" *Los Angeles Times*, March 16, 1986, pt. V, p. 1.
18. Philip Martin, Richard Mines, and Angela Diaz, "A Profile of California Farmworkers," *California Agriculture* (May–June 1985): 16–18; Rick Rodriquez, "After Twenty Years, Fruit of Their Labor Is Pockets of Progress Amid Poverty," *Sacramento Bee*, March 31, 1985, p. A1; Bob Shallit, "Mechanization Is Taking Root," *Sacramento Bee*, April 1, 1985, p. A9; Stephen Green, "Poor Health Care, Miserable Housing," *Sacramento Bee*, April 4, 1985, p. A1. See also Jim Lewis, "Top Political Contributors," *Sacramento Bee*, February 8, 1983, p. A4; Vic Pollard, "Turbulant Past, Troubled Future," *California Journal* (December 1983): 444.
19. Michael Kirst and James Guthrie, "Declining Teacher Quality: Public Schools' Toughest Problem," *California Journal* (April 1983): 141–144.

20. Vic Pollard, "Workfare: An Unusual Coalition Comes Up with an Innovative Plan," *California Journal* (March 1986): 159. See also T. Anthony Quinn and Ed Salzman, *California Public Administration*, 2nd ed. (Sacramento: California Journal Press, 1982), chap. 3; Michael Wiseman, "Workfare," *California Journal* (July 1985): 289–292; Robert Pruger and Michael Wiseman, "Workfare Wins the Right Converts," *Los Angeles Times*, August 18, 1985, pt. IV, p. 5; David Kirp, "The California Work/Welfare Scheme," *The Public Interest* (spring 1986): 34–48.
21. Elizabeth McGlynn and Joseph Newhouse, "Medi-Cal and Indigent Health Care," in *California Policy Choices*, vol. 2, pp. 96–99.
22. Quinn and Salzman, *California Public Administration*, pp. 65–66.
23. Walter T. Anderson, "Thousands Released; Few Treatment Facilities," *California Journal* (June 1984): 215. See also Kathryn Maney, "The Latest Crisis in Care for the Mentally Ill," *California Journal* (July 1981): 239–241.
24. Quoted in Sherry Bebitch Jeffee, "California: Good Aims, Bad Results," *Los Angeles Times*, March 22, 1987, pt. V, p. 3.
25. Ronald Soble, "Report Finds Rent Law's Impact Has Been Slight," *Los Angeles Times*, April 24, 1985, pt. I, p. 3. See also Patricia Rogero, "The Affordable-housing Hunt," *Golden State Report* (December 1986): 7.
26. "Proposition 8: Serving Justice or Assaulting It?" *Los Angeles Times*, May 3, 1982, pt. I, p. 3. See also Kevin Valine, "Plea Bargaining: The Real World," *California Journal* (July 1981): 252.
27. Bruce Conklin and Richard Sieden, "Gun Deaths," *Public Affairs Report*, University of California at Berkeley, 22 (October 1981): 2.
28. James S. Holliday, "California—Images and Realities" (paper presented at the Second Conference on Research Needs in California Government and Politics, Institute of Governmental Studies, University of California at Berkeley, May 2–3, 1986).
29. Carey McWilliams, "Is California Still Exceptional? A View from a Distance," in *California Perspectives: Four Leaders Look at the State of the State*, ed. Eugene Lee (Berkeley: Institute of Governmental Studies, University of California, 1977), p. 22.
30. Houston, *Californians*, p. 272.
31. Judi Hasson, "Top Issue: The Pay Putdown," *San Diego Union*, September 2, 1984, p. C1; Maria Puente, "Equal Pay," *San Diego Tribune*, May 31, 1984, p. A1; Terri E. Jonisch and Sherry Bebitch Jeffe, "Comparable Worth," *California Journal* (January 1985): 27–29. In 1986, the court gave some indication of how it might rule on comparable worth. In *Bazemore v. Friday* (106 S. Ct. 3000 [1986]), the Supreme Court decided that Title VII of the 1964 Civil Rights Act can be used to correct pay discrimination which began *before* the law took effect.
32. Mervin Field, "Living in California," *California Opinion Index* (November 1985): 1.
33. California Energy Commission, *Fifth Biennial Report*, p. 44.

2

California in the Federal System

Before considering such topics as California politics, the California legislature, or local government in California, it will be helpful to take a look at the constitutional framework in which these activities and institutions are found. We will describe the state constitution and how changes can be made in it. Because California is only one of fifty states, we will also discuss its relationships with the other forty-nine states, especially neighboring ones, and its role as a member of the federal system.

THE CALIFORNIA CONSTITUTION

In 1849, the year of the great gold rush, California drew up its first constitution. A year later, California was admitted into the Union as one provision of the historic Compromise of 1850 (September 9, 1850). The constitution of 1849 proved to be inadequate, and just thirty years later, a new constitution had to be written to meet the needs of the time. The Constitution of 1879 is the present state constitution, although it has been amended (changed in some manner) more than 460 times. The California Constitution is long (more than 100 pages of standard print) and very detailed. Some of its 22 articles are devoted to matters that might better be left to ordinary legislation. Many authorities contend that constitutions should be basic documents that briefly outline the division of powers among the state's executive, legislative, and judicial branches and between state and local governments; set forth a bill of rights specifying citizens' basic liberties; and describe a means for amending the document or calling a constitutional convention. The Constitution of 1879 as originally written was rather stingy in its grants of power to public officials (for example, legislators), especially in financial matters. It severely and narrowly limited official discretion. Therefore, the state constitution has had to be amended hundreds of times, and the amendments have made it even longer. (The use of the **initiative** by interest groups has contributed to this vicious circle. See Chapter 5.) In contrast, the United States Constitution is less than one-fourth as long as the California Constitution and has been amended only twenty-six times, even though it is twice as old.

CHANGING THE CONSTITUTION

Constitutional change can be accomplished in California by any of three processes: constitutional **amendment, constitutional revision,** and the drafting of a wholly new constitution by a **constitutional convention.** Constitutions in general can also be changed more subtly as they are interpreted by courts.

Constitutional Amendment

Most changes in the state constitution have come through constitutional amendments, which must be approved by a two-thirds vote of the state legislature. After legislative approval, these proposed amendments must be finally approved by a **majority vote** of the voters at the next statewide election. Citizens may also amend the constitution by circulating a proposed amendment to obtain voter signatures, and then placing it on the ballot. This initiative route has the same effect as if the legislature had originated the proposal.

Constitutional change by means of amendment is piecemeal and ad hoc—that is, an article or section is added here or another is dropped there. Individually, these changes may not amount to much. But over the years, the amendments that appear and win approval at statewide primary elections and general elections may cumulatively alter the constitution in basic ways.

Constitutional Revision

A constitutional revision commission is used to change substantial amounts of the state constitution at one time. This blue-ribbon commission of distinguished citizens and legislators is selected by the legislature and meets at length to revise whole sections of the constitution. The recommendations of the revision commission must be forwarded to the legislature for its approval by a two-thirds vote before being submitted to the voters. From the early 1960s to the early 1970s, a constitutional revision commission headed by Judge Bruce Sumner substantially modernized and streamlined California's constitution.

Constitutional Convention

If major alteration of the constitution or a wholly new document is necessary, a constitutional convention is called. On five occasions the legislature has asked Californians if they want to have a constitutional convention. Only once—during the tumultuous Depression—have the voters answered affirmatively, and then a surprised legislature refused to carry out the order. The calling of a constitutional convention is not likely at the present time. Constitutions are important and basic documents; although some people are mildly dissatisfied with the present constitution, few want to discard it entirely. Furthermore, many special interests benefit from the existing constitution and might not want a convention tampering with their favorite provisions. In any event, a convention to write a new fundamental law for a state as diverse and factious as California would be a major and conflict-ridden undertaking.

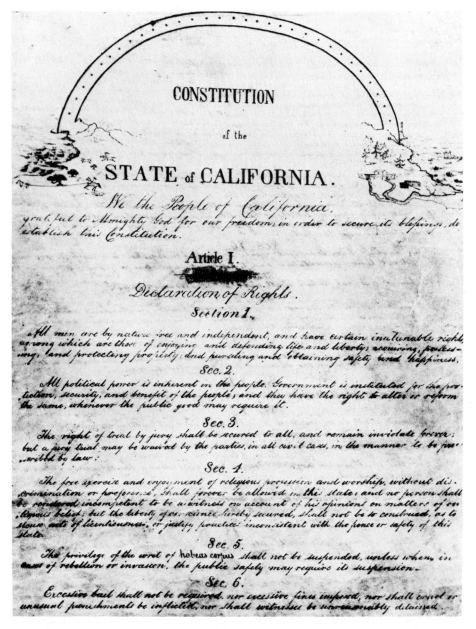

California's multi-cultural heritage is evident in its first constitution, published in 1849 in English and Spanish. Article XI decreed that all future laws be translated into Spanish. The 1879 constitution did not include this provision.

Role of the Courts

"No constitution interprets itself"; that is, no constitution says what its words mean in every situation. This crucial function is performed by the courts in a common-law country like the United States. In applying the words of a very

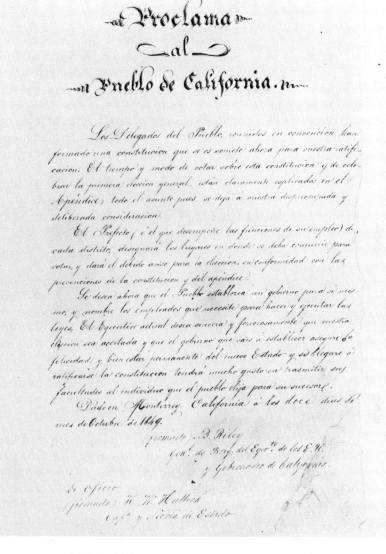

SOURCE: California State Archives, Office of the Secretary of State, Sacramento

old document to a modern situation, judges must of necessity use their own judgment and beliefs concerning what is good public policy for California.

RELATIONS WITH OTHER STATE GOVERNMENTS

Every state government must have relations with other states; even an island state like Hawaii is not exempt. California has certain obligations to other states. For example, the U.S. Constitution (Article IV, Section 1) requires that "full faith and credit shall be given in each state to the public acts, records, and judicial proceedings of every other state." The purpose of this provision (the **full faith and credit clause**) is to prevent a person from escaping his or her civil obligations (for example, debts) by moving to another state. Mortgages, leases, contracts, and wills that are enforceable in a civil proceeding in another state are enforceable in California. Moreover, according to the U.S. Supreme Court, the governor of California can be required by a federal court to return fugitives from justice in another state upon request of that state's governor. We shall discuss **extradition** in Chapter 6.

No state may discriminate against the citizens of other states in favor of its own citizens—that is, California cannot deprive citizens of other states of what the U.S. Constitution calls the "privileges and immunities" of U.S. citizenship. The exact nature of these privileges and immunities has not been spelled out by the U.S. Supreme Court, but California may constitutionally charge higher tuition to out-of-state students or require teachers certified in another state to obtain a California credential. In addition, the commerce clause of the U.S. Constitution (Article I, Section 8) forbids states from discriminating against the businesses and products of other states in an attempt to advance their own commercial interests.

States may undertake joint ventures by means of interstate compacts which usually require approval by Congress. For example, California and Nevada belong to the Tahoe Regional Planning Agency (TRPA), which attempts to provide planning and regulations to protect the environment of the Lake Tahoe area. Unfortunately, the agency has not been effective in preventing over-development, pollution, and smog around the lake.

NATION–STATE RELATIONS

California deals not only with the other forty-nine states, which are its constitutional equals, but also with the federal government, which is California's constitutional superior. The U.S. Constitution and all federal laws or treaties made under its authority are "the supreme law of the land" (Article VI, Section 2). Any state constitution, state statute, or state executive action violating federal law must yield. However, federal power is not limitless. As the U.S. Supreme Court has said, "Congress may not exercise power in a fashion that impairs the states' integrity or their ability to function effectively in a federal system."[1]

The U.S. Constitution places certain restrictions, in addition to the supremacy clause, on the states. States may not make treaties with foreign nations, may not coin money, and may not tax foreign imports. The vitally important Fourteenth Amendment declares that no state shall "deprive any person of life, liberty, or property, without due process of law, nor deny to any person within its jurisdiction the equal protection of the laws." The U.S. Supreme Court has ruled that according to the Fourteenth Amendment, nearly all of the Bill of Rights (the first ten amendments to the U.S. Constitution) applies to state and local governments. Of note is the fact that should California and the federal government have a dispute, the arbiter will be an organ of the federal government, the Supreme Court of the United States.

'LAKE Tahoe? Let's see, I think it used to be around here
somewhere. It was blue, wasn't it?'
SOURCE: Dennis Renault, *Sacramento Bee*

Because of U.S. Supreme Court decisions since 1937, there is hardly any subject matter which the federal government cannot regulate. Two students of federalism have argued that the court no longer views federalism as a "constitutional bulwark against tyranny."[2] Since Franklin Roosevelt's New Deal, both the federal government and the state governments have increased in power, but the federal government has increased much more than have the states. Although the number of domestic programs run *directly* by the national government has not increased much recently, many more new programs are run by state and local governments but funded and controlled by the federal government.

The U.S. Supreme Court has generally rejected the doctrine of dual federalism, which held that the federal government and the states operate in independent and autonomous spheres of influence or centers of power, with each making its own decisions about public policy. The current view is that all levels (federal, state, and local) must jointly implement important public policies in a dynamic partnership. For example, in Chapter 1 we noted extensive federal–state–local involvement in AFDC, SSI/SSP, and Medi-Cal. Long since discarded by the court is the view that the functions of government can be neatly parceled out among the three levels. Today, the federal government's constitutional power to undertake some activity is seldom challenged successfully. Instead, those who question federal authority may claim that some other level of government can perform an activity more effectively or that the activity is not necessary in the first place. As the constitutional aspects of federalism have declined in importance, the fiscal aspects of the relationship have moved to center stage.

FISCAL RELATIONSHIPS

Through more than 400 **grant-in-aid** programs, the federal government annually funnels over $10 billion to California state and local governments. However, in terms of federal grants per capita, California is ranked near the bottom one-third of the states and is below the national average. The objectives of grant programs are

1. to implement minimum national standards in all states in programs such as pollution control
2. to equalize resources among the states by redistributing wealth from richer to poorer states
3. to upgrade the quality of public services at the state and local levels
4. to stimulate experimentation and to demonstrate new approaches
5. to improve state–local administrative structures and operations—for example, auditing the handling of federal funds
6. to encourage social objectives favored by the national government
7. to minimize the observable role of the federal government by allowing state or local governments to deliver services actually financed by the federal government

Federal grants usually include restrictive requirements intended to further social objectives favored by federal officials. Whatever the intent of the grant program may be, Congress might attach any of sixty requirements, such as the protection of endangered animal species, the protection of historic sites, special provisions for handicapped or elderly persons, and others. Moreover, California state and local governments may even be penalized in one grant program for failing to take action desired by the federal government in a different area. For example, any state with a minimum drinking age of less than

21 years receives less federal highway funds. Former Gov. Victor Atiyeh of Oregon is very critical of the federal government's attitude toward the states. Noting that other countries receive billions of dollars in foreign aid with no strings attached, he says that state and local governments are treated "as if we are crooks who must be watched like hawks."[3] Although states and localities must meet numerous national requirements, they are receiving less money from the federal government to fulfill those standards. When state and local governments first sought funds to administer the numerous programs described in Chapter 1, they agreed to the required regulatory restrictions. But as the Reagan Administration has reduced money for these programs, Congress has allowed the restrictions to remain.

Total federal spending in California includes not only grants-in-aid to state and local governments but also federal salaries, payments to individuals (Social Security, Medicare, federal retirement benefits, aid to farmers, etc.), and especially defense spending. Total spending in California by the national government is more than $100 billion, which places this state tenth on a per capita basis. At least two conclusions can be drawn from this information. Since California has the largest representation in Congress, the Golden State should do better when spending is considered on a per capita basis. Moreover, since our defense spending income far exceeds that of other states, we are receiving an insufficient amount of payments to individuals and grants-in-aid.

California receives more than $40 billion in defense spending, which is far more than the second-ranking state, Texas, at $16.5 billion. Counties very heavily dependent on this money are Santa Clara, Los Angeles, Orange, and San Diego. Ten of the most important defense contractors in the state (and some of their recent projects) are the following: Aerojet-General (MX missile), FMC Corporation (Bradley troop transport), General Dynamics (F-16 fighter plane and Cruise missile), Hughes Aircraft (largest industrial employer in the state), Litton Industries (electronic equipment), Lockheed (Trident missile), McDonnell-Douglas (helicopters), Northrop (Stealth bomber), Rockwell International (B-1B bomber), and TRW (MX missile). Lockheed and Northrop have recently signed a contract with the Air Force to compete with each other in building a new advanced tactical fighter plane, with the winner receiving an expanded work force and billions of dollars in revenue. Not only are defense corporations major employers, but they and their employees pay state and local taxes. There are also numerous smaller subcontractors as well. In addition, there are significant military installations at Fort Ord; Travis, Vandenberg, and Edwards air bases; Camp Pendleton; and many Navy facilities in San Diego. Salaries paid to civilian and military personnel have immense "ripple" or secondary effects on the California economy in terms of enhanced commercial activity, housing, energy, transportation, education, and other policy issues discussed in the last chapter. The defense industry clearly plays a key role in California's economic life, but thoughtful observers fear that we have slipped into serious overdependence. California's future is mightily affected by decisions made in Washington, D.C.: since 1981, we have greatly benefited from the pro-defense presidential policies of former governor Ronald Reagan. But Reagan leaves office in 1989, and California's overdependence on defense dollars may have serious consequences.

Federal spending in California is significantly affected by the Gramm–Rudman Act passed by Congress in 1985. Seeking to eliminate the federal government's massive deficits, Congress voted to reduce the deficit by increments of $36 billion per year until a balanced budget is achieved by October of 1990. If Congress is unable to meet this yearly goal, automatic across-the-board cuts of federal programs are required to meet the law's objective. The automatic cuts are a uniform percentage and must fall equally between defense and non-defense spending. Exempted from the cuts are Social Security, interest on the national debt, veteran's compensation, Medi-Cal, Aid to Families with Dependent Children, Supplemental Security Income, and food stamps. Cuts in Medicare are restricted.

The Gramm–Rudman law is an admission by Congress that it is incapable of ending deficits by its own direct actions. House members and senators are afraid to say "no" to the spending demands of powerful interest groups, and this law gets them off the hook. Since legislators lack the discipline to make cuts themselves, the automatic provisions of the law will reduce the federal government's massive deficits. The law also has many important implications for California. If it is ever fully implemented, federal aid to this state will be drastically curtailed. The exempted programs noted above constitute about half of the federal budget, *and they are all in the non-defense part of the federal budget.* If it is correct that California is not receiving its "fair share" of non-defense spending, then this state is not as well protected as many other states. However, no defense programs are exempted from automatic cuts, and it is upon these programs that California is so heavily dependent. It could be argued that Gramm–Rudman protects California where it least needs protection, and exposes it to cuts where it is most vulnerable. In any event, future possible recessions in the national economy before 1990 will disrupt the law's goal of reducing the deficit by $36 billion per year and could lead to serious stalemate in the federal budget process.

Implementation of the Gramm–Rudman law is clouded by the U.S. Supreme Court's decision in *Bowsher v. Synar* (106 S. Ct. 3181 [1986]). The Supreme Court seldom declares a law of Congress unconstitutional, but it did invalidate a key provision of the Gramm–Rudman Act. The automatic cut provisions of the law are to be calculated by the Comptroller General on a program-by-program basis. The President is then required to order these cuts into effect. Although the Comptroller is appointed by the President to a fifteen-year term, he or she may be removed only by Congress. The court ruled that this arrangement violates the separation-of-powers principle because it allows the Comptroller, an officer answerable to Congress, to intrude too far into the operations of the executive branch. The court's decision still allows Congress to act without the Comptroller General playing any role, though, if Congress passes a bill specifying the spending cuts and sends the bill to the President. But it was the reluctance to make these painful political decisions in the first place that prompted Congress to pass the Gramm–Rudman law. In the long run, Gramm–Rudman can work only if Congress and the President agree to raise taxes significantly, which is an unlikely possibility.

If the $36 billion-per-year spending reductions are fully implemented,

California can count on drastically reduced federal spending. The state's fiscal future is further complicated by the Gann Spending Limit (see Chapter 10) and by the fact that Congress has also decided to end **revenue sharing,** a program in which the federal government gave substantial amounts of money to cities and counties with few strings attached.

Recent actions by various California communities have raised interesting issues of federal–local relations. By declaring themselves "nuclear-free zones" or enacting ordinances establishing themselves as sanctuaries for Central American refugees, cities and counties have intruded into foreign policy and military policy, areas which have traditionally been the responsibility of the federal government. These issues will have to be resolved by the federal courts, and it is likely that they will be resolved in favor of the federal government.

CALIFORNIA IN THE U.S. CONGRESS

With forty-five House members and two senators, California has clearly the largest congressional delegation, but California's low rankings on per capita federal grants-in-aid and on per capita federal spending indicate that this state's delegation has not converted size into clout. Although Alan Cranston is the Senate Democrat Whip and Tony Coelho is the House Democrat Whip, Californians chair only four House committees, and three of the four are very minor ones. California House members cannot work as a team because they are polarized between extreme liberals and extreme conservatives. According to a recent scorecard of liberalism compiled by the Americans for Democratic Action (ADA), California House Democrats score 88, but all House Democrats only 67; California Republicans score only 7, but all House Republicans 17.[4] The root of the problem is gerrymandered districts (described in the next chapter), which make it nearly impossible to defeat an incumbent no matter how extreme he or she may be. (On the other hand, safe districts allow Californians to amass seniority that someday may lead to committee chairmanships.) The conclusion seems inescapable that California's delegation in Congress is much more ideological than effective.

A good example of the ineffectiveness of the state's representation in Congress is the on-going struggle over oil drilling on the outer continental shelf (OCS). The state government owns mineral rights for three miles out to sea, which is known as the state tidelands. Beyond that is the outer continental shelf, and the U.S. Supreme Court has ruled that states may not block oil drilling there. A congressional moratorium of drilling on the OCS expired in late 1985 without California's congressional delegation nailing down an agreement with the pro-drilling Reagan Administration. With the expiration of the moratorium, California lost all of its bargaining leverage. The Interior Department intends to conduct a northern California offshore lease sale in 1989. A difficult balancing of state interests and national interests needs to be achieved. On the one hand is the need to protect California's scenic coastline and also the fear of an oil spill as happened in the Santa Barbara Channel in 1969. On the other hand, there is the economic well-being of a nation seriously dependent on foreign oil and the concerns for national security that this dependence implies. Moreover, the national government says that California should contribute its share to the country's energy supply and not leave this task to states such as Texas or Louisiana. As California's U.S. House members, U.S. senators, and governor negotiate with federal officials, there is a long-term petroleum problem which will not go away: "When the next oil crisis hits, there will be incredible pressure to drill off the California coast in the cheapest and fastest possible way—in areas closest to shore and among the most environmentally sensitive."[5]

California receives fees and royalties from oil companies for tidelands oil and gas exploration if it chooses to grant leases for that area. However, oil pools may begin in the tidelands but extend into the outer continental shelf. When the federal government allows the OCS to be pumped, oil (and oil revenue) are drained from the tidelands. Therefore, Congress has given California 27 percent of the money the federal government receives from tracts three to six miles offshore. The tidy sum of $627 million will be paid over the years 1986 to 2001.

Other resources' revenues still in dispute, regarding which the California congressional delegation might assist the state, are receipts from logging operations and on-shore minerals. The 39 California counties in which trees are felled on federal land receive money from these logging operations. The counties are afraid that the U.S. Forest Service will reduce these payments. In addition, the state receives money from leases of on-shore minerals such as oil, gas, sodium, potash, phosphate, and even geothermal steam. California says that the Interior Department is underpaying it for these leases.

The immigration reform law recently passed by Congress is extremely important for California because in the past so many undocumented workers came to this state rather than to other states. California agriculture has been heavily dependent on illegal immigration. For example, 100 percent of the pole tomato work force in San Diego County is foreign workers, 80 percent of the Monterey strawberry work force, 60 percent of the Tulare citrus and deciduous workers.[6] Urban restaurants and the garment industry in Los Angeles depend on this labor as well. In 1986, Congress responded to public demands that it stem the tide of illegal workers entering the United States by passing an immigration reform law. This complex law is a carefully crafted compromise intended to placate, if not completely satisfy, the many powerful and contending groups concerned with the issue. For example, agricultural interests, which had fought previous attempts to deal with the problem, need a dependable labor supply for harvesting seasonal crops. Latino groups, on the other hand, opposed a return to the bracero program ended two decades earlier, in which imported foreign workers were mistreated. The root of the problem is the lure of American jobs, whether in the fields or in urban areas. Hence, the law provides for employer sanctions ranging from fines to jail sentences for knowingly hiring undocumented workers not on the payroll in 1986. The law covers growers, factories, construction companies, hotels and restaurants, and even employers of household laborers and gardeners. Employer sanctions will undoubtedly increase job seekers' use of phony identification such as false Social Security cards, driver's licenses, and birth certificates. Will employers avoid foreign-looking applicants? The immigration law forbids employers to refuse to hire a job seeker because he or she is not a citizen, but the employer may choose a citizen over a legal alien if both are equally qualified.

A central provision of the law grants legal status and eventual citizenship to those persons who can prove that they have lived continously in the United States since 1982. This stipulation is intended to end the extensive "shadow society" of illegal aliens living in poverty, subject to exploitation, and in continual fear of deportation. More generous legalization rules apply to alien farm workers who can receive temporary resident status (and eventually permanent resident status) by demonstrating ninety days of field work during 1985 and 1986. The federal government will provide aid to California state and local governments to pay for increased welfare and school costs resulting from legalization, but newly legalized aliens may not receive most federally funded welfare benefits for five years.

Congress had wrestled with the immigration problem for more than five years, and it was four California legislators who played key roles in finally bringing the struggle to conclusion. Rep. Howard Berman (Democrat, Panorama City) vigorously opposed a guest worker program and negotiated for months with Rep. Leon Panetta (Democrat, Carmel Valley), who eventually developed the accelerated residency status for farm workers. Sen. Pete Wilson (Republican, San Diego) sought to ensure a stable labor supply for California growers. Rep. Dan Lungren (Republican, Long Beach) pressed all parties for compromise to keep the hard-fought bill alive and to keep the delicately balanced coalition intact. Congress eventually passed the immigration reform bill primarily because it was tired of wrestling with the issue year after year and because it did not want to have to go through the whole matter one more time.

SUMMARY

At least since the end of World War II, American politics has become increasingly focused on the national government's resolution of issues. This development has resulted from the increase in the power of the federal government, U.S. Supreme Court decisions, America's position as a world power, presidential visibility, the national emphasis of the electronic media generally, rapid social change, and other factors. Three decades ago, Leonard White, an eminent political scientist, wrote that "if present trends continue for another quarter century, the states may be left hollow shells, operating primarily as the field districts of federal departments and dependent upon the federal treasury for their support."[7] When White wrote those words, the California state budget was slightly over $1 billion. For fiscal year 1988, California state government will spend more than $39 billion. The state constitution has marked its centennial, state government is alive and well in Sacramento, and local governments are providing services for their citizens at an unprecedented rate.

The California Constitution of 1879 remains the basic law of the state. By means of more than 460 amendments and the work of a revision commission, the state constitution has been altered to meet the needs of the times and the ever-changing balance of political forces. But whatever the California Constitution may provide now or in the future, one factor will remain constant: the U.S. Constitution, federal laws and treaties, and decisions of the U.S. Supreme Court take precedence over the state constitution. This is the nature of our federal system. The constitutional or legal relationships between the federal government and California state and local governments are complemented by fiscal relationships, such as grants-in-aid. This chapter has stressed the dynamic interaction among all three layers of government and between our state government and other states in providing services for the public.

DISCUSSION QUESTIONS

1. What are some of the characteristics of the California constitution, and how have these characteristics stimulated alterations in the document? Of the three processes for changing the constitution, which is most commonly used?
2. Does it seem peculiar to you that the federal government should raise large amounts of money *in* California (by means of the income tax) and then return it *to* California (through grants)? Would it be wiser for the federal government just to keep the money or not to raise it in the first place?
3. Some commentators on the federal system view the future of federalism as the federal government raising the money but states and communities spending the money. Other observers stress the "golden rule of politics": "He who has the gold makes the rules." Can these two views be reconciled?
4. Depending upon whom you talk to, defense spending in California is either a sacred cow or a white elephant. Choose one of the animals and argue that side.
5. Congressional delegations from other states, even when they have equal numbers of Democrats and Republicans, can work together more effectively than can California's delegation. What is the matter with this state's legislators, especially House members, and what effects has it had on California's welfare?

NOTES

1. *Fry v. United States,* 421 U.S. 542 (1975). On the commerce clause, see *H. P. Hood & Sons, Inc. v. DuMond,* 336 U.S. 525 (1949), and on interstate compacts, see *Virginia v. Tennessee,* 148 U.S. 503 (1893).
2. Michael Reagan and John Sanzone, *The New Federalism,* 2nd ed. (New York: Oxford University Press, 1981), p. 15. See also pp. 12, 60–65.
3. Quoted in "Mandates without Money," *National Journal,* October 4, 1986, p. 2369. See also Michael J. Ross, *State and Local Politics and Policy: Change and Reform* (Englewood Cliffs, NJ: Prentice-Hall, 1987), chap. 2.

4. Jeff Raimundo, "Fanatic Doves Room with Macho Hawks," *Sacramento Bee*, January 7, 1985, p. A1. However, the report cards issued by various groups can be very misleading. See "The Ratings Game," *National Journal*, April 30, 1977, p. 686.

5. "Offshore Dilemma " (editorial), *Los Angeles Times*, July 31, 1986, pt. II, p. 8.

6. Richard Mines and Philip Martin, "Foreign Workers in Selected California Crops," *California Agriculture* (March–April 1983): 7. See also "Congress Clears Overhaul of Immigration Law," *Congressional Quarterly Weekly Report*, October 18, 1986, p. 2595; "Main Features of Conference Pact on Immigration Reform," *Los Angeles Times*, October 15, 1986, pt. I, p. 18.

7. Leonard D. White, *The States and the Nation* (Baton Rouge: Louisiana State University Press, 1953), p. 3.

P A R T

2

California government, like American national government, is government "of the people" and "for the people." Popular wishes should be reflected in public policy, or the public may soon be looking for new policymakers: "The only really effective weapon of popular control in a democratic regime is the capacity of the electorate to throw a party from power."[1] What ultimately keeps politicians responsive to public opinion is the presence of another group of politicians waiting in the wings to seize their jobs. "Ambition must be made to counteract ambition" was good advice once, and it still is.[2]

In Chapter 3, we examine the selection and retention or rejection of California politicians. Keep in mind the matter of competition, because in competition lies responsiveness. Statewide races (for example, for the office of governor) are generally more competitive than legislative races (for example, for membership in the assembly or senate). Some regions of California are more competitive than others. Two legacies from the past characterize California's politics: antipartyism and the spirit of reform.

In Chapter 4, we consider interest groups. Californians can influence their

Political Organizations
and Processes

government not only by participating in elections, but also by joining together in interest groups. However, many interest groups tend to be very self-seeking. We make note of different kinds of interest groups.

Finally, in Chapter 5 we discuss direct democracy. Should Californians become fed up with politicians and their interest group allies, they can take matters into their own hands through the initiative, referendum, and recall. But, paradoxically, evidence also shows that these direct democracy devices can be the tools *of* (not against) interest groups.

NOTES

1. V. O. Key, Jr., *The Responsible Electorate* (Cambridge, MA: Harvard University Press, 1966), p. 76.
2. Alexander Hamilton, James Madison, and John Jay, *The Federalist Papers* (New York: Mentor Books, 1961), p. 322. Madison's famous quote is from Federalist 51.

C	H	A	P	T	E	R

3

Politics, Parties, and Elections

In the first chapter we noted numerous California policy issues. The means for resolving these issues is at hand: politics flourishes in California. Candidates and parties eagerly press their claims of being best able to provide the needed leadership. A change of policymakers (officeholders) often means a change of policy, although voters make their decisions not only on the basis of issues but on the basis of candidate characteristics and party affiliation as well.

This chapter describes the robust, no-holds-barred politics of the Golden State. Californians are frequently independent-minded voters who refuse to hew to a party line. Such antipartyism is a major theme of the chapter. Paradoxically, this independence may be more prevalent in statewide races, such as the election of the governor, than in local legislative-district races, in which members of the assembly and state senate are selected. This disparity implies that there are really two arenas of California politics; we will point out the characteristics of each.

Other factors that affect the electoral behavior of Californians are the type of election—primary election, general election, or special election—and the local traditions of the voter's area (political region). In addition, Californians have shown a long-standing preference for political reform, especially when they feel that politicians have become corrupt or unresponsive.

In politics, as in many other fields, California often acts as the pacesetter. Trends and styles gaining acceptance here are frequently adopted throughout the nation. California has a political style, or political culture, that was once thought unique but is now increasingly becoming the national norm.

ANTIPARTYISM

The key element of California's political style is antipartyism—that is, California parties are weak as organizations, they are ineffective in directing the government, and they prompt few stirrings in the hearts of their members. The state's voters like to say that they vote for the person and not the party. Californians are chronic **ticket-splitters,** often to the dismay of newspaper columnists, political scientists, and losing candidates. The electorate divides its ticket, choosing here a Democrat, there a Republican. The form of the California ballot facilitates, if not encourages, ticket-splitting. As we shall see, an

63

office-block ballot is the form used. In 1976, the state rejected the nation's Democratic choice for president (Jimmy Carter), ousted an incumbent Democratic senator (John Tunney) in order to replace him with a Republican with absolutely no political experience (S. I. Hayakawa), and yet voted overwhelmingly for Democrats running for the U.S. House of Representatives and the state legislature. In 1978, Californians reelected a Democrat as governor (Jerry Brown) but selected a Republican as lieutenant governor (Mike Curb). In 1980, Republican presidential candidate Ronald Reagan carried California by 1.4 million votes, but Democratic Sen. Alan Cranston was reelected by 1.5 million votes. The 1982, 1984, and 1986 elections are described later in the chapter.

Table 3.1 presents the percentage of Democratic and Republican identifiers since 1958; 1985 was the first year that the proportion of Democrats and Republicans was roughly the same. Most of the Republican Party's gain has occurred in Southern California; former Democrats who now prefer the Republican Party have many of the following characteristics: age 30 to 39, white, conservative, homeowner, attended college or trade shcool. The demographic characteristics of Democrats and Republicans in this state are generally similar, but Democrats have a higher percentage of women, Latinos, blacks, and lower-income people. See Table 3.2. Of particular importance is the sizable 25 percent of the electorate that may fluctuate between the parties. Many of those

TABLE 3.1   Trends in Party Identification

	Democrat	Republican	Democratic advantage
1986	44%	45%	− 1
1985	45	46	− 1
1984	49	41	+ 8
1983	50	40	+10
1982	51	39	+12
1981	48	43	+ 5
1980	50	38	+12
1978	53	32	+21
1976	59	32	+27
1974	57	33	+24
1972	51	33	+18
1970	53	35	+18
1968	54	38	+16
1966	58	39	+19
1964	58	39	+19
1962	58	40	+18
1960	55	39	+16
1958	56	37	+19

The question asked was as follows: "Generally speaking, do you usually consider yourself as a Republican, a Democrat, an Independent or what?" Those describing themselves as Independents or with another party were then asked: "Do you think of yourself as closer to the Republican or the Democratic Party?" Those who felt closer to either of the major parties are included as partisans.

SOURCE: Mervin Field, "Political Party Identification," *California Opinion Index*, October 1985, p.1; Mervin Field, "Independents and Primaries," *California Journal* (February 1987): 103.

*"Put me down for 'no comment' on that one . . . I really
haven't read enough polls on the subject
to form an opinion!"*
SOURCE: Reprinted by permission: Tribune Media Services

TABLE 3.2   Demographic Characteristics of Democrats and Republicans

	Democrats	*Republicans*
GENDER		
Male	46%	54%
Female	54	46
AGE		
18–29	26	29
30–39	27	21
40–49	15	15
50–59	12	14
60 or older	20	21
ETHNICITY		
White (non-Hispanic)	73	88
Hispanic	12	7
Black	12	2
Asian	3	3
UNION MEMBERSHIP		
Union household	26	16
Non-union household	74	84
INCOME		
Less than $10,000	15	8
$10,000–$19,000	22	16
$20,000–$29,000	21	20
$30,000–$39,000	15	17
$40,000 or more	24	33
Refused to state	3	6
	N = 1624	N = 1627

SOURCE: Mervin Field, "Political Party Identification," *California Opinion Index*, October 1985, p. 2.

in this group are weak Democrats who will bolt from the party for an appealing Republican. These swing voters are vitally important because they decide statewide elections in California. The rural Central Valley contains many fluctuating voters, especially nominal Democrats living in such cities as Stockton, Fresno, or Bakersfield. The candidate carrying these three cities often wins the entire state. Another group of wavering Democrats can be found in the working-class suburbs of many California cities. If these blue-collar voters cannot agree with the Democratic candidate on social issues, or if they feel that they are paying more in taxes than they are receiving in government services, they may desert the Democratic party.[1] This volatility adds to the unpredictability—and the excitement—of California politics.

Furthermore, intraparty factionalism is a permanent feature of the California political landscape. Within each party are groups, or factions, contending for power and for the right to define party principles. These factions may consist of the personal supporters of an ambitious politician, or they may be dedicated to a political philosophy such as liberalism or conservatism, or they may represent a combination of the two. Among the Republicans, conservatives usually vie with middle-of-the-roaders, or moderates, as they prefer to call themselves. Up and down the state in Republican circles, followers of Ronald Reagan square off against those who carry on the tradition of Hiram Johnson (governor, 1911–1917; U.S. senator, 1917–1945) and Earl Warren (governor, 1943–1953). Among the Democrats, liberals battle moderates for the right to say what the Democratic party stands for. In the case of the Democrats especially, tension exists between those who work for the party as volunteers because they have strong beliefs about today's controversial issues, and the party's elected officials, who have the responsibility to legislate on these issues and then face the judgment of the electorate. Party activists are particularly important because of the tireless effort they put into campaigns and because they sustain the political party as an organization between elections. Republican and Democratic activists tend to be middle-class professionals for whom issues or ideology are vitally important. The activists reject compromise and bargaining, and believe that advocating correct principles is more important than winning elections. Not only may party activists be at odds with their party's elected officials, but they may also be unrepresentative of rank-and-file members of the party. The potential for conflict is described in the boxed newspaper article on page 67.

Bitterness is often greater *within* parties than *between* them. Pent-up antagonisms burst forth during primaries when factions struggle to secure the party's nomination for their own candidates. In 1976, both parties had bruising primary fights in selecting their nominees for U.S. senator. The 1982 Republican primaries for governor and U.S. senator featured angry contests among candidates representing the GOP's conservative and ultraconservative factions. Such intraparty hostility and factionalism not only weaken California parties, but also do little to endear the parties to an electorate that already views them with a jaundiced eye.

Voters and Party Leaders Far Apart on the Issues

On issues, on candidates and in personal ideology, there are big differences between rank-and-file California voters and those who run the state's political parties, according to a unique survey by the Los Angeles Times Poll.

The study provided startling evidence that the activists and the givers are significantly out of step with the voters, especially on the Democratic side.

Results of the poll, conducted from July 12–22 under the direction of I. A. Lewis, showed that:

—Democratic Party activists view themselves as more liberal than rank-and-file Democrats, while Republican activists see themselves as more conservative than the GOP member.

—Most Democratic voters take conservative positions on such issues as voluntary prayers in schools, the death penalty and Proposition 13, the property tax-cutting initiative passed in 1978, whereas the Democratic Party activists take the liberal view.

—Most Republican voters line up in support of the equal rights amendment while the party officials are overwhelmingly against it.

—Contributors to both parties generally took more moderate positions than party activists. . . .

A long list of questions was presented to 1,304 Californians in telephone interviews. Then the same questions were presented to a cross section of the 1,193 members of the Republican State Central Committee and the Democratic State Central Committee's 1,683 members. . . . Researchers also interviewed a cross section of political contributors who gave $100 or more last year. . . .

Respondents were asked whether they would classify themselves as conservatives, moderates or liberals.

A clear majority—65%—of the Democratic Party activists said they were liberals, while only 26% of the Democratic rank and file said they were liberal. Only 39% of the Democratic contributors said they were liberals.

On the Republican side, ideological differences also showed up, though to a lesser degree. A whopping 81% of the activists and 79% of the contributors said they were conservatives while 60% of the GOP voters put themselves in that category.

Differences also cropped up on issues.

On the Democratic side, party activists and rank-and-file voters split over such issues as busing and the death penalty.

With Democratic activists about evenly split for and against school busing, the party's rank and file solidly opposed it.

And, while a majority of Democratic Party activists said they opposed the death penalty, an overwhelming 70% of the Democratic voters said they favored it.

Republicans were less divided on the issues, although a number of stands taken by party leaders drew dissent from the GOP ranks.

While Republican activists and the GOP membership were united in strong opposition to school busing, they split decisively on the equal rights amendment, with a solid majority of the party leaders opposed to it and the majority of GOP voters for it.

SOURCE: "Voters and Party Leaders Far Apart on the Issues," by R. Bergholz, *Los Angeles Times*, August 2, 1981, pt. I, p. 1. Copyright 1981, Los Angeles Times. Reprinted by permission.

In addition to voter independence and intraparty factionalism, weak party organization is another aspect of antipartyism. Organizational weakness characterizes the California lifestyle. Heavy immigration and the mobility of the state's population hamper stable, locally based party organizations.[2] In fact, one-third of the population changes its address every year. Faced with such mobility, parties cannot maintain the kind of frequent contact between organization and voter that will enable the local party organization to turn out the faithful on election day. The political party organization is weak at its base, so that not surprisingly, the whole structure is shaky. But organizational frailty did not just happen; it was planned.

Until the early part of this century, the Southern Pacific Railroad dominated California politics. This virtually complete control was assured by the company's manipulation of both political parties. In order to break Southern Pacific's control over the state's politics, the **California Progressives,** a group of reform-minded Republicans, decided to break the state's parties. They succeeded, and the wreckage is still strewn across the state. Party organizations that wield significant power in other states, such as the Republican or Democratic state central committees or the parties' county central committee, have little influence in this state. Here these party organizations either have few functions prescribed by law or, as in the case of the state central committees, they may be so large (about 1,200 to 1,700 members) as to be ineffective. These official party organizations can make no preprimary endorsements; that is, prior to the election in which party members choose the party's nominee, the state committees or county committees cannot indicate which person running in the primary they would prefer to have receive the party's nomination.[3] In order to perform this and other functions that cannot be performed by the official party organizations (organizations recognized by state law), unofficial, or extralegal, party organizations have come into being. The California Republican Assembly (CRA), California Democratic Council (CDC), and others are not regulated by the state's election laws, hence they are extralegal and may make endorsements before the primary. Since each of the organizations promotes a point of view (CDC, liberal; CRA, conservative), they can point out to party members their view of the true bearer of party principles. Furthermore, they back their endorsements with money and campaign workers. Since these volunteer organizations are to some degree immoderate, they add a little color to the state's politics and often increase its temperature. They also fill an important void purposely left in state law.[4]

The ultimate in antipartyism would be elections free from party affiliation, or **nonpartisan elections,** which are precisely what California has at the city and county level. There are also nonpartisan elections for governing boards of special districts, judges, and the state superintendent of public instruction. Holding nonpartisan elections does not mean that political parties cannot be found working behind the scenes; it simply means that a candidate's party affiliation is not revealed on the ballot itself. However, since most voters do not know the party affiliations of candidates running for the city council or county board of supervisors, or do not take the time to find out such affiliations, considerations of party are kept to a minimum.

Other aspects of state government that contribute to antipartyism and weak parties are California's civil service system and the direct democracy devices of initiative and referendum. A civil service system in which state employees are selected and promoted on ability and merit may go a long way toward promoting more efficient public service, but such a merit system also substantially eliminates one of the best means for building a strong political party—**patronage.** The promise of a state job as a reward for working for a party can be a potent ingredient in making vigorous parties. In New York, the governor has 40,000 jobs at his disposal; in Illinois, 14,000; but in California, only 2,000.

Initiative and referendum are often thought of as devices for increasing citizen control of the political process. But such increased control can also be had at the expense of political parties. Political parties take positions on current issues and are frequently rewarded or punished on election day for their decisions. But the initiative and referendum are means whereby the electorate can directly resolve current issues without the assistance of political parties. Should the initiative come to be the principal means of dealing with the most dramatic issues of state politics (issues such as capital punishment, farm labor laws, obscenity, discrimination in housing, water, and taxes), political parties would have only a bystander role in those matters that might concern citizens the most.

Antipartyism is also fostered by the way campaigns are conducted. California candidates seldom stress loyalty to their party while campaigning, nor do a party's candidates run as a team or slate. Instead, each candidate has his or her own precinct workers, fundraisers, and strategy. Campaigns are run independently of the party and other party candidates. In fact, many a candidate has run *for* office by running *away from* his or her party. Republicans running for statewide office frequently downplay their party affiliation. Much of the electoral success of Earl Warren and Ronald Reagan was due to their images as citizen–politicans, rather than partisan politicians. In legislative districts with high registration of one party, the voter will search in vain through the campaign literature of the minority party candidate for any mention of his or her party.

Since little help may be forthcoming from the official party organization, candidates run personalized campaigns. Instead of saying, "Vote for me because I am a Democrat (Republican)," the candidate simply says, "Vote for *me.*" This tactic, made necessary by the tendency of California voters to vote for the person, not the party, in turn encourages that tendency. Such a lone-wolf strategy is fostered by two indispensable tools that go hand in hand, the media campaign and campaign management firms.

All statewide election candidates depend on television and radio in their campaigns. With little party machinery on which to rely, the aggressive candidate has to take to the airwaves to get his or her message across. The electronic media are well suited to the California political style of antipartyism. The candidate can use the media to emphasize himself, his personality, his most effective issues, his tailor-made appeal. The radio, moreover, can reach millions of voters made into a captive audience twice daily by the state's morning and evening snarled freeway traffic.

Television and radio spots, those nuisances that seem to be necessary for the conduct of modern democratic politics, require expertise in their making. Campaign management firms supply this expertise. These private corporations, which provide the services that California's feeble parties cannot supply, can do almost everything for a candidate, from writing the press release announcing that the candidate has entered the race to planning the election night party. The firms can even do the fundraising that helps to pay for their services. However, the candidate may want to purchase only a few services, rather than contract for complete campaign management. He or she may want advice on strategy, speech preparation, direct mailing, phone banks, polling, press relations, media arrangements, or other services. In any event, candidates for offices such as governor or U.S. senator search out the most prestigious firms and rely heavily on their direction, especially regarding television and radio: "The size and geography of the state and mushrooming mobile population force [statewide] candidates to conduct the bulk of their campaigning via mass media."[5] Media consultants operate on the premise that candidates seldom lose an election by underestimating the intelligence of the voter. California media campaigns are long on image and personalities, but short on substance. On the other hand, considering the fact that this state is characterized by substantial population in-migration, weak voter party loyalty, and little electoral support from party organizations, this is perhaps the only effective strategy. Moreover, the more specific a candidate is about issues or public policies, the more likely it is that he or she will say something that someone opposes. Campaign management firms are very astute at using public opinion polls to identify "switchers," voters who are backing the opposing candidate and who might switch to their candidate or who are undecided. The bulk of television, radio, and direct mail advertising is then directed at these people. Recall the importance of the weak or nominal Democrats mentioned earlier: Republicans running for statewide office really direct their appeals to this audience. At the same time, Democratic campaigners are vigorously trying to keep these people from straying from the party fold.

Do the campaign management firms win elections for the candidates? Important races will find professionals on both sides. Candidates in less visible races would be well advised to purchase as much expert advice as their budgets allow. However, not all authorities are convinced that the campaign management industry with all its wizardry can replace the time-honored winning mix of the right candidate, the right issues, and the right year.

We have now considered the party in terms of its members and as an organization. What about the party in office? Do party members vote as a bloc in the state legislature? Legislative cohesion is not as high in California as in most urban, industrial states. After all, assembly members and senators were elected as individuals, so why should they vote as a team? Moreover, the sanctions that the party can apply against mavericks are minimal. The party voting that does occur may result primarily from the fact that the people elected as Democrats generally are like-minded people (middle-of-the-road to liberal), as are the people elected as Republicans (middle-of-the-road to conservative).

Furthermore, the assembly speaker and the senate president pro tem raise a great deal of money for the election and reelection of majority party candidates (see Chapter 7). These campaign contributions encourage majority party members to vote with their party.

THE TWO ARENAS OF CALIFORNIA POLITICS

In California, political battles between Democrats and Republicans really take place in two very different arenas, the first of these being the "competitive statewide arena in which the battles for president, governor, and senator are contested."[6] We say that the statewide political arena is competitive because in almost any election year an attractive candidate from either major party has a reasonable chance of winning. Because these races rely heavily on television and radio advertising, they are high-visibility elections that are candidate-centered rather than party-centered. Furthermore, the weak party loyalty and voter independence of so many Californians usually make these races unpredictable. By contrast, true competition is definitely not likely in the second arena of California politics, the frequently one-party districts of state legislators and U.S. representatives. These legislative districts did not become safe for one party by accident but rather by plan. These lopsided districts are the result of a **gerrymander.**

A gerrymander occurs when the majority party in the state legislature draws district boundary lines in such a manner that the party will increase its number of seats. **Redistricting** must take place after each U.S. census, which is held every ten years (1980, 1990, and so on). The state legislature draws not only its own district lines but also those of California's members of the U.S. House of Representatives.

Figure 3.1 will help to give you a very simplified but accurate example of how the process works. Let us assume that the state consists of only four districts (rather than eighty for assembly members or forty for members of the state senate or forty-five for representatives). Let us further assume that we are the Democratic majority in the state legislature and that Democrats (represented by O) tend to live near each other, as do Republicans (represented by X). Since we have been required by the U.S. Supreme Court's one person–one vote rule to make all districts of equal population (*Reynolds v. Sims*, 377 U.S. 533 [1964]), we could choose Plan 1 shown in the figure. In that way we could isolate the Republicans in one district and write the district off, and no Democrat would have to worry about a serious race in the other three districts. But a better and more profitable way to draw lines is shown in Plan 2. The tactics illustrated here force the minority party to waste its votes, either by isolating its strength or by breaking up its strength. In actual practice, both plans are used. An example of the effectiveness of the gerrymander in wasting votes of minority party members is the 1984 elections for the U.S. House of Representatives. All California Republican candidates for the U.S. House got more votes than all the Democratic candidates, but the Republicans were able to win only 17 out of the 45 seats. Such a result is a denial of majority rule.

Plan 1
XXXXXXXXXXXXXXXXXXXXXX
OOOOOOOOOOOOOOOOOOO
OOOOOOOOOOOOOOOOOOO
OOOOOOOOOOOOOOOOOOO

Plan 2			
XXXXX	XXXXX	XXXXX	XXXXX
OOOOO	OOOOO	OOOOO	OOOOO
OOOOO	OOOOO	OOOOO	OOOOO
OOOOO	OOOOO	OOOOO	OOOOO

FIGURE 3.1   Two redistricting plans

In contrast to the partisan gerrymander, an **incumbent** gerrymander establishes district lines to protect incumbents of both parties by preserving the status quo. This strategy is employed when each party has a roughly equal number of legislators—without such a compromise plan, no redistricting bill could be passed. Situations of divided control, in which different political parties control the assembly and senate or in which the governor is a member of a political party different from the one which controls the legislature, are also likely to lead to an incumbent gerrymander. However, Republican Governor Reagan and the Democratic majority in the legislature could not agree on a redistricting plan after the 1970 census, with the result that district lines were drawn by court-appointed judges.

The drawing of district lines is deadly serious business because nothing worries a politician more than the composition of his or her district. When the legislature turns its attention to redistricting, it breaks the entire state down into units of as few as 200 people, feeds data about voters into giant computers, and begins strategy making. Not only is gerrymandering a science, but it may also be an art. A political party must show great creativity to accomplish its ends. The result is that many districts have strange and unusual shapes. The author has heard of some districts bearing a distinct resemblance to a flying goose. In the fall of 1981, Democrats who controlled the legislature put eight incumbent assembly Republicans in four districts, and six incumbent senate Republicans in three districts.

Listed in Table 3.3 are percentages of registered Democrats and Republicans in fifteen state legislative and congressional districts drawn up in fall 1981. Although they are a sampling, they are not atypical. Consider the reality that these cold facts present for the minority party candidate. In these districts and in most legislative districts in this state, the minority party candidate has no chance. People are frequently outraged when they learn of this blatant attempt to stack the deck. However, a few points should be kept in mind. Unless a reform proposal, like the bipartisan reapportionment commission described below, is actually approved by the voters as an initiative, change in redistricting procedures is difficult to achieve. State legislatures draw district lines and probably will not give up this important power voluntarily. Party politicians, like most people, act out of self-interest. They are not altruistic; they do not put the welfare of others before their own. We may deplore self-interested be-havior, but we should not be surprised by it.

It is important to remember two key points. First, the party that draws district lines at the beginning of the decade can mightily affect legislative politics for the next ten years. Second, for most legislative districts in Califor-nia, the important election is not the November general election but the June primary of the *majority* party. Whoever voters select in the primary election will almost always win in November.

Why would anyone run in a district where there is no hope of winning? Robert Huckshorn did an extensive study of losers in congressional races, and he found that the most important reason was to enhance the prestige of a political party or to promote a particular political **ideology,** liberal or conservative.[7] One must "show the flag" or "give the voters a choice," not simply stand by and let an incumbent run unopposed. Many candidates view the race as an opportunity to educate (inform) the American people about liberalism, conservatism, environmentalism, and so forth.

Huckshorn indicates that another reason that many run is "for the sheer love of the game." Others "like to talk and to be listened to and there is no better forum than the political stump." A final reason is "personal prestige or per-sonal gain," especially on the part of young attorneys who hope to enlarge their practices. We could add that a candidate might run a hopeless race now as preparation for a real chance later. For example, a person might be a 1988 sacrificial lamb in a noncompetitive congressional district because he or she is eyeing a 1990 race for a competitive assembly district in the area. By means of a 1988 effort, the candidate learns how to campaign and how to put together a

TABLE 3.3   Registered Democrats and Republicans in Fifteen Districts

District number	Percentage Democratic	Percentage Republican
Assembly districts		
4	59	28
14	63	25
30	62	28
66	59	29
70	31	57
Senate districts		
2	56	30
8	62	23
23	60	28
30	67	23
21	39	53
Congressional districts		
3	57	32
10	60	25
27	56	31
44	58	27
22	37	55

campaign organization, and also increases vital name recognition in the area. By running the hopeless race, our hypothetical candidate may have paid some dues and earned the right to get a real chance.

There *are* circumstances in which an incumbent can be defeated. The demographic characteristics of the district may gradually change. The incumbent may become involved in a scandal. The incumbent's margin of victory may have been declining in recent elections just as a very strong challenger appears. The challenger might spend an extraordinary amount of money or be a particularly effective campaigner who can make his or her name well known in the district. Salient issues or political tides of the day might favor the challenger— for example, the challenger's gubernatorial or presidential candidate might be very popular. Moreover, some incumbents feel insecure or "run scared" even when there are few objective reasons for believing that they might be defeated. This behavior is prompted by stories of other incumbents who were defeated for no apparent reason.

The decreased competition which results from gerrymandering raises some serious questions in democratic theory. When California voters participate in a legislative election the outcome of which has been virtually determined in advance, are they participating in a sham? Are legislators elected in safe districts less responsive to the wishes of their constituents? The greatest worry of an entrenched incumbent may be a serious challenger in the party primary, but how frequent are these? Today's long-term incumbent may have initially achieved nomination long ago in a crowded primary field in which he or she received only a small **plurality** of the vote. Are less capable legislators selected by such a system? The gerrymander can deny majority rule: a party could win a **majority** of all votes cast in the state but win only a minority of the districts because of the distribution of votes among districts. For example, a party might win three districts 90 to 10 but lose four districts 40 to 60; it would thus win a large majority of the votes but only three of seven seats.

Concerns such as these prompted the reform group Common Cause to sponsor an initiative in 1982 establishing a bipartisan reapportionment commission to draw district lines. Fairness in commission deliberations would be promoted by requirements for partisan balance and for an extraordinary majority (two-thirds) necessary for important decisions. The ten-member commission would consist of four members chosen by the Democratic and Republican caucuses in the assembly and senate, two members appointed by the Democratic and Republican state chairpersons, and four members (two from each party) selected by courts of appeal justices. Partisan maneuvering would be inhibited by requiring that the final plan be approved by seven members, including three of the judicial appointees. Should the reapportionment commission become deadlocked in its deliberations, the state supreme court could appoint court masters to draw district lines. Common Cause, usually regarded as a liberal, reformist group, was joined in its initiative effort by an unlikely ally, the California Republican Party. The Republicans wanted to increase competition after having been on the losing end of a Democratic gerrymander. The reapportionment commission initiative was defeated, as was another sponsored by Gov. Deukmejian in 1984.[8]

VOTER REGISTRATION, ABSENTEE VOTING

Two administrative procedures associated with politics are voter registration and **absentee** voting. A person who meets the citizenship, residence, and age requirements must register with the county clerk or county registrar of voters at least twenty-nine days before an upcoming election. This may be accomplished by filling out a voter registration postcard and dropping it in the mail. Once registered, a person stays on the voter rolls until he or she moves to another county, has a name change, becomes ineligible because of insanity or conviction of a felony, or fails to vote in a general election.

In order to keep voter rolls current, California once conducted a **positive purge** of the rolls. Those who did not vote were notified by mail, and if they did not respond, their name was removed from the list. In 1975, the state changed to a **negative purge**, in which nonvoters are contacted by mail and removed from the voting list only if the post office returns the cards as undeliverable or if the cards are returned by the person now living at the address. In many respects, the accuracy of the state's election rolls depends on the efficiency of the U.S. Postal Service, which is somewhat of an unnerving thought. Secretary of State March Fong Eu would like to return to the positive purge because she believes that the present registration system carries on the rolls deadwood or phantom voters amounting to more than 8 percent of all those registered, or at least 1 million people. Moreover, the cost of mailing election materials to those who have died, moved, or no longer care to vote costs about half a million dollars. It is generally agreed by campaign specialists that those persons incorrectly remaining on the voting rolls are overwhelmingly Democrats. If this is correct, the fact that there are currently about five registered Democrats for every three registered Republicans is very misleading. The data in Table 3.1 give a much more accurate picture of party strength in California. Finally, the frequently asserted claim that too low a percentage of the state's registered voters turn out to vote is in need of revision.

Another administrative aspect of politics which can be completed by mail is absentee voting. Prior to 1978 if someone wanted to vote by absentee ballot, he or she had to cite illness, absence on election day, conflicting religious commitment, or residence at a long distance from a polling place as a reason for a mail ballot. The requirements were dropped in 1978, and candidates soon started urging the public to "vote in the convenience of your own home" and started sending absentee voter applications along with campaign literature. Some recent elections have seen heavy absentee voting: in 1982, 6.5 percent of all voters used absentee ballots (previously only 3 to 4 percent had used this method). The Republican party sent preprepared absentee ballot applications with the voter's name printed on it to *every* Republican household in the state. All the voter had to do was sign the application and return it. Sixty percent of all 1982 absentee voters selected George Deukmejian for governor, which greatly assisted him in winning a very close election. In 1983, San Francisco Mayor Dianne Feinstein defeated a recall attempt, and 36 percent of all votes cast in the election were by absentee. In the 1984 election, 9 percent of all votes (or 900,000 votes) were absentee.

The present use of absentee ballots raises some serious concerns in election administration. For instance, in addition to distributing absentee ballot applications, political party workers take absentee ballots to the voter and can even be present when the voter marks the ballot. In this situation, there is no poll judge present to ensure the integrity of the ballot; moreover, the voter can be coerced into voting a certain way by relatives, friends, employers, union leaders, interest group officers, or of course party workers who happen to be on the scene. In these circumstances, it also cannot be ascertained for sure who actually marked the ballot. There have even been instances of party workers asking for absentee ballots on behalf of people who were unaware of the request, and then forging the signature. In other words, there is great potential for fraud; Secretary of State March Fong Eu has described the situation as a "time bomb waiting to explode."[9] On a less serious level, there is also the very real opportunity for human error. People often sign absentee voter applications without knowing exactly what they are requesting. When the absentee ballot arrives, they throw it away thinking that it is campaign literature. Then these unfortunate people cannot vote at the polls because the poll record indicates that the person has received an absentee ballot.

When we combine registering by mail and absentee voting by mail, we have the potential for vote fraud on a massive scale. It is possible for votes to be cast for years without election officials ever seeing a flesh-and-blood person.

PRIMARY, GENERAL, AND SPECIAL ELECTIONS
Primary Elections

In a **primary election,** held in June, each party selects a person to represent it in November's general election. California primaries are "closed," which means that only registered Democrats may vote in the Democratic party primary, only registered Republicans may vote in the Republican party primary, and so forth. If a person indicated "decline to state" when registering to vote, he or she will receive on primary day a ballot containing only initiative and referendum propositions, the names of candidates for nonpartisan offices such as judgeships and for county offices, and the names of candidates for the office of California superintendent of public instruction (this four-year office was on the ballot in 1986.).

Turnout (the percentage of people who actually vote) is lower in the primary than in the general election. This low turnout is unfortunate because, for reasons already cited, the primary is often more important than the general election. As a result, party factions (liberal, middle-of-the-road, conservative) are encouraged to fight it out in the primary.

However, most primaries are not very dramatic. Incumbents (persons already holding the office) have a distinct advantage. Especially for the minority party, the "primary campaign is brief, the candidates are not well known, and the issues, if any, are often unclear."[10] Low interest in primaries has led to the emergence of a strange political creature—the "Republicrat"—which is thought to inhabit California only. In a district dominated by one party, the majority incumbent may ask friends in the other party to write in his or her name on primary day. Especially if no one has bothered to run in the minority party primary, the incumbent can thus get the nomination of both parties. A Republican following this route would be listed on the general election ballot as a "Republican–Democrat." In recent general elections, there have been from two to four "Republicrats" on the ballot. The possibility of getting the nominations of both parties is reminiscent of **cross-filing,** a practice abolished in the late 1950s. California is the only state to have tried cross-filing extensively. By cross-filing, a candidate could seek the nominations of both parties without having to reveal which party was actually his or her own. Republicans frequently captured both nominations. This practice, established by the California Progressives, had the intended effect: it seriously weakened political parties. Candidates with cross-party appeal became very important in the state's politics.

Although our discussion has concerned party, or partisan, primaries, California also has nonpartisan primaries for all officials elected on a nonpartisan basis. Municipal (city) officials usually have their primaries in March or April. County officers, all judges, and the state superintendent of public instruction have their primaries in June on the same day as the partisan primaries. This part of the ballot is the same for everyone, whether registered as a party member or as "decline to state." All candidates who receive a majority vote in the primary are elected outright. Should no one gain a majority, a runoff must be held between the two top vote-getters.

Some small units of government such as rural special districts have long held mail-ballot elections, but in 1981 the city of San Diego conducted a special election on the single issue of constructing a convention center. The election was conducted by mail, and a record-high 61 percent of the voters participated. The city also saved a substantial amount of money by holding the special election in this way.

General Elections

Politics comes alive for most people at the time of the general election. Names of political heroes may be on the ballot, issues are discussed (often heatedly), politics is in the air and on the airwaves. California's elections for governor and state constitutional officers such as controller or treasurer are held in the even-numbered years in which no presidential election is held (see Table 3.4). All of the state assembly and one-half of the state senate are elected every two years. As for federal officials elected from this state, all members of the House of Representatives are elected for two-year terms. U.S. senators serve six-year terms—one ending in 1988 and the other in 1992.

The **office-block** form of the California ballot is consistent with the spirit of antipartyism and independence discussed earlier. Such a ballot groups candidates according to the office sought, rather than listing party members in columns as a party-column ballot does. The California ballot and punch-card voting machines force the voter to make a new decision before voting for each *office*. With a **party-column ballot**, the voter is initially given an opportunity to vote for an entire party by simply marking the circle at the head of the list of party candidates. The office-block ballot, if only by the way it appears to the eye, suggests picking and choosing between candidates of different parties.

Special Elections

Should a vacancy occur in the state legislature or in California's House of Representatives delegation because of death, resignation, or another reason, the governor must call a **special election**.[11] In a special election all candidates of all parties are listed on a single ballot, and the voter votes for one. A candidate who receives a majority of the votes cast is automatically elected. If no one receives a majority, the top vote-getters of *each* party face each other in a runoff. This procedure, however, may result in a curious situation. If the percentages of the vote are as follows, the runoff ballot will list candidates C, D, E, and G, although more voters in this district clearly favored candidate A than E:

- 26%   Candidate A   Democrat
- 11%   Candidate B   Republican
- 31%   Candidate C   Democrat
- 2%   Candidate D   Libertarian
- 17%   Candidate E   Republican
- 8%   Candidate F   Democrat
- 5%   Candidate G   Peace and Freedom

Republicans tend to do better in special elections than Democrats. The GOP is better able to mobilize party workers from throughout the state for election day canvassing in the contested district. Although special elections are low-turnout elections, Republican voters are more likely to vote than Democrats.

TABLE 3.4   Timing of General Elections

Office	Year					
	1988	1990	1992	1994	1996	1998
FEDERAL						
President	yes		yes		yes	
U.S. senators	yes[a]		yes[b]	yes[a]		yes[b]
Members of House of Representatives	yes	yes	yes	yes	yes	yes
STATE						
Governor and all state constitutional officers		yes		yes		yes
Assembly members	yes	yes[c]	yes	yes	yes	yes
State senators	1/2	1/2	1/2	1/2	1/2	1/2

[a]Seat "A."
[b]Seat "B."
[c]Congressional and state legislative districts redrawn after this election.

THE 1982 ELECTION

As the 1982 primary season opened, the state and the nation were in the worst economic slump since World War II: unemployment was dangerously high, interest rates were even higher, and the housing construction industry was in a depression. Sensing victory in November, the Democrats had few significant primary contests as Tom Bradley, mayor of Los Angeles, was nominated for governor, and Gov. Jerry Brown was nominated for U.S. senator.

Media attention and public attention focused on the Republican primary, where there were bitter contests for governor and U.S. senator. Wealthy Republican fundraisers, dubbed "kingmakers" by their opponents, forced San Diego Mayor Pete Wilson out of the gubernatorial primary and into the primary for U.S. senator. However, the support of these same fundraisers for Lt. Gov. Mike Curb's gubernatorial candidacy was not enough to deter Attorney General George Deukmejian from entering the gubernatorial race. Curb made a strong appeal to conservative Republican primary voters by pledging to restrict welfare benefits and to seek the recall of liberal Chief Justice Rose Bird of the state supreme court. He also opposed the Peripheral Canal, suggested a freeze on utility bills for present customers with future customers paying higher bills, and attacked Deukmejian's party loyalty. The attorney general stressed his long experience in state government, supported the Peripheral Canal, and said that voters should wait until Bird came up for reelection in 1986 to defeat her. Pointing out that Curb had said "I'm going to get you" to a reporter who had written critical stories about the lieutenant governor, Deukmejian called Curb immature and irresponsible. Pollster Mervin Field said that he had never seen such wide swings in candidate preference in thirty-five years of polling, but in the end Deukmejian defeated Curb.

The Republican field for U.S. senator consisted of nine candidates, including incumbent S. I. Hayakawa, whose popularity was very low. Hayakawa eventually declined to seek renomination, leaving Wilson, Congressmen Barry Goldwater, Jr., and Pete McCloskey as the main contenders. All the candidates aligned themselves with President Reagan, perhaps in recognition of the fact that 78 percent of the state's Republicans considered themselves to be conservatives, and only 22 percent middle-of-the-road or liberals. Goldwater's early lead, based on name identification with his famous father, soon faded, and McCloskey was perceived as too much of a maverick. Mayor Pete Wilson won the nomination because he was, in the words of Mervin Field, the "remainder man": after primary voters rejected each of his rivals, Wilson was the candidate who remained. Mayor Wilson followed the classic Republican strategy in statewide elections: adopt a conservative posture in the primary in order to appeal to Republican voters, but move to the broader middle ground for the general election. (Democrats, on the other hand, usually appear far more liberal in the primary than they do in the statewide general election.)

As Jerry Brown began his general election campaign for senator, it was evident that he was in deep trouble. Brown had received only 51 percent of the Democratic primary vote against weak opposition, and he trailed far behind Pete Wilson in public opinion polls. Wilson's lead eventually shrank as a result both of Brown's charges that the San Diego mayor would weaken the Social Security system, and of revelations that wealthy friends had once supplied Wilson with rent-free housing. In the end, however, Wilson defeated Brown, carrying fifty-three of California's fifty-eight counties. Wilson's victory was more a rejection of Brown than an endorsement of Wilson. In eight years as governor, Jerry Brown had accumulated numerous negative images. For example, his handling of the Medfly crisis angered many voters, especially in farm areas, and his two unsuccessful runs for the presidency made him look like just another ambitious politician. Perhaps Brown lost because his novelty wore off. His initial popularity as governor was partly due to his being different and unconventional—but it is very hard to be distinctive for very long in this media-oriented state.

In the race for governor, George Duekmejian turned back Tom Bradley's attempt to become the nation's first black elected governor. It was the closest gubernatorial election in almost a century, as the attorney general defeated the Los Angeles mayor by only 93,000 votes out of more than 7.5 million cast. Spending heavily on media campaigns, both candidates were against crime and for more jobs (at a time of 10.7 percent unemployment); both sought ways to improve the state's business climate. Neither was very specific about how to deal with the state's fiscal crisis. One issue on which the candidates differed sharply may have cost Bradley the election—although in such a close race almost any factor can tip the scales. Bradley favored and Deukmejian opposed a bitterly contested initiative proposition to require the registration of handguns. Democrats and independents drawn to the polls to vote against the measure also voted against Bradley, while Republicans overwhelmingly backed Deukmejian. Deukmejian was also aided by an extremely effective Republican program encouraging Republicans to vote by absentee ballot. In terms of campaign spending, Deukmejian spent $9.06 million and Bradley spent $9.48 million in his losing effort.

Democrats swept all other statewide offices, including lieutenant governor, and Wilson Riles was defeated for the nonpartisan office of superintendent of public instruction after twelve years in office. Calling for more rigorous academic standards, more student homework, and tougher discipline, Bill Honig defeated Riles in a race in which the wealthy challenger vastly outspent the incumbent. Spending imbalances also played a key role in three ballot proposition contests. Opponents of the handgun registration initiative raised large sums of money from the National Rifle Association (NRA) and firearms manufacturers to defeat the measure. Proponents of an initiative to require a $.05 deposit on beer and soft-drink containers were widely outspent by the beverage and bottling industries, and the measure went down to defeat. Finally, sponsors of an advisory vote on freezing nuclear weapons raised over $3.4 million, much of it from Hollywood entertainment personalities, while opponents could spend only $6,000; the measure passed 52 percent to 48 percent. Total spending by candidates for the state legislature and for all statewide offices was a record $83 million, nearly double the amount spent in pursuit of the same offices only four years earlier.[12]

THE 1984 ELECTION

Since incumbent President Ronald Reagan had no renomination challengers in the 1984 election, attention focused on the Democrats. Former Vice President Walter Mondale soon became the acknowledged front-runner after receiving the endorsements of the AFL–CIO, the National Education Association (NEA), the National Organization for Women (NOW), and many incumbent Democratic elected officials. Long a friend of labor, Mondale's endorsement by the AFL–CIO meant that he would be the beneficiary of labor's extensive financial and organizational resources. (Unions in 1984 were particularly concerned about placing foreign imports at an economic disadvantage [protectionism] and requiring that foreign cars sold in the United States contain some American parts and labor [domestic content legislation].) The NEA, the nation's second largest labor union, endorsed Mondale because he favors increased federal aid to education; every state has many teachers, especially California, who could be very valuable to Mondale as telephone callers, envelope stuffers, and convention delegates. The feminist NOW favored Mondale because of his pro-Equal Rights Amendment and pro-abortion positions. These endorsements, plus those of prominent Democratic House members, senators, governors, and mayors, clearly made Mondale the "establishment candidate of the Democrats." Mondale's strongest supporters among the voters were people concerned with the health of the economy and those who felt they were personally economically insecure. However, Mondale soon received a strong challenge from Sen. Gary Hart of Colorado, who won the nation's first primary (New Hampshire). Saying "I am the Democratic Party's future, Mondale is its past," Hart claimed to offer a fresh approach to old problems, new ideas, and new leadership. Hart ran on a strong platform against American military intervention in foreign conflicts, criticized protectionism as a policy of having consumers bail out weak industries, argued that Mondale cannot say "no" to special interests, and said that Mondale's economic program "is a collection of old and tired ideas held together by paralyzing commitments to special interests and constituent groups." Hart's strongest supporters were "yuppies" (young, urban professionals): white, aged 25–44, holding professional or technical or managerial positions, earning high incomes. In response, Walter Mondale said that the Democratic Party has a "special responsibility" to blacks, teachers, women, and the elderly, and that his struggle with Hart was for "the soul of the Democratic Party and the future of our country." Many of the issues raised by Hart and Mondale in 1984 are likely to arise again in the 1988 Democratic presidential primaries: one or more candidates may follow the classic Democratic strategy of assembling a coalition of different interests ("you support organized political interests and they support you"), while one or more other candidates follows an "outsider" strategy stressing independence and new approaches to public problems.

Other presidential contenders running were California's senior senator, Alan Cranston, who based his campaign primarily on the issue of freezing the number of nuclear weapons, and black civil rights leader Jesse Jackson, who sought to assemble a "rainbow coalition" of blacks, whites, Latinos, Native Americans, old people, young people, homosexuals, lesbians, and others who felt neglected by other candidates. However, Jackson soon became controversial for his criticism of Israel, his support of the Palestinians, his acceptance of donations from Arabs, and his references to Jews as "Hymies" and New York City as "Hymietown."

At the time of the California primary, which was on the last primary day, Walter Mondale had 1,627 delegates and Hart had 962, with other candidates far behind. A total of 1,967 delegates was needed for nomination. The importance of the California primary was that 345 delegates were at stake (the largest block in any state), that a late win in such an important state could give Hart a big advantage with the numerous uncommitted delegates in other states who were looking for a winning candidate, and because the California unemployment rate was not as high as in other states (thus depriving Walter Mondale of one of his best issues). On the other hand, California's labor unions were making an all-out effort for Mondale. Hart won the California primary with 38 percent of the vote and received 205 delegates; Mondale had 35 percent and 72 delegates; Jackson 21 percent and 29 delegates; Cranston had withdrawn by the time of the primary. Democrats in each congressional district voted for a specified number of delegates whose names were on the ballot pledged to a particular presidential candidate—the length and complexity of the Democratic primary ballot caused many voters to incorrectly mark their ballot. A total of 6.8 percent of all Democratic ballots in Los Angeles County had this part of the ballot disqualified. Turnout statewide was only 48 percent of registered voters, the lowest in 44 years, but this outcome can probably be attributed to the lack of a Republican contest and the presence of only one significant ballot measure.

Although Gary Hart won the California primary, Walter Mondale received enough delegates in New Jersey and West Virginia on the same day to secure the Democratic nomination. At the Democratic Convention, Mondale selected Congresswoman Geraldine Ferraro as his vice presidential nominee, the first woman chosen by a major party for that position. In his acceptance speech, Mondale outlined a plan to raise taxes in order to reduce the nation's huge deficit and charged President Reagan with having a concealed plan to do the same thing.

A prominent feature of the fall campaign was the two nationally televised presidential debates. Walter Mondale clearly won the first debate, and President Reagan's poor performance prompted speculation that he was too old to handle another four years in the White House. However, Reagan's improved showing in the second debate substantially defused that issue. An early October ABC News poll showed Mondale behind by 18 percent and losing in every state. At the same time, Mervin Field's California Poll had Reagan 50 percent, Mondale 40 percent, and 10 percent undecided. A serious failing of the Mondale campaign was that the former vice president was unable to land a serious blow on Ronald Reagan: the latter's numerous misstatements did not hurt him, and Reagan was jocularly called a "Teflon candidate." Moreover, Mondale was unable to score with what he had hoped would be his big issues, for example, the issue of nuclear war (the voters favored a freeze on nuclear weapons,

Reagan was charged by Mondale as leading the country closer to war); the nation's huge budget deficit; and the "fairness" issue (Mondale charged Reagan with being the candidate of wealthy people). On the Republican side, President Reagan ran what is sometimes called a "feel good" campaign: because his media commercials were upbeat, positive, and optimistic, they made people feel better. In addition, the country was at peace and appeared to the voters to be militarily strong, the economy was thought to be fairly healthy, and Ronald Reagan was perceived by the voters as a decent person. All of these factors, plus the fact that Walter Mondale was not that popular with the voters from the start (note his difficulty in turning back the challenge of the relatively unknown Gary Hart) led to a smashing Reagan victory. The president received 59 percent of the popular vote and 525 out of 538 electoral votes including

- 63 percent of the votes of men and 56 percent of the votes of women (despite much discussion of a "gender gap").
- 67 percent of the votes of white people, 47 percent of the Latino vote, but only 9 percent of the black vote (Latinos were being courted by President Reagan and responded by an unusually high Republican vote).
- 61 percent of the votes of Protestants, 59 percent of the Catholic vote, and 32 percent of the Jewish vote (despite the fact that Geraldine Ferraro was supposed to draw Catholic votes).
- about 60 percent of the votes of all age groups, including the youngest and the oldest voters.
- 48 percent of the votes of labor union families despite the fact that almost all union leaders endorsed and worked for Mondale.
- 97 percent of the votes of Republicans, 16 percent of the Democrats, and a very high 67 percent of independents.

In California, President Reagan won 57.3 percent of the statewide vote, and Mondale won 41.3 percent; Mondale carried only 5 of 58 counties (San Francisco, Alameda, Marin, Santa Cruz, and Yolo). Four of the counties won by Mondale were also 4 of the 5 counties carried by Jerry Brown in his devastating loss to Pete Wilson years earlier. California turnout was 72.7 percent, the lowest in a presidential election in 60 years. The perception that President Reagan was a sure winner, plus an early media projection of his victory, may have decreased turnout. Absentee voting was an extraordinarily high 885,000 votes, up from the already large 1982 total of 528,000.

Despite the Reagan landslide in California, Democrats lost only one House of Representatives seat in this state, and only one seat in the California legislature. The power of the Democrats' gerrymander is demonstrated by the fact that California Republican candidates for the U.S. House of Representatives received a majority of the statewide vote but only 18 out of 45 seats. Republican candidates for the state senate also received a majority of the statewide vote, but could gain only a single seat. On the other hand, voter turnout is usually lower in heavily Democratic legislative districts.

On the ballot proposition front, an initiative to establish a state lottery (described in Chapters 5 and 10) passed, as did a measure to require the governor to write federal officials urging that voting materials be printed in

English only. A proposal by Howard Jarvis to limit local government's ability to charge new service fees failed, as well as a proposition by Gov. Deukmejian to establish a reapportionment commission of retired judges to draw district lines. The opposition to the reapportionment commission came from the Democratic party, which charged that it would politicize the courts and enhance the power of party politicians. Speaking in a lighthearted mood after the election, Democratic Speaker of the Assembly Willie Brown said that the television campaign against the reapportionment commission was "the most extensive collection of con jobs I've ever seen." An initiative by a Republican member of the assembly to limit welfare payments to no more than 10 percent of the average of the other 49 states and to reduce Medi-Cal payments to welfare recipients was defeated. The measure was opposed by the California Medical Association and the California Hospital Association, who receive millions of dollars in Medi-Cal payments. Their substantial campaign contributions were instrumental in defeating the proposal.

THE 1986 ELECTION

In 1986, Los Angeles Mayor Tom Bradley sought a rematch after his narrow 1982 defeat at the hands of George Deukmejian. In the second election, Bradley altered his position on the issue that may have cost him the 1982 election: he now opposed handgun control. However, the Bradley campaign got off to a slow start as the mayor had great difficulty dealing with the issue of whether controversial Chief Justice Rose Bird should be retained. Bradley said that he had never endorsed Bird although he was the cochair of a committee supporting her election in 1978. Finally, Bradley said that he would neither support her nor oppose her in 1986. George Deukmejian responded that Bradley ought to take a stand on Bird because the public has a right to know what kind of justices Bradley would appoint as governor. Bradley hammered away on the issue that Deukmejian had taken one-quarter of a million dollars from the toxic waste industry and had done favors for that industry. As the primary campaign ended, Bradley trailed Deukmejian badly in public opinion polls.

As Alan Cranston began his reelection race, he looked vulnerable: Cranston's 1984 run for the presidency had emphasized his liberalism, especially his opposition to nuclear weapons. Although elected U.S. senator three times, Cranston had never faced a serious opponent. Each of his three previous opponents had been unelectable right-wingers. The Republican primary field consisted of ten candidates, but two eventually broke away from the pack. Los Angeles television commentator Bruce Herschensohn represented the very conservative wing of the party and was supported by ultraconservative U.S. Senator Jesse Helms of North Carolina. Herschensohn emphasized themes such as "get the U.S. out of the United Nations, and the U.N. out of the U.S." Ed Zschau was a Silicon Valley congressman with the capacity to raise large sums of money from the high-tech industry where he had been a computer entrepreneur. As a political unknown, Zschau used his campaign contributions to buy television time and to make his name known to the public.

Although generally a supporter of President Ronald Reagan, Zschau was clearly in the moderate Republican tradition of Hiram Johnson and Earl Warren. For example, Zschau took the following positions (which are unusual for a Republican): favorable to abortion, the Equal Rights Amendment (ERA), and a nuclear arms freeze; opposed to prayer in the public schools, offshore oil drilling, and the MX missile. On primary election day, Republican voters exhibited an interesting pragmatism—they chose Zschau by 37 percent over Herschensohn at 30 percent because they believed that the former would be a stronger opponent for Alan Cranston. Overall primary turnout was less than 40 percent, the lowest in more than half a century. Martin Smith, the astute political editor of the *Sacramento Bee,* judged television to be the real winner of the 1986 primary. Zschau had risen from near total political obscurity by raising large sums of money and then using TV to make his unusual name known. Moreover, Zschau's closest rival was also a creature of the tube, Bruce Herschensohn the television commentator.

The only significant ballot proposition in the primary was the hotly contested "deep pockets" initiative to change the state's tort liability law. The legal issues involved were highly complex, but the campaign featured emotional and misleading slogans by each side. On one side were insurance companies, physicians, and local governments; on the other was the California Trial Lawyers Association. With the exception of city and county governments, all of the interests involved were very wealthy, and they spared no expense to further their cause. In the end, the insurers, doctors, and local governments won, probably less because of the persuasiveness of their case than because of the extravagant television commercials of the other side.

In the general election, Gov. Deukmejian scored a stunning 61-percent to 37-percent victory over Tom Bradley. The winning margin was the largest in thirty-six years, with Deukmejian carrying every county except Alameda and San Francisco, and also receiving the votes of one out of every three Democrats. Most voters were inclined to back the incumbent governor before the race had even begun: not only was the state's economy healthy, but Deukmejian had made no serious mistakes and thus gave the voters little reason to throw him out of office. The race for U.S. senator, on the other hand, was extraordinarily close as Alan Cranston defeated Ed Zschau by 1.6 percent, the slimmest senatorial vote margin since 1920. In the gubernatorial and senatorial elections, Californians again displayed their penchant for ticket-splitting on a massive scale. Cranston's victory marked the fourth consecutive time that he was elected U.S. senator, a feat matched in this century only by the legendary Hiram Johnson. The race was very bitter, since Zschau employed an expensive television campaign claiming that Cranston voted against major drug control bills and against antiterrorist legislation, and that Cranston was against the death penalty and for controversial Chief Justice Rose Bird. Cranston also flooded the airwaves, hitting hard at Zschau as a flip-flopping opportunist on issues such as the MX missile and aid to anti-Communist forces in Nicaragua. Each candidate tried to get the public to vote against his opponent for negative reasons, rather than building a positive case for himself. In 1986 (if not in other years), voters responded to negative rather than positive appeals and were more ready to believe them. In any event, Zschau was never able to define clearly what principles he stood for, while Cranston was able to claim that his nearly two decades in the Senate gave him the experience and influence to further California's interests.

The absence of a close race for governor and the recriminatory tone of the U.S. Senate campaign may have been contributing factors to a low voter turnout of only 58 percent, the smallest turnout ever in a gubernatorial election year. The voters also defeated a ballot proposition to quarantine victims of aquired immune deficiency syndrome (AIDS), approved a toxics measure (described in Chapter 1), and denied reelection to Chief Justice Rose Bird and two other supreme court justices (which will be analyzed in Chapter 8).

CAMPAIGN SPENDING

Campaign spending in California is increasing at a dizzying rate, with each election year's total far surpassing the last, especially for state legislative races. Between 1958 and 1986, spending in campaigns for the state legislature rose by 4,000 percent, a rate much higher than both the inflation rate and the state's population increase.[13] Between 1984 and 1986, it increased by 31 percent alone. The largest item in legislative campaign budgets is direct mail, for example computer-written letters and full-color brochures. The prohibitively high cost of campaigns has discouraged new candidates from running and presenting their ideas to the public. Incumbents usually outspend their challengers by overwhelming amounts; in 1982, the ratio was eight to one; in 1984, it was fourteen to one; but in 1986, it was more than thirty to one. Not surprisingly, more than 95 percent of all incumbents are reelected. Incumbents raise massive amounts of money for many reasons: to deter potential challengers from running against them; to hedge against the possibility of a personally rich opponent or one who received large contributions from interest groups, legislative leaders, or party sources; to protect themselves against a last-minute surprise blitz. Moreover, money is often raised to be transferred to other candidates. Because an incumbent wants to be a party leader or a powerful committee chair, or by virtue of the fact that he or she already is, some incumbents raise a great deal of money to give to other candidates of their party.

Two particularly troublesome issues are off-year fundraising and out-of-district contributions. Off-year fundraising occurs during a year when the incumbent is not running for reelection and usually takes place in Sacramento. Legislators solicit lobbyists for contributions, frequently scheduling fundraising events such as receptions on the eve of important votes affecting substantial economic interests. This activity receives very little public scrutiny because it takes place when fewer contribution disclosure reports are required, the incumbent does not have an announced opponent, and the attention of the press may be diverted to the more visible business of government such as hearings and legislative votes. Off-year fundraising must be contrasted with fundraising during an election year. In the latter case, money is given to *candidates*, often because the contributor likes the candidate's ideology or point of view on many issues or because the contributor dislikes the opponent's ideology. The purpose is to support a point of view and to win a specific election. In contrast, off-year contributions go to *incumbents,* but this time to gain access or influence for the contributor. The purpose now is not to influence an election but to influence pending legislation. Two important off-year contributors are the California Trial Lawyers Association and the California State Employment Association (CSEA). Off-year contributions are almost always out-of-district money: the interest groups and Sacramento lobbyists giving the money are usually not located in the legislator's district. These out-of-district forces lessen the importance of the legislator's own constituents. Transfers of funds from legislative leaders or other candidates also are out-of-district contributions and have the same effect of tying the legislator more toward outside interests and less toward the people back in the district.

Two trends which are not widely known are the increasing importance of partisan contributions and the decreasing importance of very large contributions by individuals or interest groups. Partisan contributions include the candidate transfers noted earlier but also contributions from party caucuses in the state legislature and from state party committees. Democrats stress money transferred from legislative leaders such as the assembly speaker and senate president pro tem (as long as the Democrats control the state legislature), while Republicans emphasize money from the Assembly Republican Caucus, the Senate Republican Caucus, and the Republican State Central Committee. The California Commission on Campaign Financing notes that transfers from incumbents, party leaders, and party caucuses and committees

> have disrupted the electoral process in several respects. First and perhaps foremost, transfers inject a psychologically destabilizing element into campaigns. Candidates know that at any moment their opponents may suddenly receive as much as $200,000 in last-minute money. This threat encourages candidates to stockpile large cash reserves. Transfers thus contribute to an "arms race" mentality between candidates.[14]

Very large single contributions by individuals or interest groups could have the same effect; these are influential when they occur yet are infrequent.

The California system of privately financed elections has many unfortunate consequences, not the least of which is that locally made decisions are frequently overruled. For example, a city government may turn down the building request of a wealthy developer or may enact a zoning ordinance that the developer does not like. The developer then asks the state legislature to overturn the city's decision while at the same time making generous campaign contributions to influential legislators. Decisions that should really be made at the local level, for example property zoning disputes, are increasingly being made in the state legislature.

The California Commission on Campaign Finance has suggested expenditure ceilings, contribution limits, and limited public financing of campaigns to reform the state's election finance system. Expenditure ceilings reduce some of the destabilizing elements mentioned earlier, such as the fear of last-minute contributions, and they also lessen the fundraising advantages of incumbents.

Candidates accepting matching funds and expenditure ceilings would not need to be constantly searching for ever-increasing amounts of money in an attempt to ensure an election victory. Contribution limits reduce special-interest influence over the legislative process and encourage candidates to seek a larger number of smaller contributions. Limited matching funds would be provided until the expenditure ceilings are reached; within-district contributions would be matched at a ratio of five to one, but out-of-district contributions matched only at a ratio of three to one. Matching funds are derived from a voluntary individual state income tax checkoff of $3. The commission's reform package is a comprehensive one that also includes

- prohibition of transfers by candidates or incumbents to other candidates
- prohibition of non-election-year fundraising
- a requirement that gifts and honoraria for speaking engagements count as part of contribution limit
- limitation on contributions by political parties and legislative caucuses
- limitation on the total amount of contributions that a candidate may receive from political action committees (PACs), corporations, and labor unions

Nearly any far-reaching change in the status quo is likely to have drawbacks. Candidates now spend an inordinate amount of time searching for money; if contributions were limited to $1,000 as suggested by the commission, would they spend even *more* time on fundraising in an attempt to raise the $400,000 or more needed for a race? Rather than spending ceilings, should spending floors (minimum necessary expenditures) be established to enable all candidates to get their message to the voters? Also, the commission's reform plan covers only money contributions; what about in-kind contributions of manpower or equipment that can be used for election day phone banks or get-out-the-vote drives? If political contributions are a form of political expression, are contribution limits a violation of the First Amendment to the U.S. Constitution? Moreover, for those persons who have very little free time, campaign contributions may be their only chance for political activity other than voting. Finally, there is the issue of whether the commission's reforms treat only symptoms and not causes. The heart of the problem is that the taxing, spending, and regulatory policies of government have vast economic and social consequences. As long as Californians want large-scale government, the affected groups (business, labor, farmers, doctors, lawyers, teachers, state employees, utilities, gun owners, and countless others) will find some way to influence the process and protect their interests.

In conclusion, campaign spending needs to be put in perspective. Because of characteristics of this state noted earlier, campaign spending in California calculated on a cost-per-vote basis has to be higher than in other states. The size and diversity of this state (see Chapter 1), antipartyism, weak political parties, low party loyalty among voters, personalized appeals by candidates using media and direct mail, campaign management firms—all of these drive up campaign costs. Also, the availability of money means that more money will be spent: interest groups and wealthy individuals are able to contribute money and are inclined to do so. On the other hand, Sears, Roebuck and Co. or General Motors or Proctor & Gamble may annually spend more money for product advertising in California than it costs to elect a legislature and statewide officers.

POLITICAL REFORM

We cannot conclude our discussion of California politics without mentioning recent political reforms. Reform has been a tradition in this state since the early 1900s. In 1974, California voters, spurred by Watergate revelations, approved an initiative (Proposition 9, the Political Reform Act) with far-reaching consequences. The act, as amended, applies to both state and local candidates. Its election provisions include the following:

1. *Public reports:* A candidate must report the names of everyone contributing more than $100 in money, goods, or services, along with the amount contributed and other details. Anonymous contributions above $100 are illegal. Reports of all amounts received and all expenditures above $100 must be filed both prior to and after an election. No contributions or expenditures above $100 may be made in cash.
2. *Conflict of interest:* Any financial holdings that might bias an official's judgment must be reported; for example, this could include income, real estate, or investments.
3. *Ballot pamphlets:* Citizens are given the opportunity to challenge in court any information in ballot pamphlets that they believe is false or misleading. This challenge may be made before the pamphlets are printed and mailed to the voters.
4. *Fair Political Practices Commission (FPPC):* A five-member commission was established to enforce the act. No more than three members of this commission can be of the same political party. The governor may appoint two members; the attorney general, the secretary of state, and the controller each appoint another.

It is clear that the Political Reform Act has not decreased either overall spending or contributions. Although the act has opened up the election process by compelling disclosure of who is contributing how much to whom, it has also had one ironic result. A report commissioned by the Fair Political Practices Commission concluded that the disclosure provisions made fundraising more difficult, especially for challengers of incumbents. The report described a contribution to a candidate or campaign as a "personal political statement. . . . The individual is more likely to hesitate at the possibility of public disclosure of the personal statement."[15] Since they are already in office and can vote to further a group's goals, incumbents can more easily receive financial contributions from organized interests. Challengers, on the other hand, may have to rely on the personal contributions of people reluctant to reveal their name, address, occupation, and employer's name.

Two other reforms were passed in 1982. After being prodded repeatedly by the FPPC, the legislature forbade personal use of campaign funds. Prior to 1982, candidates could use campaign contributions for non-campaign expenses as long as they paid income taxes on the money. Campaign contributions were used to pay for sports cars, vacations, or divorce proceedings. Now, campaign contributions may only be used for campaign-related expenses or be given to charity. The state legislature also established a procedure through which Californians can contribute up to $25 to the political party of their choice when they fill out their state income tax form. Those taxpayers due for a refund may designate that up to $25 of their refund by given to their favorite party, and those who owe additional taxes may increase their payment by up to $25. All money paid into the fund is disbursed by the chair of each party's state central committee acting with each party's legislative leaders.

SUMMARY

In this chapter, we have discussed antipartyism, the two arenas of California politics, voter registration and absentee voting, types of elections, campaign spending, and political reform. Antipartyism has many manifestations in California, but it can be seen principally in ticket-splitting on the part of voters, weak organizational structures on the part of political parties, and independent campaigns and personalized appeals on the part of candidates. Manifestations of antipartyism are quite striking in races conducted in the competitive statewide arena, but these manifestations are not absent in local legislative races as well. For example, incumbents with strong name identification have an advantage in district races, regardless of party. Furthermore, we can find evidence of antipartyism in any type of election, whether a primary, general, or special election. Antipartyism is a statewide phenomenon, but some political regions will abandon it for an attractive candidate. Antipartyism, a product of early-twentieth-century political reform, has in turn spurred contemporary reform, especially in the area of the corrupting influences of money in politics.

It has frequently been said that political parties in California are electoral mechanisms and not policy mechanisms, that is, they are more effective in winning elections than in formulating public policies. Some cynics even contend that public policy is a means of furthering politics and is not a product of politics; they also argue that public policy is really made by interest groups and not political parties. In any event, we turn to interest groups in Chapter 4.

DISCUSSION QUESTIONS

1. Pretend that you are a candidate for the California legislature. Bearing in mind what this chapter has said about antipartyism, how would you conduct your campaign?
2. Suppose you are a Republican candidate in a district with at least five Democrats for every three Republicans. What would be your approach in this situation?

3. Whether or not reform is motivated by the best of intentions, it some-times goes awry. Why is the absentee voting law a "time bomb waiting to explode"? Would you change how nonvoters are purged from the voting lists?
4. Describe the two arenas of California politics. Why is one noncom-petitive?
5. Is it a contradiction that incumbents in gerrymandered districts have an insatiable demand for campaign funds? Why are off-year fundraising and out-of-district contributions a problem?
6. The Political Reform Act of 1974 reflects the California reform tradition. Name some of its provisions.

NOTES

1. Tony Quinn, "Anatomy of an Electorate," *California Journal* (March 1982): 100–102.
2. John R. Owens et al., *California Politics and Parties* (New York: Macmillan, 1970), p. 4. This book has influenced much of our discussion of antipartyism.
3. A federal appeals court has ruled that the state law prohibiting preprimary endorsements by party committees violates the First Amendment of the U.S. Constitution. It has also struck down requirements that the state central commit-tees elect a new chair every two years (and that the chair be rotated between Northern and Southern California) and has denied the legislature the power to establish criteria for membership on the state central committee. The court's decision is a defeat for members of the state legislature, who now dominate the state central committees. If the ruling is ultimately upheld, it will make both state and county party committees much more powerful, because having the power to make preprimary endorsements will give them something valuable to award or withhold. Moreover, members of party committees are much more liberal (in the case of the Democrats) and much more conservative (in the case of the Republi-cans) than are members of the state legislature. This would make state politics more ideological. In any event, the state attorney general has appealed the decision, and the U.S. Supreme Court will probably decide the issue sometime in the future.
4. Three other Republican organizations of note are the Young Republicans (YRs), the California Federation of Republican Women, and the California Republican League (CRL). The first two groups consist of dedicated campaign workers and the latter embodies the party's Johnson–Warren tradition. In recent years, the Republican state central committee has made substantial campaign contributions to Republicans running for the state legislature. Whether this indicates a revitali-zation of party organizations remains to be seen.
5. Owens, op. cit., p. 158. Campaign strategy is described in greater detail in John Goldbach and Michael J. Ross, *Politics, Parties, and Power* (Pacific Palisades, Ca: Palisades Publishers, 1980), chaps. 4–6.
6. Eugene C. Lee, "The Two Arenas and the Two Worlds of California Politics," in *The California Governmental Process,* ed. Eugene C. Lee (Boston: Little, Brown, 1966), pp. 47–48. The discussion of California's two political arenas does not apply to low-visibility statewide races such as those for state treasurer or secre-tary of state.
7. Robert J. Huckshorn, "Political Defeat," in *Practical Politics in the United States,* ed. Cornelius P. Cotter (Boston: Allyn & Bacon, 1969), pp. 173–196.
8. In 1986, the U.S. Supreme Court ruled that gerrymanders are subject to challenge on constitutional grounds (*Davis v. Bandemer,* 106 S. Ct. 2797 [1986]). However,

those who challenge a gerrymander in court must prove at least three things: there was both the intent to and the effect of discriminating against an identifiable political group, the gerrymander "consistently degrades" the influence of a group of voters on the political process, and there has been a pattern of several lost elections by that group.

9. Robert Studer, "Is Liberalized Absentee Ballot Fraud-prone?", *San Diego Union*, December 12, 1984, p. C6.

10. Frank Sorauf, *Party Politics in America*, 5th ed. (Boston: Little, Brown, 1984), p. 375.

11. Examples of a different kind of special election are the balloting on Gov. Reagan's 1973 tax-limitation initiative, the 1979 votes on busing and on spending limits, and the 1981 San Diego vote on a convention center.

12. Further information on the 1982 election may be found in the *Sacramento Bee*, November 4, 1981, p. A30, June 13, 1982, Forum p. 2, and February 26, 1983, p. A12; the *Los Angeles Times*, October 24, 1982, pt. V, p. 3, and November 7, 1982, pt. I, p. 1. Further information on the 1984 election may be found in the *Sacramento Bee*, December 9, 1984, p. AA5; the *Los Angeles Times*, November 19, 1983, pt. I, p. 1, March 7, 1984, pt. I, p. 1, March 25, 1984, pt. IV, p. 1, April 1, 1984, pt. IV, p. 1, April 25, 1984, pt. I, p. 14, November 8, 1984, pt. I, p. 24, November 22, 1984, pt. I, p. 3; Tony Quinn, "Johnson and Jarvis Lost After Alienating Would-Be Allies," *California Journal* (January 1985): 21. Further information on the 1986 election may be found in the *Sacramento Bee*, June 5, 1986, p. B6; William Endicott, "Trash Clash: Candidates Seek Victory at Bottom of the Barrel," *California Journal* (December 1986): 583–585.

13. California Commission on Campaign Financing, *The New Gold Rush: Financing California's Legislature Campaigns* (Los Angeles: Center for Responsive Government, 1985), pp. 3, 37. See also pp. 2–14, 47, 56, 102–104, 115–120, 134–135, 143; Goldbach and Ross, *Politics, Parties, and Power*, chap.3; and Dan Walters, "The Dark Side of Government," *Sacramento Bee*, March 5, 1986, p. A3. The California Commission on Campaign Finance is a distinguished group of private citizens.

14. California Commission on Campaign Financing, *The New Gold Rush*, p. 102.

15. Allen D. Putt and J. Fred Springer, *Impacts of Campaign Disclosure and Lobbying Provisions of the Political Reform Act of 1974* (Sacramento: Evaluation Research Consultants, November 30, 1977), "Conclusions and Recommendations," pp. 23–24.

4

Interest Groups

California is a diverse state. Californians have an amazing number of interests, ideas, and aims that they would like to see reflected in public policy. Therefore, people organize—they form interest groups. Most interest groups exist to protect the economic self-interest of their members, but some groups have formed because they want to move California in the direction of their notion of a good society. Consider the variety of interests represented by the following interest groups:

1. Business
   - California Chamber of Commerce
   - California Manufacturers Association
   - Association of California Life Insurance Companies
   - California Retailers Association
   - California Bankers Association
   - Mobil Oil
2. Labor
   - California Labor Federation
   - American Federation of Labor–Congress of Industrial Organizations (AFL–CIO)
   - California State Employees Association
   - California Teamsters Public Affairs Council
   - United Farm Workers
3. Agriculture
   - California Farm Bureau Federation
   - Agricultural Council of California
   - California State Grange
4. Professional associations
   - California Medical Association
   - State Bar of California
5. Education
   - Association of California School Administrators
   - California School Boards Association
6. Government officials and local governments
   - County Supervisors Association
   - League of California Cities
   - Association of California Water Agencies
   - City of San Jose

7. Public utilities
    Pacific Gas and Electric Company
    General Telephone Company
    California Railroad Association
8. Ideological organizations
    American Civil Liberties Union (ACLU)
    John Birch Society
9. Racial, ethnic, or religious organizations
    National Association for the Advancement of Colored People
      (NAACP)
    GI Forum (Latino veterans organization)
    California Catholic Conference
    Mexican American Political Association (MAPA)
10. Miscellaneous
    California Taxpayers Association
    Sierra Club
    Los Angeles Dodgers
    Arthur Murray Dance Studios
    Girl Scouts

Although many interest groups have people who speak for them in Sacramento, not everyone speaks with an equally loud voice, nor do the voices fall on equally receptive ears. Spokespeople for local governments, school districts, and government officials are the most numerous, although private business organizations (corporations) are probably the most influential. Groups are usually not concerned with all public questions, only with those issues affecting the group's own interests. Many governmental actions "do not concern many people directly . . . [but] they do concern a few vitally."[1] Interest groups can exert maximum influence on issues that do not significantly touch the interests of a large number of people and that do not receive extensive media coverage. Industries that are under fairly close state regulation, such as the liquor industry, railroads, and trucking, must *lobby*—attempt to influence public officials—rather heavily. Groups whose welfare is dependent on state aid and state legislation must also make their influence felt; for example, many observers rate the California Teachers Association (CTA) as extremely powerful. Interest groups can be considered as a kind of representation, but it is self-interested representation to be sure.

LOBBYISTS

Men and women who speak for interest groups in Sacramento are known as **lobbyists,** or **legislative advocates.** Currently about 750 lobbyists are officially registered, although many lobby part-time or only occasionally. Lobbying is still primarily a male occupation, but about one-fifth of the lobbyists are women. The public's rating of lobbyists is quite low, "somewhere between a used car salesman and a piano player in a house of ill repute."[2] The 750 legislative advocates can be identified by five broad categories:[3]

1. *Private interest lobbyists* who work for a single corporation, industry, or labor union.
2. *Contract lobbyists,* engaged to represent clients in various fields. A famous multiclient lobbyist is James O. Garibaldi, who represents the Association of Talent Agents, Blue Chip Stamps, California Association of Highway Patrolmen, Hollywood Turf Club, Leslie Salt, Pacific Outdoor Advertising, Signal Companies, and Wine and Spirits Wholesalers. Conflict of interest sometimes becomes a problem for the multiclient contract lobbyist or lobbying firm. For example, one firm represents both tobacco interests and health care interests which are opposed to smoking.
3. *Lobbyists for governments or public utilities,* such as lobbyists for the Public Utilities Commission, regional governments, or local governments. We could include here lobbyists for state agencies (these people are usually called legislative liaisons and need not officially register). The governor also has legislative aides, who have been referred to as the governor's lobby; they are very influential. Lobbying of this sort is paid for by taxpayers rather than by interest groups.
4. *"Public-interest" lobbyists,* who represent consumers, environmentalists, children, and poor people.
5. *"Hobbyists,"* or people who like to state their opinions before legislative committees.

TECHNIQUES OF INTEREST GROUPS

Interest groups attempt to influence opinion through television, radio, and newspaper advertising. These public relations efforts can be either short-term (to support or oppose a particular piece of legislation) or long-term (to generate broad support for an organization, industry, or ideology).

In addition, interest groups attempt to influence legislative opinion. Because thousands of bills are introduced each session, no legislator can be informed about all or even most of them. Therefore, lobbyists provide information for legislators on this myriad of bills. Lobbyists or leaders of interest groups also testify at legislative committee hearings. Participation at such hearings is an important activity because many crucial decisions are made at the committee stage of the legislative process described in Chapter 7. Interest groups can inform legislators concerning the actual effects of a bill under consideration— that is, interest groups can say how the bill will work in practice. When many different groups appear before a legislative committee, it is evident which interest groups are for the bill and which are against it. Legislators determine not only the worthiness of the arguments made, but also which interest groups might attempt to injure them should they vote against the interests of those

SOURCE: Dennis Renault, *Sacramento Bee*

groups. The membership of committees with jurisdiction over a group's interests is of vital concern to lobbyists. Interest groups want "friends" assigned to these committees, and to keep hostile legislators off them. These groups frequently draft bills and ask friendly legislators to introduce these bills.

Lobbyists also meet informally with legislators on the so-called wine-and-dine circuit. By entertaining legislators, lobbyists hope to establish favorable social relationships with them. The lobbyists' aim, of course, is to increase their access to, and influence over, decision makers. The wine-and-dine technique has been somewhat curtailed in California under the restrictions of the Political Reform Act, described at the end of this chapter.

A discussion of the entertaining of legislatures brings us to the controversial subject of bribery. Do lobbyists bribe legislators? Of course they do, but not so frequently as the American public might be inclined to believe. Two respected political scientists have written realistically about bribery: "Very simply, it is risky business, for legislator as well as lobbyist; it is costly; it is hard to conceal, for to be effective it must involve a number of lawmakers. . . . The prevalence of bribery in any form is grossly exaggerated."[4] All things considered, California is a relatively honest state. It is not so scandal-free as Wisconsin or Minnesota—each is usually described as "cleaner that a hound's tooth"—but it has avoided the excesses of Illinois, New York, and many states in the South.

Campaign Contributions

Interest groups also make campaign contributions, which some commentators have considered a form of legal bribery. Campaign contributions go overwhelmingly to incumbents because incumbent candidates are most likely to win; the failure of an interest group to contribute to an incumbent legislator may result in the defeat of legislation favored by the interest group or the passage of legislation opposed by the group. In the 1984 elections, the 10 interest groups contributing the most money to legislators gave 96 percent of their contributions to incumbents.

Since campaign contributions are the most effective technique of interest groups, we will examine contributions in some detail. Which interest groups are the biggest givers? The 20 largest contributors to state legislative candidates in the period from January 1975 through the 1982 general elections are listed in Table 4.1. Contributions increased every election in a manner similar to an arms race: for example, total contributions of the groups listed in Table 4.1 increased by 23 percent between 1980 and 1982.

There are three strategies for giving campaign contributions.[5] The first is to give money to incumbents, regardless of party, in order to gain access. Politicians listen more intently to those groups or individuals who are paying for their reelection campaigns. Needless to say, those who make few or no contributions have greatly reduced access. A second strategy is to give money to candidates of the political party closer to the giver's point of view. Good examples are gun owners (Republicans), United for California (Republicans), autoworkers (Democrats), Teamsters (Democrats), AFL–CIO (Democrats), and teachers (Democrats). This strategy is intended to affect the ideological makeup of the legislature. The third strategy is to combine the first two and to try to have it both ways: give to incumbents of either party for access, but also contribute to the candidates of only one party in **open-seat races** when no incumbent is running. Furthermore, larger contributions can be given to candidates of one party. Good examples of the having-it-both ways givers (with the party getting more) are doctors (Republicans), bankers (Republicans), and state employees (Democrats).

Interest groups are also active at the local level. Important campaign contributors in the city of Los Angeles are real estate developers, lawyers and bankers, entertainment industry executives, unions for police and fire fighters, unions

TABLE 4.1   Twenty Largest Contributors
to State Legislative Candidates, 1975 to 1982

California Medical Association	$1,945,157
California State Employees Association	1,589,198
United for California (various large corporations)	1,423,600
California Real Estate Association	1,370,276
California Teachers Association	1,170,990
Gun Owners of California	904,884
California Dental Association	888,646
California Trial Lawyers Association	876,589
California Bankers Association	860,800
AFL–CIO	748,042
Teamsters	682,839
Association of California Insurance Companies	647,382
United Auto Workers	578,481
California Farm Bureau Federation	523,645
Nursing Homes Association	515,435
California Retailers	463,925
Western Growers	460,295
California Automobile Dealers Association	401,940
Southern California Edison	311,432
Housing Council (developers and landlords)	264,620

SOURCE: California Common Cause, *Twenty Who Gave $16 Million* (Los Angeles: California Common Cause, 1983), p. 2. Reprinted by permission.

for city engineers and architects, Atlantic Richfield and Southern California Gas Company, and a homosexual rights organization. Similar organizations have "clout" in nearly all cities, as do the Chamber of Commerce, Kiwanis, Lions, Rotary, League of Women Voters, homeowners groups, and construction unions.

The impetus for ever larger campaign contributions does not always come from the donating interest groups. As the boxed newspaper article makes clear, the recipients likewise apply pressure. If campaign contributions by interest groups are a form of legal bribery, what is described there is a form of legal extortion or shakedown.

Other Lobbying Tactics

In addition to making campaign contributions, interest groups also publicly endorse candidates and give them favorable coverage in publications sent to group members. For example, on the eve of elections, union newspapers give extensive coverage to candidates considered to be friends of labor.

A different tactic used to influence a legislator through his or her constituency has been called the rifle approach—asking people who are influential with an assembly member or senator to talk to the legislator. Another tactic is the shotgun approach, the practice of encouraging **constituents** to write or wire their legislators. In an extreme case, an interest group might threaten to support an opponent in the legislator's next primary or general election. Experienced lobbyists seldom resort to threats because legislators may be around for a long time, and their help may be needed in the future. The words of former Speaker of the Assembly Jesse Unruh are pertinent here: "If I'd slain all my political enemies yesterday, I wouldn't have any friends today."[6]

Another legislative strategy is to form coalitions with other interest groups. The purpose of these temporary alliances might be to pass or kill a specific bill.

Lobbyists Get Word: "Give"

The leadership of the Senate has given some of Sacramento's top lobbyists a not-so-subtle hint to make larger campaign contributions to upper house Democrats or face a less hospitable reception in the Senate.

No one has been harder hit by the toughened stance than California savings and loan associations. Their lead lobbyist, Larry D. Kurmel, was called into the office of Senate Democratic Caucus Chairman Paul D. Carpenter, D-Cypress, Tuesday night and told that in the last election far more money was given to Assembly members.

The meeting came hours after a controversial bill to allow state-chartered financial institutions to make variable rate loans was temporarily derailed by Senate President Pro Tempore David Roberti. Roberti ruled the measure would have to be sent to the Senate Finance Committee, thus delaying possible passage until August.

The bill, which would allow home mortgages to rise or fall with prevailing interest rates, had been awaiting a Senate floor vote.

Both Carpenter and Roberti denied the meeting with Kurmel had anything to do with delay of the measure.

Carpenter said he had been holding discussions with lending industry lobbyists for "more than a month" about increasing financial contributions.

Nonetheless, the meeting with Kurmel was the latest in a series Carpenter has held with lobbyists. And, Carpenter said in an interview, there will be more with other lobbyists in the future.

"Senate Democrats were receiving a disparate amount," Carpenter said.

"People who make contributions apparently feel it doesn't cost any money to be re-elected in the Senate. I don't think it's fair."

The first public indication Senate Democrats were unhappy with the level of contributions came about 10 days ago at a Sutter Club $500-a-plate dinner to benefit the Democratic Caucus. During the dinner, with Roberti and other Senate leaders present, Carpenter told lobbyists he realized large contributions went to Assembly members last year because of a battle over the speakership, according to two lobbyists who attended.

But, he said, Senate Democrats need money too. And he was serving notice they would ask for more.

In the Tuesday meeting, Carpenter said, he worked from a black three-ring binder filled with an analysis of savings and loan and lobbyist-controlled political contributions in Sacramento for the past two years.

"I felt they ought to know I had that kind of data," Carpenter said. He added he did not know whether Roberti had the information.

Kurmel refused all comment. "I don't know nothing," he said. "I don't recall any meeting with Sen. Carpenter."

But several other lobbyists say Kurmel has complained of what he called extortion by the Senate leadership.

SOURCE: "Lobbyists Get Word: 'Give,'" *Sacramento Bee,* July 3, 1981, p. A1. Reprinted by permission.

This process may also involve trade-offs or support of other bills. Coalitions of *diverse* interest groups are very effective because the different elements of the coalition can lobby different legislators, that is, they can piece together a majority composed of different minorities. For example, a coalition of corporations, labor unions, and farm groups would be a force to be reckoned with.

Once a bill has been passed by the legislature, an interest group may urge the governor to sign it or to veto it. If the bill becomes law, it must be administered; therefore, interest groups also attempt to influence administrators. Although the subject matter of many laws may be quite complex, laws are typically general and undetailed because legislators want to give administrators flexibility to deal with unforeseen problems and because the interest groups which favored or opposed the bill during the legislative process were unable to work out a satisfactory compromise. Legislators therefore grant substantial authority to administrators to issue rules and regulations necessary to carry out a law. Interest groups want a law carried out in a manner favorable to them. To this end, interest groups often have been instrumental in establishing a new agency or department. Likewise, the interest group may have persuaded the governor to appoint sympathetic department heads or commissioners. Sometimes the interest group *is* the agency, as in the case of state boards that license chiropractors, embalmers, and barbers. The legislature has attempted to correct this problem by requiring the appointment to boards and commissions of more members who are not linked to established interest groups, so-called "public" members.

Although economic interest groups often loudly oppose government regulation of their activities, they also frequently seek regulation. When the state government licenses such diverse professionals as court reporters, geologists, dry cleaners, architects, cosmetologists, income tax preparers, and even professional wrestlers, the state in effect is limiting access to these professions, thus benefiting those already licensed. Moreover, the state cannot always guarantee that the licensed person is competent. In 1980, large trucking firms fought a bill for increased deregulation of intrastate trucking, expressing great concern that the measure would destabilize the industry, destroy smaller companies, and reduce service to rural areas. Proponents argued that deregulation would lead to greater competition, lower rates, and hence lower costs for consumers. In 1986, the legislature finally abolished the Board of Fabric Care, which was supposed to regulate dry cleaners. Legislators had tried four previous times over two decades, but had been unsuccessful. Although created to eliminate incompetent practitioners, the board had canceled only one dry cleaner's license in the last decade. In fact, it set artificially high licensing standards having no plausible relationship to quality. In the words of a *Sacramento Bee* editorial, all of the board's actions were intended to "keep competition down and prices up" and the board was "taking the public to the cleaners."[7]

Many people wonder why laws seem to be weakly enforced after they are passed. This problem occurs because the administrative process is an extension of the legislative process and because the struggle for power and influence among interest groups has shifted from the legislative to the administrative arena:

> Once the legislation is enacted, the supporting coalition tends to lose interest in the matter, assuming that with the enactment of legislation the problem is adequately cared for. The groups that opposed the law and perceive themselves as bearing the brunt of it remain concerned and active. . . . Much more is heard from them by the enforcing agencies and the legislature concerning the undesirable effects of the legislation. The result may be administrative action and legislative changes tempering the original legislation. Conversely, it may become very difficult for supporters of the original legislation to get together again to secure amendments to strengthen the law.[8]

The intermeshing of public agencies and private groups has long been decried by reformers. The close ties between the public utilities commission and telephone and power companies, between the department of education and the California Teachers Association, between the department of food and agriculture and agricultural interest groups have led many observers to compare this nexus of groups and government to the much-discussed military–industrial complex at the federal level.

After trying to sway legislators, the governor, and administrators, interest groups will seek to influence judges. However, it must be understood that approaching judges necessitates a specific kind of interaction. The medium of interaction is the court case. Groups that have not been influential with the institutions we have mentioned might seek to have a court declare a law unconstitutional by means of the court's power of **judicial review.**

Nor is litigation (bringing suit) the final stage. Interest groups also circulate and campaign for initiative laws and constitutional amendments (see Chapter 5). As a last resort, groups may engage in marches or protest demonstrations to dramatize their grievances.

REGULATION OF LOBBYING

In the last chapter we mentioned that California voters passed a Political Reform Act (Proposition 9) containing many provisions, some of which relate to lobbying. Passed in 1974, the act, which has since been amended about 100 times, requires that every lobbyist—a "person employed or retained . . . to influence legislative or administrative action"—register with the secretary of state and keep detailed records of lobbying expenses. Employers of lobbyists and any person spending more than $5,000 per quarter must also report payments. Furthermore, lobbyists may not make gifts of more than $10 to a state officer in any one-month period. The provisions of the Political Reform Act also apply to lobbyists at the city–county level and to local candidates.

Despite its apparently stringent provisions, Proposition 9 has not significantly altered lobbyist activity in Sacramento, although wining and dining has been somewhat curtailed. The Political Reform Act has decreased personal contact between lobbyists and legislators, but enhanced in importance are written communications to legislators, testimony before legislative and administrative hearings, and especially contacts with legislative staff. However, entertainment is not so important in the influencing of public officials as are campaign contributions, and limiting these is beyond the scope of the Political Reform Act.

How California Podiatrists Won 'Battle of the Ankle'

SACRAMENTO—The fight over the bill could properly be called "the battle of the ankle."

Medical doctors and podiatrists fought one another with intensive lobbying and sizable campaign contributions over legislation that gave podiatrists, who are trained to care for the foot and do not have medical degrees, the legal authority to perform surgery on the ankle.

The California Orthopedic Assn., representing the state's orthopedic surgeons, fears that the medical turf war is not over and that podiatrists will in future sessions try to advance on up the leg.

The podiatry bill was singled out earlier this month by the state Fair Political Practices Commission as the most clear-cut example this year of the effect of big spending in influencing the Legislature.

For seven years, the California Podiatry Assn., representing about half the state's 1,600 podiatrists, had unsuccessfully labored to include the ankle in the legally defined scope of practice of its members—an issue with powerful economic consequences.

This year, after pouring $90,000 into the campaign chests of legislators in less than six months, the podiatrists finally prevailed. The ankle bill, after a close call in the Senate, won legislative approval and became law in July, without the signature of Gov. George Deukmejian.

Deukmejian allowed the bill to pass quietly into law without his endorsement because of "strong opposition from the medical fraternity" on the one hand and no "overwhelming evidence to support a veto" on the other, according to his assistant press secretary, Kevin M. Brett.

Although the podiatrists won the contest that pitted them against the affluent and powerful California Medical Assn., representing about 30,000 medical doctors, and the California Orthopedic Assn., representing half the state's 1,500 orthopedic surgeons, the fight is not over.

The podiatrists' political action committee still had $146,000 on hand after the ankle bill was enacted and have other bills before the Legislature that would give them "parity" with medical doctors in prepaid health plans and on hospital staff committees.

Representatives of both sides deny publicly that money was the deciding factor with this year's bill. Legislators cannot be bought, they say, a point insisted on by several of the legislators themselves.

But at least one orthopedic surgeon said privately: "I think they (the podiatrists) bought the bill, but you can't prove that."

And the chairman of the state Fair Political Practices Commission, Dan Stanford, pointed out that the podiatrists, who were pushing for similar legislation in past years, won only when they began making heavy political contributions.

SOURCE: "How California Podiatrists Won 'Battle of the Ankle'," by P. Jacobs, Los Angeles Times, September 9, 1983, pt. I, p. 1. Copyright 1983, Los Angeles Times. Reprinted by permission.

ATTRIBUTES OF EFFECTIVE INTEREST GROUPS

Some combination of the following factors make an interest group effective: size (number of members), money, unity (an interest group divided against itself will not be effective), members who are willing to devote time to achieve the group's goals, prestige (the group must be accepted as legitimate by public officials), good leadership and good organization, and a skillful and experienced lobbyist.[9] It also helps interest groups to have weak opponents. The article on page 102 not only describes a clash between three powerful groups, but it also shows that the legislative process can be distorted by the inordinate amount of time that is spent on bills that have the potential for campaign contributions. The substance of these bills may not be important for society, but if large campaign contributions are at stake, such bills can rivet the attention of the legislature.

In recent years, California state and local government has seen the rise of intense interest groups with fairly small membership but with influence far out of proportion to their numbers. Legislators cast thousands of votes each session; however, these groups focus on only a single issue, such as gun ownership, abortion (either for or against it), some environmental matters, and other issues. By the use of direct mail, these single-issue groups can target a particular motivated audience to raise money, and then can use the money to attempt to defeat a legislator who has voted incorrectly from the group's perspective. The weakness of California political parties contributes to the effectiveness of single-issue groups. The actions of these groups reduce political compromise and the building of political consensus, and make coherent policymaking much more difficult.

SUMMARY

Interest groups come in all shapes and sizes. In this chapter, we have described their diversity. The range of techniques or strategies employed by interest groups is also quite broad. A fear of improper techniques prompted Californians to pass the 1974 Political Reform Act (Proposition 9). This act was aimed especially at the activities of interest group spokespersons, called lobbyists or legislative advocates. Interest groups and their lobbyists are especially strong in a state like California that has weak political parties. An important means that interest groups use to achieve their ends is seeking the passage of ballot measures. In Chapter 5 we turn to direct democracy.

DISCUSSION QUESTIONS

1. What kinds of interest groups have lobbyists in Sacramento?
2. Can you name some of the techniques or strategies employed by interest groups? Which of these activities were affected by the 1974 Political Reform Act? Which key activity is not significantly regulated by the 1974 act?

3. It is true that interest groups spend much of their time with legislators, but which of their activities are directed toward members of the executive and judicial branches and toward the general public?
4. What factors make an interest group effective? If a special interest had only money, would it still be effective?

NOTES

1. Charles R. Adrian, *State and Local Governments,* 4th ed. (New York: McGraw-Hill, 1976), p. 289.
2. Frank Mesplé and George Cook, "How the Lobbyist Does His Job," in *Capitol, Courthouse, and City Hall,* 6th ed., ed. Robert Morlan and David Martin (Boston: Houghton Mifflin, 1981), p. 153. Mesplé was a lobbyist for Sacramento County, and Cook is a lobbyist for the California Bankers Association.
3. Mesplé and Cook, "How the Lobbyist Does His Job," p. 155.
4. William J. Keefe and Morris Ogul, *The American Legislative Process,* 6th ed. (Englewood Cliffs, NJ: Prentice-Hall, 1985), pp. 280–281.
5. California Common Cause, *Twenty Who Gave $16 Million* (Los Angeles: California Common Cause, 1983), pp. 35–37. A word of caution is in order: money may be *more* important in primaries than in general elections. Because of California's many noncompetitive, gerrymandered districts, the primary is often the real election (see Chapter 3). Those who favor public financing of elections should note this fact.
6. California Journal, *The California Political Action Handbook,* 3rd ed. (Sacramento: California Journal Press, 1987), p. 10.
7. "Taking the Public to the Cleaners," *Sacramento Bee,* January 21, 1985, p. B6.
8. James E. Anderson, *Public Policy-Making,* 3rd ed. (New York: Holt, Rinehart & Winston, 1984), p. 157.
9. Daniel R. Grant and H. C. Nixon, *State and Local Government in America,* 4th ed. (Boston: Allyn & Bacon, 1982), pp. 171–172; John Goldbach and Michael J. Ross, *Politics, Parties, and Power* (Pacific Palisades, CA: Palisades Publishers, 1980), chap. 2.

CHAPTER
5

Direct Democracy

Initiative, **referendum**, and **recall** are forms of **direct democracy**. By means of these three processes, average citizens decide public issues directly, rather than through representatives. (American government is generally thought of as representative democracy, with citizens electing representatives to decide public issues.) The initiative involves voters making laws, referendum means voters repealing laws, and recall involves voters removing public officials before the end of their terms. Not all states have these processes, and the national government does not—having these processes is a matter of state discretion.

States that have the direct democracy devices are generally states in which the Progressives were strong early in this century. The Progressives believed in the wisdom, virtue, and public-spiritedness of the common person. Note that these direct democracy processes are means by which a wise and virtuous public may promote the public interest and control the special interests. Whether the California Progressives built better than they knew or whether they were well-meaning but naive reformers is something for the reader to decide from the information presented in this chapter.

INITIATIVE

The initiative is a means by which voters can enact laws and add amendments to the state constitution. Some initiatives appear in Figure 5.1, as Propositions 5 through 8. The initiative procedure begins with a petition that goes to the attorney general for approval of the initiative's official title and for a short summary that must appear at the head of each petition to be circulated. Those circulating the petition have 150 days to get the required number of signatures. For an initiative constitutional amendment, the required number of signatures is 8 percent of the number of votes cast for all candidates for governor in the last gubernatorial election. (595,479 valid signatures are required through November 1990). In order to get 595,479 *valid* signatures, more than that number of signatures must be collected. The secretary of state must reject many signatures because the signers do not live in California, are not registered to vote, or have moved since registering to vote. Many Californians will sign nearly anything if it sounds impressive or if they want to escape the petition-circulator. For an initiative statute (law), the required number of signatures is 5

MEASURES SUBMITTED TO VOTE OF VOTERS		
STATE		

1 FOR NEW PRISON CONSTRUCTION BOND ACT. Provides $495,000,000 bond issue to be used for the construction of the state prisons. `+`

AGAINST NEW PRISON CONSTRUCTION BOND ACT. Provides $495,000,000 bond issue to be used for the construction of the state prisons. `+`

2 PRESIDENT OF SENATE. Repeals Constitutional provision that Lieutenant Governor is President of Senate. Fiscal impact: No direct state or local impact. YES `+` NO `+`

3 TAXATION. REAL PROPERTY VALUATION. Amends "change in ownership" definition to exclude replacement of property taken by eminent domain type proceedings. Fiscal impact: Significant loss of property tax revenues and increase in administrative costs to local governments. Increased state costs to provide offsetting aid to local school and community college districts. Increase in state income tax revenues due to lower property tax deductions. YES `+` NO `+`

4 BAIL. Prohibits release on bail where court makes findings regarding likelihood of released person causing great bodily harm to others. Fiscal impact: Increase jail and bail hearing costs of local governments. Could be offsetting savings if person later sentenced to jail or prison. YES `+` NO `+`

5 GIFT AND INHERITANCE TAXES (Proponent Miller). Repeals existing taxes. Reenacts state "pickup" estate tax equal to specified federal tax credit. Fiscal impact: Reduce state revenues by about $130 million in 1982-83, $365 million in 1983-84, and higher amounts thereafter. Save state about $6 million annually in administrative costs. State revenue reductions would result in corresponding reductions in state payments to local governments and schools. YES `+` NO `+`

6 GIFT AND INHERITANCE TAXES (Proponent Rogers). Repeals existing taxes. Reenacts state "pickup" estate tax equal to federal tax credit. Fiscal impact: Reduce state revenues by about $130 million in 1982-83, $365 million in 1983-84, and higher amounts thereafter. Save state about $6 million annually in administrative costs. State revenue reductions would result in corresponding reductions in state payments to local governments and schools. YES `+` NO `+`

7 INCOME TAX INDEXING. INITIATIVE STATUTE. Provides continuing personal income tax brackets adjustments by using full Consumer Price Index percentage changes. Fiscal impact: Reduce state revenues by about $230 million in 1982-83, $445 million in 1983-84, and increasing amounts thereafter. State revenue reductions would result in corresponding reductions in state payments to local governments and schools. YES `+` NO `+`

8 CRIMINAL JUSTICE. Amends Constitution and enacts statutes concerning procedures, sentencing, and release of accused and convicted persons and regarding victims. Fiscal impact: Major state and local costs which cannot be predicted with any degree of certainty. YES `+` NO `+`

9 WATER FACILITIES INCLUDING PERIPHERAL CANAL. "Yes" vote approves, "No" vote rejects, a law designating additional Central Valley Project water facilities. Fiscal impact: Under present policies, no increase in state taxes or reduction in funds for other state programs required. Potential construction costs at 1981 prices are in excess of $3.1 billion plus unknown additional costs to be financed by increased user charges. YES `+` NO `+`

10 REAPPORTIONMENT. CONGRESSIONAL DISTRICTS. "Yes" vote approves, "No" vote rejects, statute enacted by 1981 Legislature adopting boundaries for 45 Congressional districts. Fiscal impact: If approved, no state or local costs. If rejected, state costs of $250,000 and county costs of $350,000. YES `+` NO `+`

11 REAPPORTIONMENT. SENATE DISTRICTS. "Yes" vote approves, "No" vote rejects, statute enacted by 1981 Legislature revising boundaries of 40 Senate districts. Fiscal impact: If approved, no state or local costs. If rejected, state costs of $370,000 and county costs of $500,000. YES `+` NO `+`

12 REAPPORTIONMENT. ASSEMBLY DISTRICTS. "Yes" vote approves, "No" vote rejects, statute enacted by 1981 Legislature revising boundaries of 80 Assembly districts. Fiscal impact: If approved, no state or local costs. If rejected, state costs of $400,000 and county costs of $650,000. YES `+` NO `+`

FIGURE 5.1 The June, 1982 state ballot included a number of significant measures. Proposition 4 (see Chapter 1) is the state legislature's constitutional amendment on bail rights. Propositions 5 and 6 (Chapter 5) both passed, but Proposition 6 received the higher number of votes, so it became law. Proposition 7 is discussed in Chapter 10, and Proposition 8, the "Victim's Bill of Rights," is examined closely in Chapter 1. Propositions 9 to 12 (Chapter 5) are the only referenda to appear on a statewide ballot since 1952.

percent of the number of votes cast for all candidates for governor in the last gubernatorial election (372,174 valid signatures required through November of 1990). If the required number of signatures have been obtained within the 150-day period, the petitions go to the secretary of state so that he or she may verify the signatures. The initiative constitutional amendment or initiative statute then goes on the ballot at the next statewide election. How have the initiatives fared? Since 1912, voters have approved about 29 percent of the initiative constitutional amendments and initiative statutes on the ballot.

Some examples of recent initiatives are the following: the Coastal Zone Conservation Act of 1972, the Political Reform Act of 1974, the nuclear power safety initiative of 1976, the Jarvis–Gann property tax initiative (Proposition 13 in 1978), the initiative of 1978 prohibiting school employees from advocating homosexuality, the tax-big-oil initiative of 1980, handgun control and deposits on bottles and cans in 1982, the 1984 welfare and reapportionment initiatives, and "deep pockets" (tort liability) and acquired immune deficiency syndrome (AIDS) in 1986. It is clear that many of the most controversial issues in state government have been thrashed out in the form of initiatives. Sponsors of initiatives (usually interest groups) prefer constitutional amendments to statutes because once legislation has been written into the state constitution, a two-thirds vote of the legislature and another vote by the people (or a completely new initiative amendment) are required to change what has been done. On the other hand, initiative statutes may be revised or repealed by a majority vote of the legislature and can be declared unconstitutional by either state or federal courts.[1] In the event that two conflicting initiatives are approved by the voters, the one receiving the higher vote becomes law. For example, Propositions 5 and 6 (in Figure 5.1) both passed in June 1982. Since Proposition 6 received a higher number of votes, it became law. Initiatives can take effect the day after the election.

REFERENDUM

The referendum (or petition referendum, as it is sometimes called) is the electorate's means of stopping a recently enacted law from going into effect. Except for **urgency laws**, state laws do not take effect for at least ninety days after passage. During this ninety-day period, opponents of a recently enacted statute circulate referendum petitions, trying to obtain the required number of signatures—5 percent of the votes cast for all candidates for governor in the last gubernatorial election, the same number required for initiative statutes. If enough signatures are gathered, the law is suspended until the next statewide election, when voters may approve or reject the law. Certain laws are exempt from the referendum procedure, however:

1. urgency statutes, which are passed by a two-thirds vote of each house and take effect immediately
2. statutes providing for taxes
3. laws for appropriating money
4. laws calling for special elections

In 1982, a referendum to prevent construction of the Peripheral Canal and three referenda to invalidate legislative reapportionment plans appeared on the ballot. (See Proposition 9 and Propositions 10, 11, and 12 in Figure 5.1.) These were the first referenda presented to Californians since 1952.[2] The petition referendum is used more frequently at the local level.

Another kind of referendum—the compulsory referendum—is seen frequently at all levels of government. When the state legislature has passed an amendment to the state constitution or has issued a bond over $300,000 (that is, has proposed that the state go into debt over $300,000), the electorate must approve each of these actions by majority vote. Local bond issues—in cities, counties, and school districts—must receive a two-thirds vote. This requirement means that local bond issues are frequently defeated, although they have received a majority vote.[3] Referenda take effect the day after the election. The state legislature may amend or repeal referenda.

PROS AND CONS

When we discuss the arguments for and against the initiative and referendum, we do not do so because Californians are considering abandoning these devices. By noting that initiatives and referenda have both virtues and vices, we can better understand them.

Arguments in Favor

Strengthen popular control over government   If American government is government by the people, then initiative and referendum processes allow average citizens to express their will, especially if representative institutions are not reflecting public opinion. Theodore Roosevelt said that "the movements in favor of [initiative and referendum] were largely due to the failure of the representative bodies really to represent the people."[4] Contemporary proponents of direct democracy argue that "the very essence of democracy [is] the right to decide issues."[5] California received such worthwhile improvements as the merit system of state employment and the executive budget by means of the initiative. Without this device, the legislature might have held up these reforms for many years. The political theory of direct democracy was summarized by John Dewey: "The cure for the ailments of democracy is more democracy."[6]

Control special interests   If moneyed interests have excessive influence in the legislature (as happened in California during the Artie Samish era of the 1940s), direct democracy allows citizens to regain control over their own government. Indeed, direct democracy was first introduced to break the pervasive control of the Southern Pacific Railroad over California politics in the early twentieth century.

Make legislature responsive   The initiative spurs a lethargic legislature to action, and the referendum serves as a check on unpopular legislation. Moreover, if elected officials are evading or sidestepping vital public issues, these issues can be *publicly* resolved by the initiative process.

Resolve emerging issues   Because of the weakness of political parties and the public's lack of confidence in elected officials, the initiative and referendum are the best way to resolve emerging or nontraditional issues in such areas as the environment, energy, health, lifestyle values, and others. Writer John

Naisbitt sees direct democracy as the wave of the future and as a direction that will transform our lives.[7]

Aid civic education   As vital questions receive a public airing, Californians' understanding of the issues of the day is furthered: "In the discussion and controversy over popular issues may be found the vitality of California government."[8] Furthermore, as citizens rule themselves directly through these processes, election turnout will be increased and public apathy decreased.

Arguments Against

Impair representative government   The crucial decisions of American government are supposed to be made by representatives elected by the people. Devices such as initiative and referendum were precisely what the founders of this nation wished to avoid.[9] Furthermore, the existence of the initiative allows the legislature to turn over controversial issues to the voters and to abdicate responsibility. Legislators and the governor are elected (and paid) to make decisions, and they should make them.

Lengthen the ballot   Californians already elect a bewilderingly large number of officials at the state, county, city, and special-district levels. Added to this total are numerous ballot propositions. How many citizens can adequately inform themselves on these matters?

Aid special interests   The intent of the California Progressives was to control special interests, but initiatives and referenda have become the *tools* of special interests. In 1912, 85,000 signatures were needed to put a constitutional amendment on the ballot; now more than half a million signatures are needed. Only a wealthy group can get that many signatures. A special-interest group does not need a large membership (although that helps), but rather money. It can hire a petition-circulating firm to gather the signatures (at about $1.00 to $1.50 per valid signature). Not only is money necessary to get an initiative on the ballot, but even more money is also needed to hire a campaign management firm to run the initiative campaign and to buy the television and radio time for advertising. The eight most expensive initiative campaigns in California history are as follows (note not only the large amounts, but also the imbalances):

- *Tort liability (1986):* $11.1 million ($6.2 million spent in favor, $4.9 million in opposition)—the most expensive ballot campaign in the state's history.
- *Property taxes (1984):* $10.4 million ($8.7 million spent in favor, $1.7 million in opposition).
- *Reapportionment (1984):* $10.3 million ($6 million in favor, $4.3 million in opposition).
- *Handgun control (1982):* $9.8 million ($2.6 million spent in favor, $7.2 million in opposition); more money was spent on this ballot proposition than was spent by either candidate running for governor in the same year.
- *Regulation of indoor smoking (1978):* $7.1 million—tobacco companies outspent their opponents by a margin of ten to one.

- *Rent control (1980):* $6.8 million—landlords and developers spent over $6 million trying to restrict rent control.
- *Public employee salaries (1986):* $6.7 million—public employees spent $5.8 million to defeat a cap on their salaries.
- *Mandatory deposit on bottles and cans (1982):* $6.3 million (less than $1 million spent in support of the proposition, and almost $6 million spent in opposition).

However, when we adjust spending totals for the effects of inflation, the "award" for the highest spending must go to a 1956 oil and gas conservation measure, followed by a 1958 right-to-work proposition.

It is important to caution that the side that spends the greater amount of money in an initiative campaign is not guaranteed success. For example, the side spending more on each of the 1984 measures noted above lost anyway; during the 1970s the higher-spending side lost eight out of twenty-one times. Lavish spending is probably more effective in defeating a measure than in promoting it. The fact that money can be more effectively used to defeat an initiative than to pass one may give wealthy interest groups a virtual veto over initiative measures. This effect is the exact opposite of the intended purpose of the initiative process. Opponents can hammer away at weak points or inconsistent parts of an initiative. Californians seem to be guided in initiative voting by the premise, "When in doubt, vote 'No.'" The inclination to vote negatively is strongest when ballot measures are complicated or confusing. Well-financed initiative opponents can play on this disposition. All of these factors taken together may help to explain why almost three in four initiative campaigns fail.

Allow poorly drafted legislation   Since an initiative is drawn up by an interest group to further its own goals, the measure may be more the product of ideological zeal than of careful legal drafting. (This is not to say that statutes passed by the California legislature are without fault. But laws passed by the legislature have been drafted by the legislative counsel and have survived the give-and-take compromises of the legislative process.) Whatever their merits or defects may be, all initiative and referendum proposals must be accepted or rejected in their entirety. Many initiatives are ruled unconstitutional by the courts.

Contribute to civic miseducation   Groups do not enter the direct democracy arena because they want to educate the public in a great political science seminar. They usually have financial ends in mind. Misleading claims and emotional propaganda may be more effective than the truth in furthering the aims of these groups. A favorite tactic is to stress slogans that the groups know are false but that they believe will be effective. For example, opponents of the 1972 coastal conservation initiative advertised, "Don't let them lock up our coast," although the initiative was designed to prevent just that. In 1976, opponents of the farm-labor initiative claimed that the proposition's access rule violated private property rights, despite the fact that the state supreme court, with the silent concurrence of the U.S. Supreme Court, had ruled that private property rights were not violated. In 1980, realtors and apartment owners placed on the ballot an initiative to restrict rent control, but advertised their measure as furthering rent control. The article on the next page describes trickery on *both* sides of an issue.

The essence of the problem is twofold. Voters are asked "to make policy decisions on questions that are often complex, technical, and minutely detailed."[10] At the same time, "voters seldom have clearly defined opinions about most measures even on the eve of voting. . . . Opinions of this type are often subject to quick change under the pressure of massive propaganda and emotional appeals."[11] The situation favors highly skilled public relations firms which can severely simplify complex issues.

There has been a remarkable tendency in some recent elections for voters to begin the election year strongly in favor of a particular measure, but after an intensive and expensive media barrage by the opponents, to defeat the initiative overwhelmingly on election day. The 1978 measure to regulate indoor smoking and the 1982 propositions on handgun control and mandatory deposits on bottles and cans are good examples. Victory usually goes to the side that can define the issues. Opponents often train their media weapons only on a small part of a ballot proposition, and then hammer away on that point. For example, opponents of the 1978 clear indoor air initiative succeeded in confining the debate to a discussion of intrusion by "big brother government," rather than of research on the harmful effects of secondhand smoke and nonsmokers' rights. (The fact that they could outspend their opponents ten to one was also a key factor here, too.) Had the debate revolved around the latter issue, the result might have been different. Speaker of the Assembly Willie Brown was the principal force behind the successful 1984 campaign against a reapportionment initiative; after the election was safely over, Brown described the media campaign as "the most extensive collection of con jobs I've ever seen."[12] He also went on to say "I firmly think the initiative process in California is the single greatest threat to democracy in California."

THE DISTORTION OF THE PROCESS

The initiative is undergoing a gradual but significant transformation in California. It was originally thought of as a gun behind the door, to be used only in extraordinary circumstances, but now it has become a *regular* part of the political process. In fact, a member of the state legislature may imply, as he or she is introducing a piece of legislation, "If this bill is not passed into law, I will immediately start circulating initiative petitions." When Howard Jarvis qualified his income tax-cutting initiative for the June 1980 ballot, he did not rely on volunteers to circulate his petition. Instead, Jarvis replaced volunteers with a carefully worded computer-printed letter. The letter contained not only an initiative petition but also a stamped envelope for financial contributions. The experiment was a stunning success. Of the 6 million mailers sent out, 400,000 came back with 820,000 signatures, far more than needed to qualify the measure. Half of the returned envelopes contained contributions totaling $1.8 million. According to Butcher–Forde Consulting, the direct mail firm employed by Jarvis, the average contribution was under $10, and only 1 percent of the $1.8 million came in amounts over $100.[13] The whole effort paid for itself.

Butcher–Forde advertises that computer-assisted mailing is cheaper than paid petition-circulators. The company will rent to clients a list of people who have contributed to initiative campaigns. This list can be used repeatedly and refined, paving the way for successive campaigns by groups or wealthy individuals with an interest or cause to promote. Hiram Johnson and the California Progressives would have a difficult time recognizing their brainchild: nowadays the initiative is viewed not as an extraordinary remedy for political abuses but rather as a regular method for accomplishing political aims. Moreover, instead of concerned citizens asking other citizens face to face to support an initiative that will shatter special-interest influence, a computer cranks out clever letters for those who can pay the price.

Butcher–Forde Consulting is an integral part of what has come to be known as the "initiative industry." This industry consists of profit-making firms which are in the long-term business of promoting initiatives. Such firms can draw up the initiative using staff lawyers aided by campaign consultants who will word

Proposition 37 Has That Layered Look

Remember that oath that witnesses in court are required to take, the one where they promise to tell the "truth, the whole truth and nothing but the truth?" It doesn't apply to politics.

Take, for example, the campaign for and against the state lottery (Proposition 37) on the Nov. 6 ballot. This is a measure with the layered look.

Ostensibly, a group of Californians worried about the fate of the schools—calling themselves, of course, Californians for Better Education—gathered their collective energies and in the true spirit of volunteerism sponsored a measure to provide more money for education.

Their solution to the perennial needs of the schools would be a lottery that, they said, would provide a half-billion dollars a year.

By and by, it became known that Californians for Better Education was just a front for a corporation called Scientific Games, which is a major supplier of materials for state lotteries and which put up a million bucks for the campaign that put Proposition 37 on the ballot. That was one layer peeled back.

Those who analyzed Proposition 37 carefully concluded that its provisions meant that it would be difficult for any-one other than Scientific Games to obtain the very lucrative contracts to supply materials for what could be a multi-billion-dollar lottery in the nation's largest state.

And then it was revealed that Scientific Games is a subsidiary of the Bally Manufacturing Corp., which is into gambling in several ways, including its domination of the slot machine-making market. Another layer.

Californians for Better Education ran around lining up school board members and others who would place their names on the measure as supporters, trying to provide some legitimacy to the contention that it was all for the kids.

Why education? Because Californians support the public schools. In reality, it would be difficult to guarantee that the proceeds from the lottery would go to education because there is nothing to prevent the governor and the Legislature from "backing out" the money they otherwise would have spent on increases in school aid in the future. That, in effect, would allow the lottery proceeds to go for other state programs. But, as one can readily see, a lottery promoted under the name of "Californians for Higher Welfare Payments" wouldn't get very far. Educa-

the proposition for maximum political appeal. The firm can then gather the required signatures, manage the subsequent media campaign, and later use its attorneys to fend off any legal challenges to the successful initiative. The initiative industry is a peculiarly California brand of "one-stop shopping." Since firms like Butcher–Forde plan to stay in business for a long time, they are always looking for creditworthy customers with an idea to promote. It is also not inconceivable that firms in the industry might think up a winning idea and then search out a group with seed money to fund the campaign. The basis is laid for nonstop initiative campaigns.

RECALL

The **recall** is a means by which state or local elected officials—from the governor to local school board members—may be removed from office before the end of their terms. (Members of the U.S. House of Representatives and U.S.

---

tion is simply a marketing tool to sell California voters on a lottery. It's just another layer.

The opposition to Proposition 37 has some layers of its own. Out front, the opponents are political leaders such as Gov. Deukmejian and Attorney General John Van de Kamp, who worry about the impact of expansion of gambling, and the traditionally antigambling churches.

Organizationally, however, the chief opposition is something called Californians Against the Eastern Lottery Fraud, which is conducting a sophisticated media campaign against Proposition 37.

The campaign makes much of the fact that Scientific Games and Bally are bankrolling the pro-lottery campaign.

One TV spot uses two shady-looking characters who chortle over their use of Californians for Better Education as a front to hide that "we had organized crime connections . . . " That is a reference to a never-proven-in-court allegation that Bally's executives had some dealings with organized crime figures.

That's hardball politics, perhaps, but within the parameters of legitimacy.

It turns out, however, that Californians Against the Eastern Lottery Fraud is not exactly a grassroots citizens group either.

Campaign finance statements reveal that virtually all of the money for the slick anti-Proposition 37 campaign comes from the state's horse racing tracks. Another layer.

Now why would the horse racing people care whether there is a state lottery?

One theory is that there's only so much gambling action available and at least some of the money that would be spent on lottery tickets would be money that otherwise would go for $2 bets on horse races.

But it's also interesting to note that the horse racing executives who are putting up cash for Californians Against the Eastern Lottery Fraud had a lottery proposal of their own in the Legislature. Called a "special sweepstakes," the horse racing lottery would have provided daily payoffs based on results of specified races—with much of the money going to the tracks and the breeders.

If Proposition 37 is passed, the horse people can kiss their "special sweepstakes" goodbye.

Another layer.

SOURCE: Dan Walters, "Prop. 37 Has Layered Look," © *The Sacramento Bee*, October 17, 1984, p. A3. Reprinted by permission.

Senate, because they are federal officials, cannot be recalled.) The recall, like other direct democracy devices, begins with a petition.

To initiate the recall of an officer elected statewide, a group must obtain valid signatures equal to 12 percent of the votes cast for that office in the last election, and signatures must come from at least five counties (to prevent a single large county like Los Angeles from recalling state officials). The number of signatures in each of these five counties must equal at least 1 percent of the votes most recently cast for the office in that county.

The recall of other state officials—such as judges, members of the legislature, and members of the board of equalization—requires signatures equal to 20 percent of the last vote cast for the office. The petition must state the grounds for removal, but this statement typically is couched in vague terms. Officials need not do something illegal in order to be recalled: the grounds for recall may amount to no more than personal animosity.

Recall supporters must file their petitions with the California secretary of state within 160 days after they begin circulating them. If the required number of signatures has been secured, the governor must call a recall election within 60 to 80 days after the petitions have been certified by the secretary of state. The ballot in this election requires two distinct choices. First, the voters decide a question similar to the following: "Shall Joe Zilch be recalled from the office of _____ ? Vote yes or no." A majority of "yes" votes is needed to recall the incumbent. Next follows a list of candidates, excluding the incumbent, who would like to serve the rest of the unexpired term. Only a plurality vote is needed for victory in the second step of the process. If a majority of votes were negative in the first step on the ballot, all votes for candidates in the second step are disregarded. Figure 5.2 shows the ballot used in the successful 1979 recall of the chair of the Los Angeles School Board.

Although it thrives at the local level, recall has never been a realistic threat at the state level in California. From time to time, the opponents of a governor or state supreme court justice will circulate recall petitions, but this gesture is not a serious attempt: it is more a form of harassment, a ploy to embarrass the governor or justice. If an official's opponents get the required number of signatures (an unlikely event, considering the 12–20 percent requirement) but the recall attempt fails, the state will reimburse the official for all expenses incurred in defeating the recall. Therefore, he or she is encouraged to make every effort because as far as spending is concerned, the sky is the limit. But, of course, the official had better beat the recall attempt.

In closing our discussion of recall at the state level, we give one word of caution: recall should not be confused with impeachment. Recall is done by the *voters*, but impeachment is done by the *legislature*. Impeachment requires allegations of serious lawbreaking; recall does not.

DIRECT DEMOCRACY AT THE LOCAL LEVEL

Referendum and recall are rare at the state level but frequent at the local level. The initiative occurs frequently at both levels. Recalls of local officers such as mayors, city council members, and especially school board members, occur

3

300

MUNICIPAL BALLOT
SPECIAL RECALL ELECTION
Tuesday, May 29, 1979

Shall Howard Miller be removed from the office of Member of the Board of Education of the Los Angeles Unified School District, Office Number Two by the recall?

| YES | 41 ➡ |
| NO | 43 ➡ |

FOR MEMBER OF THE BOARD OF EDUCATION
OFFICE NUMBER TWO

Candidates nominated to succeed Howard Miller for the remainder of the term in case he is removed from the office of Member of the Board of Education of the Los Angeles Unified School District, Office Number Two by the recall are listed below.

Vote

for

One

DOLLY J. SWIFT Accountant	50 ➡
DAN DANKO Retired Police Sergeant	51 ➡
JUDY KELLY Concerned Parent	52 ➡
JOSE P. GALVAN Community Affairs Specialist	53 ➡
ROBERTA WEINTRAUB Director, Miller Recall	54 ➡
JOSEPH B. HENDERSON Medical Doctor	55 ➡
ELEANORE PARKER State Central Committeeman	56 ➡

FIGURE 5.2   Sample ballot, May 29, 1979

quite frequently. During the 1970s, 375 local officials were on recall ballots, and 187 (one-half) were recalled. In small communities particularly, recall elections can be terribly bitter and divisive and may lead to recriminations and counter-recalls. In the aftermath of a recall, residents may not cooperate with each other for many years, and divisions within the community may deepen. In some communities, the recall may be used to remove incompetent officials who fail to act or who act wrongly. In other communities, recall might be used to remove competent officials who have pursued unpopular policies too energetically.

The Coro Foundation studied use of the local initiative in the San Francisco Bay Area during the 1974–1984 period.[14] A total of 110 initiatives appeared on ballots in 94 cities, but nearly one-half of these were in Berkeley and San Francisco alone. Forty percent were approved, a higher approval percentage than at the state level. The most frequent initiative subjects are development (both for and against) and rent control. As at the state level, campaign spending in opposition to a measure is more effective than spending in favor of it.

SUMMARY

Initiative constitutional amendments, initiative statutes, the referendum, and the recall are instruments of direct democracy to serve the public when elected representatives fail to act. For example, California's Proposition 13, the Jarvis amendment, was the opening gun of a nationwide tax revolt. Property tax relief had been a prime legislative and gubernatorial concern for more than a dozen years, but not until Californians reached for the gun behind the door were results obtained.

Beyond the merits or demerits of any specific measure such as Proposition 13, we have considered pro and con arguments about the wisdom of direct democracy itself. However one evaluates direct democracy—and sensible men and women can be found on either side—the process reflects something of the self-confident spirit of California itself. Initiative use is on the rise, partly as a result of the efforts of the initiative industry and partly as a result of a public policy gridlock in state government, especially in the state legislature, in which powerful interest groups seem to have checkmated each other. If gerrymandered districts have produced insulated and unresponsive legislators, one alternative for dissatisfied individuals and groups is to "go the initiative route."

DISCUSSION QUESTIONS

1. Resolved: Direct democracy has worked about as well as the Progressives believed that it would work. Argue one side of this issue, then argue the other side. In this exercise, you need not become like the ancient Greek Sophists, who would argue any side of any question because they did not believe in the possibility of truth. Rather, by knowing the strongest and weakest elements of an argument, you can better understand the issues involved.

2. Neal Pierce, a writer on state government, suggests that California return to the indirect initiative. Under an indirect initiative process, a minimum number of signatures can force the legislature, not the general public, to vote on a measure. The legislature may pass the measure, amend it, or reject it. If the legislature chooses either of the latter two, the measure's sponsors can require that the original measure go on the ballot. Evaluate this proposal.

3. As you answer the following questions, consider what your answers reveal about the theory and practice of direct democracy. Why are more signatures required on a petition for an initiative constitutional amendment than on a petition for an initiative statute? Have most initiatives been approved by the voters? Why are some laws exempt from the petition referendum? Do you favor extending the petition referendum to laws that levy taxes and spend public money? Are the signature requirements for recall of state officials too high? If state officials could be forced into a recall election with fewer signatures, how would the conduct of state government be changed?

NOTES

1. Changes made by the legislature in an initiative statute must be approved by the voters unless the initiative permits such changes without voter approval. Furthermore, initiative constitutional amendments may be declared in violation of the U.S. Constitution. For examples of initiatives declared unconstitutional, see *Mulkey v. Reitman,* 64 Cal. 2d 529 (1966), affirmed in *Reitman v. Mulkey,* 387 U.S. 369 (1967).
2. A group that does not move quickly enough to qualify a referendum during the ninety-day period before a law goes into effect can try to overrule the law by means of an initiative. Proposition 14 in 1964 repealed the Rumford Fair Housing Act of 1963.
3. Another provision in the state constitution (Article 34) prohibits the building of federally financed low-rent housing without majority approval of those voting in a local election. This section was upheld by the U.S. Supreme Court in *James v. Valtierra,* 402 U.S. 137 (1971), a case originating in the city of San Jose.
4. Quoted in Winston W. Crouch, *The Initiative and Referendum in California* (Los Angeles: Haynes Foundation, n.d.), p. 3. The discussion of pros and cons also draws on Russell Maddox and Robert Fuquay, *State and Local Government,* 4th ed. (New York: D. Van Nostrand, 1981), pp. 181–187.
5. Laura Tallian, *Direct Democracy* (Los Angeles: People's Lobby Press, 1977), p. 2.
6. John Dewey, *The Public and Its Problems* (Chicago: Gateway Books, 1946), p. 146.
7. John Naisbitt, *Megatrends: Ten New Directions Transforming Our Lives* (New York: Warner Books, 1982), chap. 7.
8. Crouch, *Initiative and Referendum in California,* pp. 10–11.
9. See James Madison, Alexander Hamilton, and John Jay, *The Federalist Papers* (New York: Mentor Books, 1961), and Herbert Croly, *The Promise of American Life* (New York: Macmillan, 1914), p. 320.
10. Charles Adrian, *State and Local Governments,* 4th ed. (New York: McGraw-Hill, 1976), p. 137.
11. "Initiatives: A Question of Control," *Los Angeles Times,* March 26, 1982, pt. I, p. 20. The quotation is from Mervin Field, who operates the respected California Poll, or Field Poll.
12. John Balzar, "Brown Labels Anti–Proposition 39 Ads 'Con Jobs,'" *Los Angeles Times,* November 22, 1984, pt. I, p. 3. See also David Magleby, *Direct Legislation* (Baltimore, MD: Johns Hopkins University Press, 1984), pp. 59–60, 168.
13. Maureen Fitzgerald, "Computer Democracy," *California Journal* (June 1980): 4.
14. Coro Foundation, *Local Initiative* (San Francisco: Coro Foundation, 1984).

PART

3

The major institutions of government in California are the executive branch, the state legislature, and the state court system. These institutions of government determine and resolve questions of policy.

In Chapter 6, we will study the office of governor and other executive offices such as those of the attorney general and the state controller. Various boards, commissions, and agencies are also part of the executive branch, but the towering figure in the executive branch and in all of state government is the governor, the person who provides the leadership for California government. The governor's position is preeminently a policy position. The one policymaker most likely to have a significant effect on the issues we mentioned earlier—in the areas of energy, jobs, education, and so forth—is the governor.

We will consider the California legislature in Chapter 7. In the legislature, the great issues of state government are debated and voted upon, and the state budget is passed. Competent observers have rated California's as one of the

Major Institutions

best state legislatures in the country. It can be a formidable adversary for the governor.

The state court system is the topic of Chapter 8. A wise political philosopher once wrote, "Scarcely any political question arises in the United States that is not resolved, sooner or later, into a judicial question."[1] Controversial issues such as environmental protection, school finance, the death penalty, water rights, and integration have all been ruled upon by the state courts.

NOTE

1. Alexis de Tocqueville, *Democracy in America*, ed. Phillips Bradley (New York: Vintage Books, 1945), vol. 1, p. 290.

6

Executive Branch

In this chapter, we consider the executive branch of state government, which consists of the governor, the governor's cabinet, other state constitutional officers, a wide array of agencies and departments, and various boards and commissions.

The public expects the governor to be *chief* executive, or head of the executive branch, and holds the governor accountable for the performance of the executive branch. However, for reasons we will examine, the state constitution really invites the governor to *strive* to be the chief of the executive branch. Some governors are more successful than others.

Despite limitations of the office, the governor of California is the most important person in state politics and one of the most important people in national politics as well. California's governors have often been individuals of great stature or personal magnetism who have left indelible marks on the state's history and have influenced national events. A sketch of **gubernatorial** powers follows. The reader should bear in mind that whether a governor uses these powers creatively or perfunctorily is largely determined by the governor's conception of the office.

POWERS OF THE GOVERNOR

Each year, the governor delivers a State of the State message, a report to the legislature about the condition of the state. This message typically is rather general, but it is soon followed by a package of specific bills—the governor's legislative program—which may constitute the legislature's agenda for much of the upcoming session. The aphorism "the executive proposes and the legislature disposes" is simplistic but accurate: the person who most influences what the legislature produces does not even belong to the legislative body. The extent of the governor's legislative success depends upon many factors: public popularity, especially as gauged by respected public opinion polls such as the Field Poll; how many seats his or her party has in each chamber of the legislature; the loyalty of members of the governor's party; the governor's ability to work with the legislative leadership; and the issues on which the governor chooses to take a stand.

In any case, we have noted that one of the ways the governor can exercise power is by vetoing bills passed by the legislature. Although recent governors have vetoed only about 7 percent of all bills passed on the average, the *threat* of a veto is nearly as important as the act itself. By using this threat, the governor can prevent laws or parts of laws from passing the legislature in the first place. The veto can also crucially affect the many bills, often the key ones of the session, that are passed at the very end of the session.

The legislature can override a governor's veto by a two-thirds vote in each house, but the chances of this happening are slim indeed. Since 1946, there have been only seven successful overrides of a governor's veto. The unfortunate governors were Earl Warren (once), Ronald Reagan (once), and Jerry Brown (five times). In July 1979, after relations between Brown and the legislature had seriously deteriorated, he was overridden three times in a single month! (Two bills would have allowed retroactive pay increases for state employees; the third prohibited banks from selling automobile, homeowner, and casualty insurance.)

The governor's most significant duty is to submit the state budget to the legislature in the first ten days of each year. The governor recommends expenditures, estimates revenues, and sometimes proposes new sources of revenue. When the legislature has modified and returned the budget bill, the governor may exercise an **item veto**. This weapon allows the governor to reduce or eliminate, but not raise, any item in an appropriations bill. The item veto is a powerful tool because it prevents the legislature from presenting the governor with take-it-or-leave-it spending bills. Rather, the governor can use the threat of an item veto to pressure the legislature. (The president of the United States does not have an item veto.)

In addition to the veto power, the governor may also call the legislature into special session, during which it must act only on the topics specified in the session's proclamation issued by the governor. By convening a special session, the governor obliges the legislators to settle specific issues thay have avoided or over which they have been deadlocked. For example, in 1986 Governor Deukmejian called a special session to address the issue of building a state prison in Los Angeles County. The last previous special session was in 1982.

Along somewhat different lines, the governor makes about 2,000 appointments, but as indicated earlier, California is not a high-patronage state. For example, the governor appoints agency secretaries and department heads, such as the secretary of resources and the director of the department of motor vehicles, and makes appointments to boards and commissions, such as the public utilities commission, the trustees of the state university system, and the board of governors of the state's community colleges. In addition, should any of the following die or resign, the governor may name a successor: U.S. senator, state constitutional officer (for example, attorney general or secretary of state), or county supervisor. As we shall see in Chapter 8, the governor also appoints judges. The characteristics of the men and women appointed to these positions are of great interest, since they provide some idea of a governor's basic beliefs. For example, many of former Governor Jerry Brown's appointees viewed themselves as agents of change, people dissatisfied with traditional practices and interested in trying avant-garde or even radical approaches in state and local government.

A recent book by Gary G. Hamilton and Nicole Woolsey Biggart describes the governor's relationships with the top nonelected officials in the executive branch and also evaluates Governors Reagan and Brown as administrators.[1] The governor's personal staff is extremely important because of all the vital issues demanding attention and because the governor's time is limited. These people make many important decisions on behalf of the governor, but they do not exercise authority in their own right—all their authority is derivative from the governor. The governor's immediate staff is characterized by personal loyalty to the governor as an individual and by a lack of independence: they tend to be younger people who do not have particularly strong personalities or established nongovernmental careers or even bases of political support outside of the governor's office. In other words, they are individuals without competing commitments who have a dependent relationship with the governor. (The staff person's power is measured by his or her amount of access to the governor.)

Typically, the appointed agency secretaries and department heads are older than the governor's personal staff, have experience in a profession, and have standing in their community and prominence among the clientele served by their agency or department. Although they have been given statutory authority to run important state programs, appointed department heads are characterized by loyalty to the governor's goals and his political philosophy.[2]

When Ronald Reagan was governor, he employed a powerful chief of staff (either William Clark or Ed Meese, both of whom also served Reagan as president). The chief of staff established formal lines of communication requiring that all communications to the governor be routed through him; the duties of other staff people were strictly defined by the chief of staff, who systematized and routinized the governor's office. Reagan's cabinet, consisting of agency secretaries and the governor's top personal aides, met twice a week to discuss the most important matters facing state government and to recommend courses of action which Reagan usually followed or ratified. Although Reagan always attended these cabinet meetings, he disliked conflict among his top people and he encouraged them to practice consensus management. Agreement was facilitated by the fact that all of his top appointees believed in Reagan's philosophy.

Governor Jerry Brown's management style contrasted sharply with that of Reagan: he encouraged disagreement among his top aides, selected advisors who advocated controversial points of view, did not delegate authority to his top aides in a systematic fashion, and did not meet regularly with his cabinet or use it as a forum for reaching decisions. Moreover, Brown frequently let issues reach a crisis stage before making a decision. His reason for holding office was to use it as a forum for articulating ideas which would foster social change. Hamilton and Biggart note the irony that despite the numerous ideas propounded by Jerry Brown, his ideas often did not become public policy because his top aides and appointees were not concerned with governing and because Brown did not have a coherent philosophy.[3]

The management style of George Deukmejian is similar in many respects to that of Ronald Reagan. In the person of Steven Merksamer, Deukmejian had a powerful chief of staff who ran a highly structured office. Moreover, like Reagan's, Deukmejian's cabinet meets twice a week.

As some of the above comments suggest, the governor is also a policy coordinator. Some federal grant programs, which we discussed in Chapter 2, designate the governor as the state coordinator and planner, and the money for the program is channeled through the governor's office. California, like over half of the states, also has a Washington, D.C., office. The office's chief of staff, who is appointed by the governor, is a spokesperson for the state and for the governor.

Several features of the legislative process hamper the governor's efforts to coordinate policy. Legislative bills come from many sources, and once these bills are introduced, numerous legislative committees and political factors further shape them. When the bills become laws, different state and local agencies must carry out these laws. The governor is the only official in a position to give a unified direction to this fragmented process:

> Aside from the office and person of the governor, there is no one in a position to provide constant and authoritative review and coordination of policy—the kind of review and coordination needed to minimize program duplication and overlap, . . . to see to it that certain vital problems are not forgotten or ignored, and to make sure that one set of state policies does not counteract others. . . . [The governor] is in a position to maintain some amount of overall perspective on state government activities.[4]

Through the power to appoint agency heads and most members of regulatory commissions, the governor can form vertical coalitions to counteract the horizontal coalitions of middle-level civil servants, their legislative allies, and influential interest groups. To achieve a consistent set of state policies, the governor must master the nexus of groups and government described in Chapter 4. The governor's executive branch subordinates—the nonappointed civil servants—may be more loyal to their agencies or to outside interest groups than to the governor. Influential legislators approve the budget requests of cooperative administrators and at the same time receive campaign contributions from interest groups regulated by those administrators. State policymaking could become dominated by discrete coalitions of administrators, legislators, and interest groups. One of these coalitions might control education policy; another, agricultural policy; another, energy policy; and so on. To prevent this development and further broader state interests, the governor must use all the appointive and budgetary power available and must also appeal for public support.

Apart from coordinating policy, the state's chief executive also has a number of specific duties related to the criminal justice system. These include **clemency powers**. The governor may grant a pardon (release from the legal consequences of a crime), a **commutation** (reduction of sentence), or a **reprieve** (postponement in carrying out a sentence). Applying the clemency power in the case of a **capital** offense can involve a governor in heated and dramatic controversies, as Governor Pat Brown discovered in the famous Caryl Chessman case of 1960.

Chessman, the "Red-Light Bandit," had been convicted in 1948 of the kidnapping and brutal rape of a teenage girl. By complicated legal maneuvering and repeated stays of execution, Chessman postponed death for twelve years. Governor Brown, who opposed capital punishment, could not commute Chessman's sentence to life imprisonment because of Chessman's prior felony conviction. According to Article V, Section 8 of the state constitution, the governor may not grant a pardon or commutation to a person twice convicted of a felony unless at least four of the seven state supreme court justices grant this permission. The state supreme court would not approve commutation of Chessman's sentence. At the last minute, Brown gave Chessman a sixty-day reprieve and called the legislature into special session to consider a bill to abolish the death penalty. The legislature was bitterly divided, and the state was in an uproar. Brown "did not exert himself on the bill's behalf," and the judiciary committee of the state senate killed the bill.[5] In May 1960, Governor Brown refused Chessman another stay, and the deathrow inmate of San Quentin was executed. Because of the many twists and turns of the case, both proponents and opponents of capital punishment were angry with Brown.

Other responsibilities pertain to extradition. As we mentioned in Chapter 2, when requested to do so by the governor of another state, the governor of California can be required by a federal court to extradite a fugitive to the state from which he or she has fled. (Although "extradition" is the popular term, **"rendition"** is legally correct.)[6]

Moreover, the governor is commander-in-chief of the state militia (the National Guard). A military officer directs the troops, should they be called out, but the governor decides when to call them into service. Natural disasters such as earthquakes or civil disturbances such as labor unrest or riots may require use of the National Guard. In 1934, a massive maritime strike occurred in the port of San Francisco. The longshoremen's union, led by Harry Bridges, stalled traffic into and out of the port for ninety days. When other dock workers left their jobs, employers tried to break the strike. Violence followed, and more than one hundred people were wounded. A general strike was called and "the entire San Francisco area was paralyzed in the most severe disturbance the city had undergone since the earthquake and fire of 1906."[7] Governor Frank Merriam called out 5,000 National Guard troops to protect state property and preserve order. In the summer of 1965, the Watts area of Los Angeles erupted in six days of gunfire, arson, and looting. When police were unable to restore order, national guardsmen were ordered into action by Lieutenant Governor Glenn Anderson. By the time the turmoil was controlled, thirty-four people were dead, more than a thousand were injured, and property damage of $40 million was sustained.

On a more positive note, as chief executive, the governor symbolizes the state, so that it is not surprising that there are also ceremonial duties to be performed. Cutting ribbons at dam-opening ceremonies and riding in parades may seem trivial compared to the previously mentioned responsibilities, but the politically astute governor will use ceremonial events as a kind of nonpolitical, interelection campaigning. When representing the state itself before the state's citizens, the governor has the chance to publicize his accomplishments, to garner goodwill, and to influence recalcitrant legislators and other opponents. On the other hand, attending ceremonies can consume a great deal of valuable time, of course.

Usually the governor is also the acknowledged leader of a state political party or at least a faction of it. This recognition assists in negotiations with legislators and other state officers of the same party. It can be an asset, too, on the national political scene. The governor of California has better presidential prospects than governors in most other states: Ronald Reagan made one attempt for the White House while he was governor, and Jerry Brown made two attempts. Yet the California governor cannot too openly treat state office as a stepping-stone to the White House. In 1958, William Knowland, then a U.S. senator, gave up his Senate seat in order to run for the governorship. This maneuver was supposed to enable Knowland to run for the presidency in 1960. The move resulted in the Republicans' losing both the governorship and the Senate seat and in Knowland's ruining his political career.

Unlike the president of the United States, the governor is not limited to two consecutive four-year terms. (The governors of about half of the states have unlimited reeligibility.) Although no *constitutional* bar exists to three or more terms, a *political* limitation may exist. Only the immensely popular Earl Warren was thrice chosen by Californians. Pat Brown, not nearly so popular, was overwhelmingly defeated by Ronald Reagan when Brown sought a third term. Heeding this unwritten two-term rule, Reagan left the statehouse after eight years.

In summary, we can say that the governor is the hub of state politics. The media give this official far more coverage than they do anyone else on the state political scene, and this attention is an important source of power: "Skillfully used, the power of publicity can be more influential than any formal power. Legislators must respect the governor's greater access to the communication media and hence to the minds of their constituents."[8] The key role of the chief executive has led one scholar to call state (and national) political parties "executive-centered coalitions."[9] The governor speaks with one voice, not with the 120 voices of the legislature, and this person represents the party and its programs in the minds of Californians. When Californians think of the state's Democratic (or Republican) party, what comes to mind is usually the governor who leads the party. Not surprisingly, the party that does not control the governor's chair must often struggle for identity in the public mind.

GEORGE DEUKMEJIAN AS GOVERNOR: AN ANALYSIS

When George Deukmejian became governor in 1982, it capped two decades of preparation as an assemblyman, state senator, and attorney general. A low-key person intensely loyal to his family and his Armenian heritage, Deukmejian stands in sharp contrast to his two more glamorous predecessors, Jerry Brown and Ronald Reagan. In the words of columnist William Kahrl,

> Brown and Reagan, of course, were big idea men with even bigger ambitions and little interest in the details of administration. Deukmejian, in contrast, is reticent by

nature, adores the details of running the government, and defines his vision of the future in terms of greater efficiency, better schools, safer streets and a host of similar objectives that warm the heart without stirring the blood. [10]

According to pollster Mervin Field, the steady and stolid Deukmejian "is not flashy—he's a good, gray, sober-sided steward of trust."[11] These characteristics aided Deukmejian as he faced a monumental crisis immediately upon assuming office: how to deal with a massive $1.5 billion deficit left him by Jerry Brown. Deukmejian reduced state spending, raised some specialized charges and taxes (described later) but not general taxes, and carried over part of the deficit into the next fiscal year. An improving economy assisted all of these efforts.

As a conservative, two of George Deukmejian's main goals are to keep taxes down and to appoint law-and-order judges. His concern regarding crime has been an important feature of his governorship: he strongly supports the death penalty and campaigned against the retention of Chief Justice Rose Bird. He favors a mandatory seven-year prison term for adults furnishing drugs to minors, and would speed up the judicial process by having judges rather than lawyers question prospective jurors and by having juries of six persons in misdemeanor cases. One of the paramount reasons Deukmejian sought the governorship in the first place was to be able to appoint judges. His selections have been law-and-order judges, but according to Gerald Uelmen, liberal dean of the Santa Clara Law School, they have been moderate and "not knee-jerk conservatives who are going to parrot a party line."[12]

Another Deukmejian priority is to emphasize education in the state budget; his support for education is based on the belief of many state business leaders that California's deteriorating educational system threatens the state's competitive position in both the national and the international economy. Thus his budgets have increased education funding much more than funding for other items (spending in this area went up 52 percent in his first four years in office). Other items high on the Deukmejian agenda are the workfare reform negotiated by his administration (see Chapter 1), new prison construction, the construction and maintenance of highways, the creation of jobs and the stimulation of economic development, and the maintenance of a prudent budgetary reserve to promote fiscal integrity.

As with his predecessors, some of George Deukmejian's actions and policies have provoked intense criticism. He has significantly reduced the budgets of the coastal commission and the energy commission (which are described later in this chapter). Critics say that his reductions have seriously slowed state review of local coastal plans and have hampered the setting of energy efficiency standards for home appliances and office buildings. Deukmejian counters that these commissions retard economic growth and saddle business with unnecessary regulation. Responding to the pleas of his key supporters among farmers and growers, Deukmejian twice vetoed bills to require farmers of labor-intensive crops to post warning signs if pesticides sprayed on the crops remain toxic for one day or longer. The veto left in place existing state regulations requiring posting only if the chemicals remain dangerous to workers for seven days. Moreover, he did not veto a bill intended to weaken the Williamson Act (described in Chapter 1).

Probably the most serious criticism of the Deukmejian administration, though, has concerned its handling of toxic wastes. In 1986, the federal Environmental Protection Agency (EPA) briefly withdrew California's authority to issue final permits to transport, store, or dispose of toxic wastes. The EPA said that California's failure to comply with federal requirements prompted it to take over a wide range of the state's toxic programs. Federal auditors were especially critical of the department of health services' efforts at the McColl Refinery Dump in Fullerton, where state contracting procedures were ignored and a $1.4 million cleanup contract was issued to a corporation without competitive bidding. The state's auditor general (see Chapter 7) also issued a scathing report criticizing Health Services for paying over $1 million to another corporation in double payments and for work not done at McColl. The Deukmejian administration argues that it has cleaned up more hazardous waste sites, conducted more investigations, and levied more fines than did the administration of Jerry Brown, a strong environmentalist. Critics contend that, because of the expense and the technical complexity involved, cleanup of the most dangerous sites has been postponed, especially those threatening underground water supplies. These critics conclude that the administration's weak enforcement of toxic laws is not protecting public health.

As noted earlier, keeping taxes down is one of George Deukmejian's key goals as governor, and he has not raised major general taxes. However, during his first four years in office he increased specialized taxes and charges by $2.4 billion, for example, motor vehicle license fees and accelerated property tax assessments. Setbacks suffered by Deukmejian include the **electorate's** defeat of his 1984 ballot proposition to create a bipartisan reapportionment commission and rejection by the Democrat-dominated senate of four of his major administrative nominees. Moreover, he has been unable to persuade a state legislature controlled by the other party to pass his water plan. In 1984, Deukmejian vetoed 306 bills, a modern record. None of his vetoes has been overridden because Republicans in the state legislature are quite loyal to the governor.

Although he is clearly a conservative, George Deukmejian does not fit the mold of a rigid ideologue. For example, he supports complete divestiture by public employee pension funds and the University of California in corporations that do business in racially segregated South Africa. When the revenue crisis that he faced upon entering office was resolved and the state's finances improved, Deukmejian did not seek to rebate any surplus money or to reduce taxes. Instead, he spent the money on needed state projects such as education or placed it in a reserve fund for emergencies. Since his budgets for fiscal years 1986 and 1987 increased state spending higher than the rate of inflation, state government actually grew under the direction of the conservative Deukmejian.[13]

CABINET, AGENCIES, AND DEPARTMENTS

As the person charged with administering the laws, the governor directs the administrative branch of state government. This branch consists of five state agencies (see Figure 6.1): business, transportation, and housing; resources;

youth and adult corrections; state and consumer services; and health and human services. The secretary of each of these agencies is appointed by the governor. The agencies are subdivided into departments, each with a specific purpose. For example, the resources agency contains the department of conservation, department of water resources, solid waste management board, and others.

The secretaries of the five state agencies, the director of the department of food and agriculture, the director of the department of industrial relations, the director of finance, and the governor's executive assistant make up the governor's cabinet, which may be called upon for advice. The director of finance is particularly important because this person is the governor's chief fiscal advisor, and the department that he or she oversees prepares the budget that the governor submits to the legislature. (The budget will be discussed more fully in Chapter 10.) Furthermore, the department of finance assesses the financial impact of new legislation and advises the governor on the cost-effectiveness of current state programs. Most state tax **revenues** are designated for specific purposes (**earmarked**) by law or by the state constitution; for example, the gas tax must be spent to build and maintain roads. Hence, approximately three-fourths of all expenditures are beyond the governor's direct control. In reality, then, the chief executive has very little flexibility in budget planning, and an ambitious governor will find it difficult to alter the priorities of state spending dramatically.

OTHER STATE CONSTITUTIONAL OFFICERS

The governor is not the only executive officer elected statewide. The following officials are called state constitutional officers because their positions are specified in the state constitution: lieutenant governor, controller, treasurer, secretary of state, attorney general, superintendent of public instruction, members of the board of equalization.

It is important to note that the governor cannot have a unified executive administration, and cannot control the other state constitutional officers in the same sense that the president controls their federal counterparts, because the others may have different political views, be of different political parties, or even be potential opponents of the governor in the next election. Separate election of each of these officials not only discourages cooperation but also encourages one or more of them to try to cut the governor down to size before the next election. Many of these offices, especially those of lieutenant governor, controller, and attorney general, are considered to be in the line of advancement to the governorship. All of this competition could be viewed as a kind of checks-and-balances system, although we usually think of checks and balances as operating between branches, not within the same branch, of government.

Lieutenant Governor

Some people think that since the governor is the most important person in state politics, the lieutenant governor is the second most important person. This is not true. In fact, the lieutenant governor ordinarily has few significant duties to

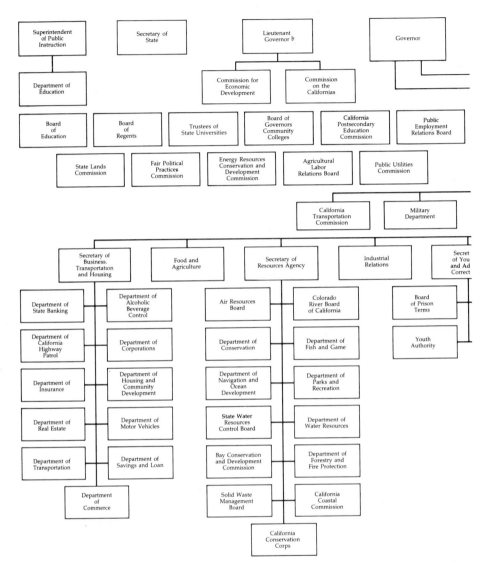

FIGURE 6.1   The executive branch of California state government

perform. For instance, he or she presides over the state senate but is not allowed to vote except in the unlikely event of a tie. "I never go there except to break ties," said a former lieutenant governor. (In 1982, a constitutional amendment was proposed to eliminate the lieutenant governor's role of presiding over the senate, but it was defeated.) The lieutenant governor also serves ex officio on certain boards and commissions, such as the state lands commission and the board of trustees of the state university system. Serving **ex officio**

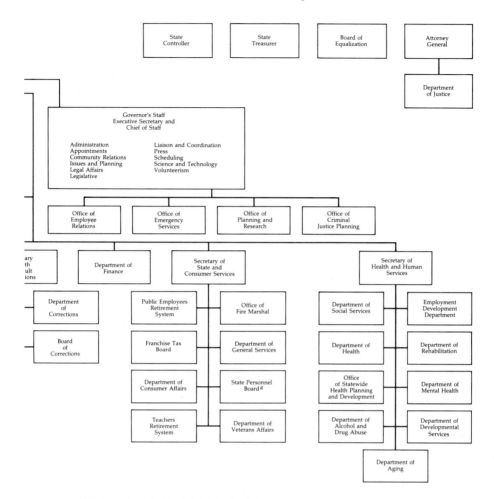

[a] Liaison established by Administrative Action.
[b] Lieutenant Governor serves as Chairman Economic Development Commission and Governor's Representative on Economic and Commerce Policy.

means that whoever holds the office of lieutenant governor automatically becomes a member of the particular board or commission. He or she does not have many other functions, and in fact, nearly everything the lieutenant governor does could just as easily be done by someone else or left undone. This may be why eight states do not have such an official.

On the other hand, in California the lieutenant governor becomes acting governor when the governor leaves the state. The state supreme court has ruled that as soon as the chief executive leaves the state's boundaries, the lieutenant governor is free to act on whatever matters may need attention during the governor's absence. For example, in 1980 as Governor Brown sought the Democratic nomination for president in primaries across the country, Republican Lieutenant Governor Mike Curb threatened to make full use of all powers temporarily in his possession. When the governor returns home, the lieutenant governor lapses back into insignificance. The state constitution could be amended to abolish the lieutenant governorship outright, and an existing constitutional officer, such as the attorney general, could take over when the governor is away.

Why would someone want to be lieutenant governor? Surely not because he or she covets the powers of the office: the position is really just a way station to better things. If the lieutenant governor is a talented person, his or her talents are wasted. To say that this person is not gainfully employed would be inaccurate, but the office does need more duties. New tasks could come from the governor, but recent governors have not especially liked or trusted their lieutenant governors. Earl Warren wrote in his memoirs that when he was governor he would lock all bills in a safe-deposit box whenever he left the state in order to prevent the lieutenant governor, Goodwin J. ("Goodie") Knight, from going on a bill-signing binge.[14] Moreover, as we have mentioned earlier, the lieutenant governor could be a political opponent or a member of the opposite party. In the 1978, 1982 and 1986 elections, the voters elected a governor and lieutenant governor from different parties.

Controller

Unlike the lieutenant governor, the state controller has a powerful position. If money talks, then the controller speaks in thunderous tones. He or she accounts for and pays our state money and is therefore the most important fiscal officer in the state. Acting as a disbursing and accounting officer, the controller audits state expenditures to make sure they are made in accordance with state law; this practice is known as a preaudit. The controller also advises local governments on financial matters and reports on their financial conditions in his or her annual reports to the public.

The controller oversees both money going out and money coming in. He or she chairs the franchise tax board, which collects state income taxes. Any Californian unfortunate enough to owe income taxes on April 15 makes out a check to this board. Taxpayers due a refund will find their checks signed by the controller. This official also sits on the board of equalization, which collects the very important sales tax.

As if all these duties were not enough, the controller chairs the state lands commission, which has charge of the state's 4 million acres of public lands.[15] California's public lands include the valuable coastal tidelands, which the commission can decide whether or not to lease for exploration by oil companies and utility companies. The need for state income must be balanced against chances of oil spills and loss of the inspiring beauty of California's coastline.

Treasurer

The treasurer has custody over state money, which he or she deposits in various banks, always in search of the highest interest rate. The treasurer also auctions state bonds, but in this case seeks the lowest interest rates that purchasers will allow. In recent years, the treasurer has been given the important duty of deciding which financial underwriters are allowed to resell lucrative tax-exempt revenue bonds to investors. This authority has prompted financial firms to contribute heavily to campaigns for treasurer. Finally, since the treasurer is given the responsibility of investing state money, he or she pools different state accounts into a single higher-yield investment program.

Secretary of State

The secretary of state's functions fall into two categories: record keeping and the supervision of elections. The secretary of state keeps the state's official records and maintains the state archives. The secretary of state is also the keeper of the Great Seal of the State of California and affixes it to all documents requiring the governor's signature. Additionally, business corporations are granted charters from this office.

In a more important and influential role, the secretary of state is chief election officer for the state. He or she must enforce the state's election laws; print the state ballot pamphlets; certify and publish election results; and check initiative, referendum, and recall petitions for the proper number of signatures. It is somewhat of an anomaly that the person who must enforce the election laws is himself or herself elected. In fact, the election is on a partisan basis. Finally, the secretary of state must also compile a list of potential presidential primary candidates. Early in the presidential election year (1988, 1992, and so on), the secretary of state places on the California presidential primary ballot the names of generally recognized contenders. By this means, the secretary of state can smoke out any candidates who would prefer not to contest the California primary. Of course, a candidate can ask the secretary of state to take his or her name off the ballot. The net result is that the secretary of state's actions prevent a favorite son from dominating California's presidential primary and discouraging other candidates from taking part in our primary.

Attorney General

The attorney general—the state's chief law enforcement officer and head of the department of justice—is one of the most powerful figures in California government.[16] As chief law enforcement officer, the attorney general has authority over all district attorneys, police chiefs, and sheriffs in the state, but seldom supervises them directly. The attorney general must see to it that state laws are "uniformly and adequately enforced" (Constitution of the State of California, Article V, Section 13). In extreme cases, the constitution gives the attorney general all the powers of a district attorney if it becomes necessary to enforce state law in a county.

As head of the department of justice, the attorney general conducts the legal affairs of the state. Unless an agency or department is allowed to have its own lawyer, it is represented in court by the attorney general's office. When requested to do so by another state constitutional officer or state agency, the attorney general issues **advisory opinions** or legal opinions that must be obeyed until the issue in question is ruled upon by a court. Most of these opinions are not reviewed by a court. The department of justice employs many attorneys and is split into several divisions, such as those dealing with environmental issues, consumer matters, and narcotics problems. In addition to enforcing the law, the attorney general must also prepare titles of ballot propositions and summaries of these propositions before they appear on election ballots.

California voters have shown a long-standing disposition to split their ticket between the two most important executive offices in state government, those of governor and attorney general. Table 6.1 shows that in nine of the last thirteen elections, Californians have selected members of different parties for these two offices. Perhaps the voters want an attorney general who will keep an eye on the governor. Table 6.1 also shows that the post of attorney general is an excellent position from which to run for governor.

Superintendent of Public Instruction

The superintendent of public instruction is elected statewide on a nonpartisan basis. Since this office is nonpartisan, all candidates appear on all party ballots in the June primary of gubernatorial election years. Should any candidate receive a majority, he or she is elected outright, and no runoff election is held in November. The superintendent directs the department of education, but policies for the department are established by a ten-member state board of education appointed by the governor.[17] The superintendent is the secretary of the board and implements the rules and regulations it adopts. This somewhat curious arrangement of an elected superintendent and an appointed board led to much infighting when Max Rafferty was superintendent (1962 to 1970), but caused much less strife during the tenure of Wilson Riles (1970 to 1982) and Bill Honig (1982 to 1990).

The state department of education provides approximately 80 percent of local elementary and secondary school districts' budgets. The state also sets the state educational policies, especially regarding curriculum and textbooks, within which local school districts must operate. Higher education is not neglected either. The superintendent sits ex officio on The Board of Regents of the University of California, with the trustees of the state university system, and the board of governors of the state's community colleges.

Members of the State Board of Equalization

The board of equalization consists of four elected members and the state controller, who serves ex officio. The state is divided into four board of equalization districts by the state legislature; each district must have approx-

TABLE 6.1   Governors and Attorneys General since 1939

Term	Governor	Party	Attorney General	Party
1939–1942	Culbert Olson	Democrat	Earl Warren	Republican
1943–1946	Earl Warren	Republican	Robert Kenny	Democrat
1947–1950	Earl Warren	Republican	Fred Howser	Republican
1951–1953	Earl Warren	Republican	Edmund G. Brown, Sr.	Democrat (1951–1954)
1953–1954	Goodwin Knight	Republican[a]		
1955–1958	Goodwin Knight	Republican	Edmund G. Brown, Sr.	Democrat
1959–1962	Edmund G. Brown, Sr.	Democrat	Stanley Mosk	Democrat
1963–1966	Edmund G. Brown, Sr.	Democrat	Stanley Mosk	Democrat (1963–1964)
			Thomas Lynch	Democrat[a] (1964–1966)
1967–1970	Ronald Reagan	Republican	Thomas Lynch	Democrat
1971–1974	Ronald Reagan	Republican	Evelle Younger	Republican
1975–1978	Edmund G. Brown, Jr.	Democrat	Evelle Younger	Republican
1979–1982	Edmund G. Brown, Jr.	Democrat	George Deukmejian	Republican
1983–1990	George Deukmejian	Republican	John Van de Kamp	Democrat

[a]Succeeded or was appointed to the office.

imately equal population, and each is represented by one member of the board elected on a partisan basis.

The board of equalization must ensure that property throughout the state is assessed according to uniform criteria. To accomplish this, the board trains county assessors. The board of equalization also does some assessing itself, but only of the property of railroads and public utilities. In addition, the board administers certain taxes, such as the sales tax, the gas tax, the cigarette tax, and the liquor tax. In income tax matters, the board of equalization rules on appeals from franchise tax board decisions.

BOARDS AND COMMISSIONS

Two commentators have noted that "perhaps the most significant development [in the structure of California government] of the last twenty years has been the rise of appointive government."[18] The range of activities regulated by independent boards and commissions filled by gubernatorial appointment is truly amazing. Boards or commissions make regulations that affect the cost of heating your home, the size of your telephone bill, the location of new power facilities, private development along the coastline, approval of auto emission–control systems, and administration of the state's system of higher education. This development suggests some conclusions: government control over private economic activity has increased; although the governor (through his appointees) can leave his stamp on a wider range of policymaking areas, fewer decisions are being made by elected officials; because appointed officials never run for election or reelection, "decision-making power has been taken further away from the people."[19]

Public Utilities Commission

The public utilities commission (PUC) has "more impact on where Californians' dollars go every day than most elected officials."[20] It consists of five members who serve six-year terms. The terms of the members overlap; thus, at any one time different members of the commission have usually been appointed by different governors. All commissioners must be confirmed by majority vote of the state senate before taking office.

The PUC has the important task of setting the intrastate (within California) charges for gas, electricity, water, and telephone companies. In addition, it sets the rates of railroads, airlines, buses, trucks, and movers of household goods. Although all of the companies regulated by the PUC are privately owned, they must obtain PUC permission in order to increase their rates. The PUC also decides how much profit these companies are allowed to make. Furthermore, through its regulatory power, the PUC is able to encourage specific policies. For example, efforts by the commission to encourage energy conservation have received nationwide attention, especially its support for cogeneration.

Critics of the PUC charge that the commission is too generous in granting rate increases for residential gas and electricity customers. These critics further argue that the utilities are mismanaged. This charge has often been leveled at northern California's Pacific Gas and Electric (PG & E); moreover, in 1986, the

PUC charged Southern California Edison and also San Diego Gas & Electric with imprudent and lax management in constructing the San Onofre nuclear power plant. The commission required the utilities' shareholders, rather than consumers, to absorb $344 million in costs. This penalty was the largest ever assessed on a California utility for unreasonable spending on a construction project. Spokespeople for ratepayer groups want the legislature to forbid the utilities to pass on to present customers the cost of constructing new power plants, because these plants will primarily benefit future customers.

Energy Resources Conservation and Development Commission

The energy resources conservation and development commission, known simply as the energy commission, began in 1975. Its purpose is to develop contingency plans in case of future energy shortages. It also funds research and development programs on new energy sources such as solar energy and promotes energy conservation, especially by means of efficiency standards for new buildings and home appliances. An important duty of the commission is to forecast future energy needs and supplies; these forecasts have prevented California from overbuilding power plants. Finally, the commission approves the location of new power plant facilities, except those within the jurisdiction of the coastal commission.

California Coastal Commission

The coastal commission was established by an initiative, Proposition 20, in 1972. Its goal is the planned, long-range development and protection of California's magnificent 1,000-mile-long coastline. The initiative created the coastal commission to control, by means of permits, development along the coast. Among the issues for commission consideration are public access to the coast (including actually being able to *see* the coast), wise land use, space for recreation, and development and conservation of vegetation and marine life. The commission's powers and jurisdiction were altered in 1976. The state commission now supervises local governments' coastal management rather than issuing permits. The area to be protected (the coastal zone) was enlarged—it may now include recreational areas such as inland Big Sur or Bodega Bay. Since the sixty-eight cities and counties along the coast now have the permit authority, they must develop local land-use plans for approval by the state commission. After these plans have been approved, the commission must oversee the implementation of the plans, rule upon local amendments to the plans, and hear appeals from local coastal development decisions. Moreover, these local plans must be updated every five years and reviewed by the commission. Finally, federal law provides that offshore oil development that might affect the California coastline or its submerged lands must be reviewed by the coastal commission. The commission studies proposals for oil and gas drilling in the outer continental shelf and informs the federal government whether these plans conflict with state law. However, the coastal commission cannot intervene in federal oil and gas lease sales to block these sales if the tracts are more than three miles offshore.

State Water Resources Control Board

The Porter–Cologne Water Quality Control Act of 1969 created the state water resources control board (SWRCB) and nine regional water quality control boards. Each of the nine commissions develops a regional water quality plan tailored to its region's needs that takes into account population growth, land use such as agriculture, industrial development, and environmental and economic impacts. In effect, the regional boards are regional governments (as described in Chapter 9) under the ultimate authority of the state water resources control board, which assures that a statewide perspective will guide water quality policy. The state board hears appeals from decisions of the regional boards. The SWRCB also administers the Clean Water Grant Program, a massive public works plan which assists local governments in building wastewater treatment facilities to process public waste discharge.

In recent years, the state water resources control board has come under increasing criticism for its handling of poisons such as toxic chemicals and pesticides that are entering the water supply, especially into aquifers deep underground that supply an important part of state water needs. The sources of these poisons are leakage from underground chemical storage tanks and hazardous waste dump sites, as well as pesticide flows from irrigated farmlands. The SWRCB has not been monitoring the regional boards closely enough to ensure that they are preventing the contamination of state water. For example, pollution sites are not being inspected often enough, and there is insufficient follow-up to guarantee that polluters are meeting requirements. Too much pollution is handled through a system that amounts to self-monitoring. Not only have some hazardous waste disposal facilities not received regulations, but discharge regulations for many others are out of date. In essence, the state board has been charged with failing to hold the regional boards more accountable.

To correct some of the problems, the state's legislature has recently enacted some significant legislation. For example, one law requires owners of underground tanks to register their tanks with the state water resources control board, which then sends the information to counties and cities for enforcement. Another law requires the SWRCB to set leakproof rules for underground tanks, especially by establishing tank construction standards and determining proper leak detection devices. Finally, the regional water quality control boards have been required to inspect open toxic ponds, lagoons, and pits to make sure that they are safe and double-lined. Any that are closer than one-half mile to a drinking-water supply are to be closed.[21]

Air Resources Board

The air resources board (ARB) is the air pollution control agency for the whole state, and its special concern is auto emissions. The ARB surveys air quality statewide, approves vehicle emission-control systems, and may order the recall and repair of cars that fall short of emission standards. The ARB has ordered car manufacturers to replace without charge to customers any smog-control parts that malfunction during a car's first 50,000 miles. When local air pollution agencies are unable to control nonvehicular sources of air pollution such as oil refineries, the ARB will do so. (Chapter 1 describes some of the enforcement programs of the air resources board.)

California Transportation Commission

The California Transportation Commission was created in 1978 to replace the state highway commission, the state transportation board, the board of aeronautics, and the toll bridge authority. It consists of nine voting members appointed by the governor and two nonvoting members of the state legislature. In making appointments, the governor is supposed to maintain a geographic balance between northern and southern California, and between urban and rural areas. The commission annually evaluates state transportation needs and sends the budget for the California Department of Transportation (CalTrans) to the legislature. This budget does not contain money for any specific construction projects, but only has eight broad, general categories of transportation-related functions. After the legislature has adopted the Cal-Trans budget, the California Transportation Commission decides which individual projects are to be built. In addition, the commission submits a five-year program called the State Transportation Improvement Program (STIP), to which all projects must conform. The STIP is updated each year, with the first year of the plan being the current year's transportation budget.

The California Transportation Commission is an important decision-making body because it decides how to spend substantial sums of money. The commission allocates billions of dollars not only for highways but also for mass transit and aeronautics. Its decisions regarding routes affect the prosperity of cities and of whole regions of the state. The rather cumbersome process used by the California Transportation Commission to fund transportation projects is intended to prevent the state legislature from engaging in pork-barrel approval of specific projects. Were the legislature to decide which individual projects are to be built, the horsetrading would be immense. Highways would be located in the districts of powerful legislators, not where they can best serve statewide transportation needs. Moreover, interest groups would use campaign contributions to legislators to get projects in their geographical area as a way of benefiting economically that area.

Governing Boards for Higher Education

The regents of the University of California (UC), the trustees of the California State University system (CSU), and the board of governors of the state's community colleges are the governing boards for higher education in California. The University of California has twenty-seven regents appointed by the governor and confirmed by the state senate; they serve twelve-year, staggered terms. Among the ex officio members are the governor, the speaker of the assembly, and the superintendent of public instruction. The regents govern the huge UC system, but the governor and the legislature maintain substantial financial control. The CSU trustees, unlike the UC regents, were not created by the state constitution but by the state legislature, and are therefore under greater control of the legislature and the state department of finance, which can disallow any expenditure by the CSU system even after its budget has been approved by the legislature and the money has been appropriated. The board of governors of the community colleges assists the seventy community college districts in the state, each of which is locally administered. State interest in the community colleges is heightened by the fact that the state government spends more money on the community colleges than on either the UC or the CSU systems.

Commission on California State Government Organization and Economy

The commission on California state government organization and economy, usually called California's Little Hoover Commission, was established to promote efficiency and economy in state government. It issues many valuable reports on state government operations; for example, the commission's highly critical 1984 and 1985 reports on state policing of privately run board-and-care homes for elderly, mentally ill, and retarded persons prompted the legislature to pass a series of reform measures. In 1986, the Little Hoover commission documented poor state management of its real estate holdings. The state owns more than 6 million acres of land valued at $2 billion, but lacks a current, complete inventory and is losing millions of dollars in income each year. In 1987, the commission documented deficiencies in the state's programs for abused and abandoned children.

This chapter has described some of the more important appointive boards and commissions in California state government. As we saw in Chapter 4, there is a plethora of others, with many performing unneeded tasks or even functions that are detrimental to the interests of consumers. The Little Hoover commission, itself an appointed commission, regularly identifies superfluous boards and commissions.

STATE CIVIL SERVICE

Excluding those who work for institutions of public higher education, there are approximately 130,000 state employees in California. Known variously as "civil servants" or "bureaucrats," these state workers are employed in positions such as clerical workers, California Highway Patrol officers, driver's license examiners, CalTrans road crew members, fish and game wardens, state foresters, park rangers, prison guards, hospital workers, and many others. These people do the day-to-day work of running California government and are the "face" of government most frequently encountered by average citizens. Civil servants administer the programs established by the governor and the legislature,

SOURCE: Reprinted by permission: Tribune Media Services

hence they exercise a delegated authority. Elected officials use laws to identify problems, set objectives for administrators to meet, and appropriate money to finance the programs. It is left to civil servants "to fill in the details" and use their technical expertise to achieve the goals set by the law. Filling in the details may also involve filling out lots of forms, as the reading on the next page indicates.

As noted earlier, California is not a high-patronage state. About 98 percent of all state employees received their positions through competitive examinations or by demonstrating competence for their position, and not through loyalty to an elected official or political party. The California civil service system is directed by the state personnel board, which conducts examinations for initial appointment and for promotion.

In 1977, state workers won the right to select a labor union as their exclusive bargaining agent in wage disputes and other employment matters. Under the collective bargaining act, the public employment relations board was established to supervise the law and to investigate and rule on unfair labor practices. In early 1983, in one of his last official actions as governor, Jerry Brown signed an agency shop agreement which allows unions representing state workers to collect fees from nonmembers. The fees are roughly equal to union dues, and produce over $6 million more each year for the California State Employees Association (CSEA). The CSEA contributed heavily to Brown's 1982 campaign for U.S. senator and to Democratic legislative candidates, as noted in Chapter 4. At the time that the agreements were signed, the CSEA represented only 46 percent of the state workers covered by the agreement.

The 1977 collective bargaining law forbade public employee strikes, but in 1985 the state supreme court ruled them to be legal. Ten other states allow strikes by public employees, but in every state except California it has been authorized by the legislature and not the courts. The state supreme court held that "unless or until it is clearly demonstrated that such a strike creates substantial and imminent threat to the health or safety of the public," strikes by state or local workers are legal (*County Sanitation District #2 of Los Angeles County v. Los Angeles County Employees Association*, 38 Cal. 3d 564). Police and firefighters are exempted from the ruling, however. The court found the right to strike by public employees to be a basic civil liberty, but only Chief Justice Rose Bird in a concurring opinion held it to be required by the state constitution.

Bureaucracy and Paperwork

There's an old saying that the "ship of state floats on a sea of paper work."

A. Alan Post still vividly recalls the time his office nearly drowned in that sea.

It was sometime in the mid-1950s when Post, then the state's legislative analyst, asked for a copy of every report issued by every state agency. That simple request unleashed a tidal wave of paper work.

"We were inundated, absolutely flooded," he recalled some 30 years later. "It filled the room, spilled out in the halls, stacked up in piles. It was unbelievable."

There were thousands of reports— more than anyone could digest in a lifetime. And that was just for one year.

"I can't even imagine what it'd be like now," said Post, who retired after five governors and 27 years as the state's legislative analyst.

Nobody knows exactly how much paper is produced, printed and passed out every year or even every day by the state bureaucracy.

The state printer alone churns out 17 million pounds of paper a year on its presses, and it doesn't handle every piece of paper put out by the bureaucracy.

But one thing is certain: Wherever you go in state government, a piece of paper follows. From a Folsom State Prison inmate who complains about cold food on an official prison grievance form to the 16-year-old applying for her first driver's license, it's all on paper.

In fact, the proliferation of paper work is so rampant that no one knows exactly how many different memos, forms, applications and other record-keeping pieces of paper exist in state government.

Assemblyman Richard Katz, D-Sepulveda, who has attempted to count them, said the figure is about 150,000. Of those, a typical Californian may encounter any of the 11,000 different forms designed for public use, including tax forms, driver's license applications and business inventory records.

But the state's official records keeper doesn't believe "anyone can truly say how many there are. Somewhere in a department right now, someone is creating a form or deleting one," said John Brownfield, assistant chief in the Office of Records Management.

Katz thought he had made a dent in the paper work pile in 1982 when he secured passage of a bill requiring the state to index every form in existence. But three years later that bill has been largely ignored.

"The (forms management) act has never been implemented," Katz said. "There is no central cross-index of forms, no inventory, no evaluation of paper work management in the state. And paper work has proliferated—not decreased."

But the state's forms manager said it's a matter of expectations. Creating an index is not as easy as Katz believes, Brownfield said.

Of the 11,000 public forms, Brownfield said, his staff has collected 3,000 examples. They are sitting on shelves waiting to be indexed in a new computer. But even with a computer, Brownfield said, it takes one person a full year to index, update and keep track of just 400 forms. . . .

The problem, said Katz and others, is that there's no regulation, no one with the authority to dump those forms that are outdated, unnecessary or duplicative.

Post, for example, discovered 30 years ago that the then-Department of Mental Hygiene had employees in one office busily compiling reports while elsewhere in the same office another group of staffers also were busily compiling reports. The same reports.

"One didn't even know what the other was doing," said Post, shaking his head. . . .

SOURCE: "California's Longtime Love Affair with Paper Work," by Claudia Buck, © *The Sacramento Bee*, September 4, 1985, p. A15. Reprinted by permission.

SUMMARY

The executive branch of California state government is huge. It consists of approximately 130,000 state employees, as well as the governor, other state constitutional officers and their staffs, and numerous boards and commissions.

The purpose of those who work in the executive branch is to execute duties prescribed by state law and the state constitution. With the important exception of rules and regulations issued by administrative agencies, the executive branch does not make law. In Chapter 7 we turn to the lawmaking branch of the state government, the state legislature.

DISCUSSION QUESTIONS

1. All of California's governors for over 100 years have governed under a state constitution that has given them much the same powers it gives the governor now. Yet some, like Earl Warren, have been powerful and are remembered, and others are forgotten even by historians. Thus, the powers written into the state constitution do not by themselves make a governor strong, influential, or effective. What factors can make an average governor into a great governor?

2. This chapter has provided some evidence for the argument that state constitutional officers might find it more to their advantage *not* to cooperate with each other than to work as a team. At the national level, the attorney general, secretary of state, and others serve at the president's pleasure. This fact encourages harmony but does not guarantee it. Would you rather have state officials elected (so that you can say who they will be), but run the risk that they will work against each other once elected? Or would you rather give up your chance to choose in order that state officials might work together more harmoniously?

3. What are some of the boards and commissions established to regulate economic activities? What are some of the areas of regulation? Which of these boards and commissions provide environmental protection?

4. State employees are important people whose role in California government is often overlooked. Why are civil servants influential in the lives of average Californians? Because of this state's merit system of employment, state workers are usually highly qualified individuals, but it is also extremely difficult to fire those who are not. Under a patronage system, public employees are very responsive to the governor, who is supposed to be the head of the administrative branch, because he or she has hired them and can easily fire them. Should California return to the patronage system that it had early in this century?

NOTES

1. Gary G. Hamilton and Nicole Woolsey Biggart, *Governor Reagan, Governor Brown* (New York: Columbia University Press, 1984).
2. Agency secretaries and department heads often feel cross-pressured because they are also loyal to the interest groups that suggested that the governor appoint

them to their current post. For example, the head of the department of insurance may actually be the insurance industry's representative *to* the governor, rather than vice versa.

3. Hamilton and Biggart, *Governor Reagan, Governor Brown,* pp. 75, 83, 201, 205, 211, 213.

4. John A Straayer, *American State and Local Government* (Columbus, Ohio: Merrill Publishing Co., 1977), pp. 110–111.

5. Quote from David Lavender, *California* (New York: Norton, 1976), p. 203.

6. See *Puerto Rico v. Branstad,* 55 U.S.L.W. 4975 (1987). Governor Jerry Brown rejected the request of the governor of South Dakota that Brown return Dennis Banks, a militant Native American.

7. Andrew F. Rolle, *California: A History,* 3rd ed. (Arlington Heights, Ill.: AHM Publishing Co., 1978), p. 482.

8. Thomas R. Dye, "State Legislative Politics," in *Politics in the American States,* 2nd ed., ed. Herbert Jacob and Kenneth Vines (Boston: Little, Brown, 1971), p. 205.

9. Frank Sorauf, *Party Politics in America,* 5th ed. (Boston: Little, Brown, 1984), p. 375.

10. William Kahrl, "Wider Horizons Await Deukmejian," *Los Angeles Times,* January 9, 1985, pt. II, p. 7.

11. Mervin Field, quoted in George Skelton, "Deukmejian's Low-Key Style May Assure Victory," *Los Angeles Times,* November 25, 1985, pt. I, p. 10.

12. Gerald Uelmen, quoted in Claire Cooper, "Despite Pledges, Duke's Choices for Bench Are Moderate," *Sacramento Bee,* October 9, 1984, p. A12.

13. Ed Salzman, "Deukmejian's Budget: Pat Brown Revisited," *Golden State Report* (February 1986): 39.

14. Earl Warren, *Memoirs* (Garden City, N.Y.: Doubleday, 1977), pp. 256–265.

15. In fact, the controller is a member of more than two dozen boards and commissions. The controller is supposed to attend so many meetings that a deputy is frequently sent in his or her place.

16. In the executive branch of government, there are two elected heads of departments: the attorney general, who supervises the department of justice, and the superintendent of public instruction, who directs the department of education. Neither of these important departments is thus under the control of the governor, but they are still part of the executive branch.

17. At the local, school-district level, the procedure is just the opposite: the board is elected and the superintendent is appointed.

18. T. Anthony Quinn and Ed Salzman, *California Public Administration,* 2nd ed. (Sacramento: California Journal Press, 1982), p. 9.

19. Quinn and Salzman, *California Public Administration,* p. 10. The governor appoints nearly all of the members of these boards and commissions, and he usually chooses individuals who share his point of view on the matters under the boards' jurisdictions. However, once on a board, an appointee cannot be directed by the governor. In fact, a board member's term may outlast the governor's tenure. The list of commissions in the text is not exhaustive. Commissions operating in related fields are grouped together.

20. Lynn Atwood Hoff, "Brown's PUC Majority and Utility-Rate Revolution," *California Journal* (March 1977): 94.

21. Mary Ellen Leary, "The Water Resources Control Board," *California Journal* (March 1985): 110–112. See also Jim Dufur, "Boards Called Lax on Water Pollution," *Sacramento Bee,* April 5, 1984, p. A5.

CHAPTER

7

Legislature

Legislative bodies, including the California legislature, perform a number of important functions:

1. Representation of the interests of constituents and response to constituent requests for assistance on governmental matters
2. Deliberation and lawmaking
3. Resolution of conflict and the building of consensus
4. Education of the public
5. Control of the administration—that is, overseeing administrators, especially through passage of the budget and through investigations[1]

This chapter describes how the California legislature is organized to perform these functions. We will also consider the legislature's leadership, legislative procedure, and the staff of the legislature.

STRUCTURE AND CHARACTERISTICS OF THE LEGISLATURE

The California legislature is a **bicameral,** or two-chamber, body. It consists of a lower house, called the assembly, that has eighty members and an upper house, called the senate, that has forty members. Members of the assembly serve two-year terms, and senators serve four-year terms. Should a vacancy occur in the state legislature, the governor must call a special election to fill the vacant seat.

Being a senator is considered more prestigious than being a member of the assembly, and assembly members often give up safe assembly seats and forsake considerable seniority in order to run for the senate. The following are some of the reasons the senate is so attractive:

1. The senate has fewer members than the assembly. Hence, the spotlight is easier to catch, and power is easier to wield.
2. Senate terms are longer than assembly terms, so that senators run half as often as assembly members. Also, the election year that falls in the middle of a four-year term provides an excellent opportunity to run for higher office (such as attorney general, controller, or congressional representative) without having to give up the senate seat.

3. Senate districts are twice as large as assembly districts. In fact, state senate districts are even larger in population than congressional districts. Representing many people confers distinction.
4. The senate itself has more duties than the assembly. The senate confirms or rejects the governor's nominees to various boards and commissions.
5. In addition, the state senate reflects some of the glory of the U.S. Senate, after which it was patterned.

Compensation

Whatever the differences in status, the salary and benefits in both chambers are the same: $40,816 per year salary, $87 per day living expense allowance while the legislature is in session, round-trip travel expenses for official business (such as sessions of the legislature and committee meetings); credit cards for telephone and gasoline expenses; an allowance for a state-licensed automobile; and generous health and retirement benefits. Is this amount of remuneration excessive? If Californians paid their legislators too much, men and women would seek these positions for the money alone. If legislators were paid too little, successful people would not take these positions, and the caliber of the legislature would decline; also, low salaries would lead to dependence on lobbyists for favors. Some members of the California legislature (for example, lawyers, doctors, and businesspeople) take a considerable reduction in salary in order to enter public life.

Sessions

Since 1967, California has had a year-round, full-time legislature. Not much time is lost between election day and the beginning of work: sessions begin on the first Monday in December of even-numbered years. The session must end on November 30 of the following even-numbered year. Special sessions, which, as we have mentioned, are called by the governor to deal with pressing topics, can run concurrently with regular sessions.

LEADERSHIP IN THE LEGISLATURE
Senate

The lieutenant governor is the president and presiding officer of the state senate. He or she recognizes those wishing to speak and makes parliamentary decisions; for example, the lieutenant governor can rule motions out of order. Since the lieutenant governor is usually not present in the chamber—as we have explained, he or she can vote only in the unlikely event of a tie—a president pro tempore ("for the time being") presides. The president pro tem, as he or she is usually called, is elected from the majority party. The president pro tem becomes acting governor when both the governor and the lieutenant governor are absent from the state. Senate leadership is collective: the president pro tem administers the senate along with the four elected members—

usually two from each party—of the senate rules committee. The rules committee names committee chairpersons, appoints members to committees, and refers bills to committee.

Assembly

The assembly is presided over by the speaker, who may be the second most important person in California government and politics and who, therefore, is a potential contender for the governorship. (When the speaker is absent, a speaker pro tempore acts as a substitute.) As presiding officer, the speaker rules on parliamentary procedure. The speaker's knowledge of parliamentary tactics and judicious use of procedure can spell life or death for some bills. The speaker's most important power is the power to appoint the chairperson and majority party members of all committees. To aid one's constituents or to further one's policy goals, an assembly member often prefers to serve on a particular committee. For example, a member from a farm area may want to be on the agriculture committee or a teacher may want to be on the education committee. The speaker places those with similar views on favored committees: friends and supporters are rewarded, while others are brought into line or penalized.

We must also note a less-than-honorable reason for wanting to serve on a particular committee. Members of those committees that review legislation on banking, mortgage lending, insurance, horse racing, and alcoholic beverages get immense campaign contributions from those interests. A member may want to serve on these committees not out of interest in banking or insurance, but in order to squeeze money out of the interest groups. Hence, the committees are known around the capitol as **"juice" committees.**

Finally, the speaker is a powerful fundraiser. Interest groups often funnel their campaign contributions through the speaker, who distributes the money to majority party members running in close election races. The speaker benefits from this arrangement much more than do the interest groups, because the speaker decides how to distribute very large sums of money to members, who may not know how much money each interest group has contributed. The speaker's influence thus pervades the assembly. In the 1984 election, Speaker Willie Brown spent more than $2.5 million on assembly races; in 1986 he spent $3.8 million. Such fundraising takes a great deal of the speaker's time: Willie Brown has lamented that "I have to spend every day of my life raising a minimum of $3,000 a day. . . . That means almost all of my public time has to be devoted to fundraising."[2] Since the speaker, and also the senate president pro tem, contribute much more to legislative candidates than do the state's political parties, these legislative leaders have been described as "the real political parties in California."

Sherry Bebitch Jeffe has conducted a comprehensive study of state legislative leadership. Speakers of the California Assembly can be considered in terms of *interpersonal style* (how each speaker relates to peers, subordinates, rivals, advisors, the governor, the media, lobbyists) or in terms of *functional style* (how each speaker perceives the function of leadership).[3] All speakers since 1961

'Please, ladies and gentlemen, please! *A simple heartfelt
and sustained round of applause will be sufficient!'*
SOURCE: Dennis Renault, *Sacramento Bee*

have followed a "directive" interpersonal style that is firm, tough, aggressive, assertive, partisan, autocratic, confrontational, and centralized in approach. Jeffe's interviews with all surviving former speakers, the current speaker, and former legislators and staff members revealed Leo McCarthy (1974–1980) to have been the best example of a directive interpersonal style. On the other hand, a speaker's functional style must be administrative if not programmatic as well. An administrative speaker may concentrate on reforming legislative procedure and organization, as did Robert Monagan (1969–1970), or may stress raising money for campaigns, as does Willie Brown (1980 to the present). In contrast, the programmatic speaker focuses upon policy issues in order to influence social change in the future. Jeffe feels that Jesse Unruh (1961–1968) is the model of the programmatic speaker, but he was also an influential administrative speaker as well.

The speaker's chief assistant and personal representative on the floor is the majority floor leader. The minority party elects a minority leader.

The 1979–1980 Speakership Struggle and Its Aftermath

A prolonged contest for the speakership took place from 1979 to 1980. This battle resulted in part from the speaker's role as a fundraiser. Late in 1979, Democratic Speaker Leo McCarthy of San Francisco announced that he would run for either governor or U.S. senator in 1982, and he vigorously began to raise money for the race. Some assembly Democrats, fearful that McCarthy would spend more effort raising money for his own race than for their reelection races, rallied behind Majority Floor Leader Howard Berman of Los Angeles, who announced that he would challenge McCarthy for the speakership. Each man promised his colleagues chairmanships and special consideration on legislation in an attempt to get forty-one of the fifty Democrats to support him (forty-one being a majority of the total assembly). Since the thirty assembly Republicans vowed for the time being to remain neutral in the struggle, and neither McCarthy nor Berman would give up the fight, a majority of the whole chamber was needed for victory. Neither contender succeeded in capturing enough votes, and so the battle shifted to the Democratic primaries of June 1980. McCarthy and Berman backed opposing candidates in various races for the Democratic nomination to the assembly, and each raised over $1 million from lobbyists to further the effort. McCarthy was able to deny renomination to one incumbent Democrat supporting Berman, and Berman did the same to an incumbent supporting McCarthy. When the Democrats caucused after the November elections, Leo McCarthy, tired from the long ordeal and fearing defeat, threw his support to Willie Brown, the San Francisco assemblyman whom McCarthy had defeated for speaker in 1974.

The normal assembly procedure is for each party to nominate a candidate for speaker, with the majority party candidate emerging victorious. However, this speakership fight was not normal. Assembly Republicans feared a Berman speakership, believing him to be vindictive; concessions from Brown prompted them to join with Willie Brown's Democratic supporters to elect him as speaker.

In return for Republican support, Brown made significant concessions: he increased the number of minority party chairpersons, augmented Republican staff assistance during reapportionment, and allowed the minority leader to name minority members of committees. Most importantly, Brown gave up the power to refer bills to committee. The referral power now rests not with the speaker but with the assembly rules committee. This power is significant because a bill's success depends on whether the committee to which it is sent is hostile or friendly. Referral is not an arbitrary procedure: bills often treat issues that fall under the authority of more than one committee; conversely, committee jurisdictions sometimes overlap. Insofar as bill assignment can influence legislative results, Brown relinquished an important power.

The "marriage of convenience" between speaker Brown and the Republicans ended abruptly in the fall of 1981 when the Democrats unveiled their partisan reapportionment plan. By that time, assembly Democrats were solidly behind Willie Brown.

LEGISLATIVE PROCEDURE

In this section we outline the stages of the legislative process through which a bill becomes law. After a brief summary of the different stages, we will describe each step in greater detail.

1. The bill is introduced.
2. The bill is given its first reading (by number, title, and author only) and then referred to committee.
3. A committee acts on the bill.
4. The bill is given a second reading on the house floor; amendments from the floor may be considered.
5. A third and final reading is made. The house votes its approval or rejection.
6. If approved, the bill is sent to the other house, where steps 1 to 5 are repeated.
7. A **conference committee** resolves differences in the bills passed by the two chambers.
8. The bill goes to the governor for signing.

Introduction   Bills come from many sources. The subject matter may be an issue studied by the author for some time or suggested by a constituent. More good laws than many people realize are suggested by citizens with ideas for improving life in California. As we noted in Chapter 4, interest groups suggest many bills. The governor also plays a large part in setting the legislature's agenda (see Chapter 6). The governor and other state constitutional officers are an important source of legislation, as are the agencies and departments of state government. Local governments receive their powers from the state. Not surprisingly, they or their statewide organizations have many proposals for new legislation. Committee staff members, who are highly competent and influential, also have many recommendations. The judicial council (see Chapter 8) is a significant source of bills for reforming the state's court system.

Whatever the source of a bill, only a member of the legislature can introduce it (after the bill has been checked by the legislative counsel). Members introduce bills simply by giving a signed copy to the clerk of the assembly or the secretary of the senate. When bills and resolutions are introduced, they are identified by letters that designate the house in which they originated and the type of legislation they contain. Table 7.1 shows the letter codes by which bills

TABLE 7.1   Codes for Bills and Resolutions

Code	Meaning of code
AB	Assembly bill. Bills introduced in the assembly are numbered AB 1, AB 2, and so on.
SB	Senate bill. Bills introduced in the senate are numbered SB 1, SB 2, and so on.
ACA	Assembly constitutional amendment
SCA	Senate constitutional amendment
ACR	Assembly concurrent resolutions
SCR	Senate concurrent resolutions. These enable the two houses to take common action, for example, to establish a joint committee, to provide for joint rules, to recess or adjourn, or to praise important individuals.
AJR	Assembly joint resolution
SJR	Senate joint resolution. Through this resolution, the legislature states its views on a matter before the U.S. Congress.
HR	House resolution
SR	Senate resolution. This resolution is used when a single chamber wants to adopt a rule for itself or when a legislator wants to honor a constituent.

and resolutions are identified and tells what these codes mean. Bills usually cannot be acted upon for thirty days after they have been introduced.

Legislators sometimes introduce bills which they are not especially desirous of having passed. If they have been pressured by a constituent or an interest group or the media, they act to relieve that pressure. Legislators may also be trying to get notoriety or to stake out a philosophical position or to encourage campaign contributions from a particular group. Sometimes they also introduce bills in skeleton form because the bill can serve as a vehicle for dealing with related matters which may come up late in the session.

First reading and referral   The state constitution requires that each bill receive three readings. This first reading is perfunctory only. After the bill is read, the rules committee then refers it to committee.

Committee deliberation   More than six thousand measures were introduced in each of the last five sessions of the California legislature. In order to deal with such a volume of proposals, the legislature divides itself into **standing committees** (see Table 7.2). When a bill is referred to committee, the committee studies it and holds hearings at which interested parties give testimony. For example, the bill's author, representatives of the department of finance, the legislative analyst (whose duties we will describe later), and lobbyists may appear and give their views. Ultimately, the committee may (1) kill the bill by not reporting it out, (2) report it out to the whole house without recommendation, (3) report it out with a "do pass" recommendation, or (4) report it out with amendments. This committee stage can be crucial because many bills never emerge from committee. Although a bill can be forced out of committee by majority vote of the entire house membership, this tactic is rarely employed—the last successful discharge of a bill from committee was in 1960.

TABLE 7.2   Legislative Committees

Assembly committees (27)	Senate committees (22)
Aging and Long-Term Care	Agriculture and Water Resources
Agriculture	Appropriations[b]
Constitutional Amendments	Banking and Commerce[a]
Consumer Protection	Budget and Fiscal Review[b]
Economic Development and	Business and Professions
New Technologies	Constitutional Amendments
Education	Education
Elections and Reapportionment	Elections
Environmental Safety and	Energy and Public Utilities
Toxic Materials	Governmental Organization[a]
Finance, Insurance, and Commerce[a]	Health and Human Services
Governmental Organizations[a]	Housing and Urban Affairs
Health	Industrial Relations
Housing and Community Development	Insurance and Indemnity[a]
Human Services	Judiciary
Intergovernmental Relations	Local Government
Judiciary	Natural Resources and Wildlife
Labor and Employment	Public Employment and
Local Government	Retirement
Natural Resources	Revenue and Taxation
Public Employees and Retirement	Rules
Public Safety	Toxics and Public Safety
Revenue and Taxation	Management
Rules	Transportation
Transportation	
Utilities	
Veterans Affairs	
Water, Parks, and Wildlife	
Ways and Means[b]	

[a]One of the so-called "juice" committees.
[b]Fiscal committees.

After first passing a policy committee, appropriations bills (bills to spend money) must then go to the fiscal committees: the assembly ways and means committee or the senate appropriations committee.

Second reading and floor consideration   Once a committee has reported a bill out, the chamber must vote on any amendments made by committee or proposed on the floor.

Third reading and final vote   If a bill can make it through committee and through the amending process, it has a good chance of passing. An absolute majority vote of the membership (41 votes in the assembly and 21 in the senate) is needed to pass legislation. Urgency statutes, appropriations bills (such as the budget), and amendments to the state constitution all require a two-thirds majority of the *total* membership (54 votes in the assembly and 27 in the senate). The requirement that the budget be passed by a two-thirds majority allows the budget to be held hostage by the minority party or even a smaller group of legislators. Since the majority party usually does not have the 54 votes or 27 votes needed to pass the budget, the minority party can exact budgetary concessions in exchange for its votes. Individual legislators can also withhold their votes until pet projects for their districts are included in the budget. Only three other states require a two-thirds vote for passing the budget, and the U.S. Congress needs only a simple majority to pass most legislation. Interestingly, voting in the assembly is by electronic voting machine; senators vote by roll call.

A *California Journal* study of key votes in the 1985–1986 session showed the legislature to be very polarized along liberal versus conservative lines. More than one-fifth of the membership voted either 100 percent liberal or 100 percent conservative on 47 significant bills. Only 14 percent of the members could be characterized as moderate, for example, Democrats who take a liberal position less than 70 percent of the time, or Republicans who take a conservative position less than 70 percent of the time. The assembly was even more ideological than the senate. (Since the California electorate is hardly as polarized as its elected officials, the representative function of the California legislature and its function of building consensus may not be performed too well.)[4]

Second house action   A bill now follows substantially the same course of action in the other chamber. If the second house makes no changes, the bill is sent to the governor for consideration. Should the second chamber amend the bill (a strong possibility), it is sent to the house of origin with a request that the original house accept the changes that have been made. If the house of origin refuses to accept the changes that have been made in its bill, a conference committee must be called.

Conference committee   The speaker and the senate rules committee each appoint three members of their respective houses to serve on the conference committee for a bill (one member from each chamber must have voted against the bill). Conference committees have great leeway in working out an agreement between the chambers: except in the case of the budget bill, a conference committee may change other items besides those disputed by the chambers. When a majority of each delegation has approved the conference committee's work, the delegations return to their respective chambers and present the conference committee's bill to their houses on a take-it-or-leave-it basis. If the two houses accept the bill exactly as presented to them by their conferees, the bill goes to the governor for his consideration. Should one or both of the houses refuse to accept the conference committee's actions, a new conference committee must be appointed (three conference committees on the same bill is the limit).

Governor considers the bill   If the governor signs the bill, it usually takes effect on the following January 1, once a ninety-day waiting period has elapsed from the date the bill was signed. The governor has twelve days in which to sign or veto the bill. If the governor does nothing, the bill becomes law without the governor's signature. If the governor vetoes the bill (which happens only about 7 percent of the time), the legislature may override that veto by a two-thirds vote (which rarely happens).

Legislative procedure for passing the budget bill follows a similar, but somewhat different, course. Introduction of the governor's budget proposal—something required by the state Constitution by January 10 each year—is the beginning of a lengthy process that is supposed to result in adoption of a budget by July 1, the start of the new fiscal year.

Here is a step-by-step guide to the process:

- *January:* The proposal is introduced separately in the Senate and Assembly, usually by the chairmen of the Senate Appropriations Committee and the Assembly Ways and Means Committee.
- *February:* Those fiscal committees usually take no action until late February, to allow the state legislative analyst—the Legislature's nonpartisan fiscal adviser—time to review the proposal.
- *March–April:* Budget subcommittees in the Senate and Assembly conduct independent hearings on spending proposed for areas including health, welfare, labor, government services and prisons.
- *May:* The state Department of Finance offers its final estimates of revenues for the coming fiscal year to the budget subcommittees.
- *May:* Subcommittee reports are collected by the Appropriations Committee and the Ways and Means Committee and incorporated into separate versions of the state budget adopted by the full committees.
- *June:* Budgets are adopted by the two houses by required two-thirds majorities. Differences are worked out in marathon sessions of a two-house conference committee, which is working under the pressure of a June 15 deadline for the Legislature to adopt a final spending plan, a deadline missed more often than it is met.
- The compromise version of the budget is adopted by the two houses, again on two-thirds votes.
- The Legislature sends the budget to the governor, who has 12 working days to sign it. The governor can veto any individual line item appropriations that the Legislature has added to his proposal, but he cannot restore proposals that the Legislature deleted. The Legislature, by a two-thirds vote, can override the vetoes.

SOURCE: "The Budget Process," by David Puckett, *Los Angeles Times,* January 11, 1985, pt. I, p. 28. Copyright 1985, Los Angeles Times. Reprinted by permission.

EMPLOYEES OF THE LEGISLATURE

Highly qualified advisers, such as the legislative counsel, legislative analyst, and auditor general protect the legislature from depending excessively on the executive branch and on lobbyists for vital information.

Legislative Counsel

The legislative **counsel,** a lawyer, helps members of the legislature draft bills. No bill may be introduced unless it is accompanied by a digest prepared by the legislative counsel. The digest shows the changes the proposed bill would make in existing law. The legislative counsel's office, which consists of 225 employees, including over 60 lawyers, also advises members on the constitutionality of bills.

Legislative Analyst

Though unknown to most Californians, the legislative analyst is one of the most influential figures in California government and politics: he or she "provides advice to the legislature on anything with a fiscal implication, which can cover virtually every major bill."[5] The legislative analyst's most important task is to analyze the budget bill presented by the governor. Since this examination is done item by item, the analyst's annual *Analysis of the Budget Bill* is a massive document, more than 1,600 pages long. The legislative analyst and a staff of about 100 people have enough technical knowledge to serve as the legislature's counterweight to the governor's department of finance. Because the legislative analyst's chief aim is to make government more efficient, he or she usually recommends cuts in the governor's budget: this office is basically oriented toward economy in state government. The legislative analyst also prepares analyses of all ballot propositions to be submitted to the voters. These analyses appear in the pamphlet sent to each voter before the election.

Auditor General

The auditor general, who must be a certified public accountant, audits state agencies to make sure that money appropriated by the legislature has been spent for the purposes intended. The auditor general frees the legislature from reliance on the department of finance for the accomplishment of this task. Some commentators argue that this postaudit is more important than the preaudit performed by the state controller. The auditor and a staff of 115 people also evaluate the administration of programs authorized by the legislature, especially with an eye to efficiency, economy, and the possibility of fraud. For example, the auditor general issued a 1983 report showing that the California Department of Health Services was ineffective in supervising the handling of toxic wastes. (The toxic waste law is described in Chapter 1.) The auditor general showed that too few of the hazardous waste facilities were inspected, that too few of the toxic dumps had final permits, and that the hauling of dangerous substances was not adequately monitored.

Additional Staff

In addition to nonpartisan support available to all members from the legislative counsel, the legislative analyst, and the auditor general, three other kinds of staff support are also available: committee staff responsible to committee chairpersons and committee members, partisan staff reporting to the political parties in each chamber, and each member's personal staff.

Of the more than 2,100 people employed by the legislature, the committee consultants are among the most vital. These highly competent individuals conduct research for the committee employing them and organize the committee's hearings. Because of the extremely high volume of legislation introduced each session, the bill analyses prepared by committee consultants and read by legislators significantly affect the content of legislation. Additionally, each political party in each chamber employs about thirty professionals whose job it is to make sure that their employers get reelected. These caucus consultants develop party positions and partisan strategy, write speeches, and during election years, take leaves of absence to work in campaigns. In effect, they are publicly financed campaign organizations. Finally, each legislator has a personal staff working in his or her Sacramento office and in district offices to assist with legislative business and to respond to constituents' requests for assistance. The generally high quality of constituent service provided by these staffers is very effective in getting members reelected. As primary and general elections draw near, these individuals may take a leave of absence to become full-time campaign workers.

From this brief look at the support available to the legislature, we can conclude that (1) the California legislature is not understaffed, as are many state legislatures; (2) many employees are quite capable, especially committee consultants and those working for the legislative counsel, legislative analyst, and auditor general; (3) many are engaged in election-related rather than legislation-related activities, especially those employed by political parties; and (4) the legislative operation, which costs about $200 million per year, is expensive. Numerous factors have contributed to the present size of the legislature's staff operation: the complexity of modern issues; the election of issue-oriented legislators; constituents' increased demands for service; members' desires for reelection; and the determination, especially by past legislative leaders such as former speaker Jesse Unruh, to have a modern, professional legislature. Critics charge that staff members may add to the workload rather than lighten it. Large staffs are faulted for generating unnecessary legislation. Other commentators claim that legislators rely too heavily on staff members for information about the content of bills—that is, others do their homework for them—and consequently, legislators may not adequately understand the policies they enact into law. Finally, there is evidence that committee consultants may be changing from nonpartisan subject-matter experts into partisan aides whose main function is to assure the reelection of the committee chair who appointed them.[6]

RATING THE CALIFORNIA LEGISLATURE

Although a group of specialists on state government in the early 1970s rated the California legislature as the nation's best state legislature, the institution has come under increasing criticism in recent years. California's state legislators are said to be too responsive to interest groups, which in turn has led to two problems: a lowered moral tone of the legislature and institutional gridlock. *Sacramento Bee* columnist Dan Walters lays the blame at the foot of Speaker Willie Brown:

> The tone of the Capitol changed dramatically and nowhere is that change more noticeable than in the shift from McCarthy to Brown in the speakership.
>
> McCarthy not only established the example of focusing on legislative product but set a tone in his private life as well, giving up his San Francisco law practice and living on his salary as a legislator.
>
> Brown set a different mark. He pointedly retained his law practice and used his political clout as speaker to represent corporate clients in dealings before local agencies, especially in San Francisco. Those private interests spilled over occasionally into state affairs as well.
>
> Brown's high-flying, wheeler-dealer demeanor emitted an unmistakable signal: It's all right to trade on your political position for private gain. And when that attitude was coupled with a voracious appetite for campaign funds, the change of atmosphere was radical. . . . Brown has used his speakership to pressure special interest pleaders into coughing up millions of dollars for his own campaign war chest and those of other Democratic politicians and causes. In their private conversations, Sacramento lobbyists term the speaker's high-powered fund raising a "shakedown."[7]

On the other hand, William Endicott, capitol bureau chief for the *Sacramento Bee*, casts a wider net. He points to the huge sums of money that must be raised for California legislative races which tend to "blur the distinction between right and wrong—and between bills that are tied to campaign contributions and other favors. [Also,] the legislature has evolved over the last twenty years from a part-time collection of amateur politicians into a full-time collection of political professionals for whom politics is an end in itself and whose primary goal is staying in office."[8] The part-time citizen–legislators prior to 1967 had another occupation which provided their main livelihood; if they were defeated for reelection, they could always return to that profession. Today's full-time professional legislators usually have no other source of income, and many have known no other career than politics. For them, reelection is a major crisis—and they will do what is necessary to win.

Raising a great deal of money from interest groups is the necessary ingredient for reelection, and this has led to heightened group influence over the legislature and, according to some commentators, to institutional gridlock. California state government, especially the governor and legislature, are said to be stalemated: because of the diversity of interest groups in this state, groups can prevent significant policy change but they cannot effect new policies. Water policy is the prime example, but so are property tax relief and such recent issues as campaign finance reform and personal injury liability. On the other hand, Chapter 1 showed the legislature in a creative policy role resolving issues of the 1980s such as Medi-Cal reforms, workfare, and education reform.

A lesser but still significant problem is the wild end-of-the-session rush which closes each legislative session. In the final week of the 1983–1984 session, fully 20 percent of the bills introduced still awaited action: 600 bills in the assembly and over 700 in the senate. Legislators "deliberated" an average of three minutes per bill. In this frantic and convulsive atmosphere, the unscrupulous lobbyist sees a prime opportunity to sneak through unnoticed a questionable bill. Only years later will the public or the taxpayers get the real "bill."

SUMMARY

Many of the key issues of California politics are thrashed out in the California legislature. This point is what we had in mind when we noted earlier that a function of the legislature is resolving conflict and building consensus. When the legislature makes its decision, which is usually embodied in the form of a statute or appropriation, it legitimizes a course of action. This chapter has described the means employed to perform those ends: the legislature's structure, leadership, procedure, and staff support. But the legislature is not the *final* legitimizing agent. Those dissatisfied with the legislature's decision may carry the battle to the courts. The California court system is our next topic.

DISCUSSION QUESTIONS

1. Why would someone run for the senate rather than for the assembly?
2. What are the sources of bills?
3. Name the stages of the legislative process through which a bill progresses on the way to becoming a law.
4. The legislative process in California might be described as an obstacle course. Can you name some key points at which a bill can be killed? If so many danger points exist, why do any important bills get passed at all?
5. Why is the speaker of the assembly such a powerful figure?
6. Describe the duties of the legislative counsel, the auditor general, and the legislative analyst.
7. Who is your assembly member? Who is your state senator?

NOTES

1. Legislatures also have judicial functions such as impeachment, judging the qualifications of members, and expelling members accused of wrongdoing. In addition, they must confirm many of the executive's appointments, such as those to boards and commissions. Legislative functions are described in George S. Blair, *American Legislatures: Structure and Process* (New York: Harper & Row, 1967), chap. 3. See also John F. Bibby and Roger H. Davidson, *On Capitol Hill*, 2nd ed. (Hinsdale, Ill: Dryden Press, 1972), pp. 3–12.
2. "Willie Brown Decries Time Spent on Raising Funds," *Los Angeles Times*, May 4, 1985, pt. II, p. 6. See also "Legislative Leaders Top Campaign Contribution List," *FPPC Bulletin*, September 1, 1983, p. 4.
3. Sherry Bebitch Jeffe, "How Leadership Styles Influence Political Effectiveness," *Western City* (May 1986): 14–19. Jeffe is Project Director, Study of State Legislative

Leadership, Institute of Politics and Government, University of Southern California.

4. Andrea Margolis and Richard Zeiger, "Bleeding Hearts, Stone Hearts," *California Journal* (January 1987): 30–33.
5. T. Anthony Quinn and Ed Salzman, *California Public Administration*, 2nd ed. (Sacramento: California Journal Press, 1982), p. 17.
6. Sherry Bebitch Jeffe, "Legislative Staff," *California Journal* (January 1987): 42–45.
7. Dan Walters, "Capitol Aura: Anything Goes," *Sacramento Bee*, February 10, 1985, p. A3, and "Willie Brown and Moriarty," *Sacramento Bee*, March 31, 1985, p. A3.
8. William Endicott, "Money, Jobs Make Legislature Seem Ripe for Scandal," *Los Angeles Times*, March 22, 1985, pt. I, p. 3. Some observers have suggested that a way to reduce legislators' reliance on special interests would be to limit legislators' time in office to a specific number of terms.

8

Courts

California has a rather elaborate system of courts to settle civil disputes and to respond to violations of state laws. This court system, which is also referred to as the **judiciary** or as the judicial branch of government, consists of two types of courts: **trial** courts and **appellate** courts. Only in the former do trials actually take place. Trial courts are said to have *original jurisdiction*, because cases originate there. A party that loses in the trial court may want to appeal to a higher court. The purpose of appellate courts is to hear appeals from trial courts.

The California courts, beginning with lowest, are listed below:

1. Trial courts
   Municipal courts and justice courts
   Superior courts
2. Appellate courts
   Courts of appeal
   Supreme court

Municipal and justice courts are often called inferior courts. This term does not mean that they are necessarily of poor quality, only that they are on the lowest step of the judicial ladder. In fact, the California court system is widely considered to be one of the nation's best. Such high quality is promoted by the commission on judicial appointments, the commission on judicial performance, the judicial council, and the commission on judicial nominees evaluation.

MUNICIPAL COURTS

Municipal courts have jurisdiction in both **civil law** and **criminal law** cases. Civil law cases usually involve disputes between private persons or private organizations and are concerned with whether one of the parties has been injured and what shall be the legal remedies appropriate for compensation. Breach of contract or defamation of character are examples of civil law cases. In a civil law case, the party bringing the suit is called the **plaintiff.** The party being sued is the **defendant.** Criminal law deals with crimes; cases are always brought "by and in the name of" a unit of government. Questions to be determined are whether the defendant has injured society and what punishment is necessary.

The civil jurisdiction of municipal courts extends to cases involving up to $25,000 in contested cash or property. Because this sum is low for most civil cases in California, most of those cases are heard at the superior court level. The criminal jurisdiction of the municipal courts encompasses infractions and misdemeanors, or less serious crimes. The vast majority of municipal court criminal cases are traffic cases. (Similar courts in other states are often called traffic courts.)

Preliminary hearings in cases concerning felonies, or serious crimes, are conducted in municipal court. At these hearings, which are not trials, the judge determines whether a law has been broken and whether sufficient evidence suggests that the accused is the lawbreaker. If both of these requirements are met, the accused is turned over to a superior court. Municipal courts also act as **small claims courts**, where individuals or corporations disputing less than $1,500 represent themselves before a judge. This procedure allows minor disagreements to be settled without lawyers' fees. Some municipal and justice courts hold small claims court at night so contestants will not have to lose a day's salary. Unfortunately, small claims court often serves as a bill collection agency, where businesses try to collect allegedly delinquent bills. The defendant in a small claims suit may appeal the case to a higher court if he or she loses, but the plaintiff does not have this right.

Municipal court judges are elected in nonpartisan elections for six-year terms. The state has more than 550 municipal court judges. Vacancies (through death, retirement, and so forth) are filled by the governor. The overwhelming majority of municipal court judges originally reached the bench by gubernatorial appointment. A judge who has decided to resign or retire will usually relinquish the post before the end of the term if he or she has confidence in the governor's ability to select a satisfactory replacement. The replacement serves the last year or so of the term and then runs for reelection as an incumbent. If the incumbent is unopposed—as is usually the case—the name will not appear on the ballot. Therefore, in practice, municipal court judges (in fact, all California judges, as we will see) are appointed to a position that they hold for as long as they wish. Some judges are defeated in elections, but not many.

The role of the governor in staffing the courts is therefore extremely important. Governor Jerry Brown made more than 800 appointments, the largest number in the state's history. Ronald Reagan made 645 appointments, and Pat Brown made 621. An intensive study of factors which governors deem significant in choosing a judge found support of the local bar association to be crucial for all three governors.[1] However, each governor placed great emphasis on different additional factors. Pat Brown weighed heavily whether the potential appointee had the support of local business, labor, and political leaders, and especially if the individual was a personal friend or acquaintance of Brown's. Reagan valued the support of local business leaders and an influential legislator. Jerry Brown sought the advice of local political leaders, influential legislators, and racial and minority groups. The appointees of both Browns had been very active in party organizations or political campaigns prior to their selection, while Reagan's choices had been active in bar and business associations. Each governor selected about 80 percent of his appointments from members of his own political party.

JUSTICE COURTS

Justice courts have the same purpose as municipal courts but are located in rural areas. Their civil jurisdiction also extends to disputes of up to $25,000. Judges of the justice courts were justices of the peace prior to a 1950 court reorganization—hence the name "justice" court. Justice court judges are elected for six-year terms in nonpartisan elections. The state has about eighty justice court judges. Vacancies are filled either by county boards of supervisors or by special elections, called by the supervisors.

SUPERIOR COURTS

The superior courts are California's major trial courts. There must be at least one superior court for each county. The importance of the superior courts is indicated by the range of their original jurisdiction, which includes all civil cases over $25,000, all cases having to do with juveniles, guardianship cases, probate (wills), divorces, and felonies. In large counties with many judges, superior court judges specialize in and hear only certain kinds of cases, such as probate or juvenile ones. Superior courts also hear appeals from municipal and justice courts, but superior courts are *not* appellate courts; they are trial courts.

Superior court judges are elected for six-year terms in nonpartisan elections. California has more than 700 superior court judges (more than 220 in Los Angeles County alone). Vacancies are filled by the governor, who may wish to elevate a municipal court judge to the superior court. By filling a vacancy in this manner, the governor turns the original vacancy into two appointments.

COURTS OF APPEAL

The state is divided into six appellate districts. Each district has a court of appeal with one or more divisions to hear appeals from the superior courts in its district. The courts of appeal also review decisions of quasi-judicial bodies such as the industrial accident commission. The courts of appeal are important: the vast majority of their decisions are not reviewed by the supreme court and thus are final decisions. The chief function of these courts is to enable the losing party in superior court to appeal the case. Appellate courts filter the flow of cases going to the supreme court and thus reduce the workload of the highest court. At appellate hearings the justices consider only transcripts of superior court proceedings and listen only to brief oral arguments by counsel. Because the purpose of the hearing is to determine whether proper legal procedures were followed by the lower court, there is no interrogation of witnesses or introduction of evidence. Despite popular misconceptions to the contrary, the courts of appeal reverse few criminal convictions meted out by lower courts.

The seventy-seven justices of the courts of appeal are elected for twelve-year terms. Vacancies are filled by the governor, then the name of the appointee appears on the ballot in the next gubernatorial election. The ballot item asks, "Shall _____ be elected to the office for the term prescribed by law?" Since voters vote yes or no, no appellate court justice ever faces an opponent. If the justice receives more yes votes than no votes, he or she is elected.[2] Should the no votes exceed the yes votes, a vacancy is created for the governor to fill. (County voters could adopt this procedure to elect superior court judges, but no county has yet done so.)

CALIFORNIA SUPREME COURT

The California Supreme Court, consisting of seven justices, is one of the most prestigious state supreme courts in the nation. Its decisions in such areas as civil rights, the death penalty, abortion, product liability, and school finance have received national attention and have frequently influenced the U.S. Supreme Court's disposition of these issues. Despite a highly publicized investigation of the court's procedures (which is described below), the California Supreme Court remains a national leader because it advocates the "independent state grounds" doctrine, which was pioneered by Justice Stanley Mosk. Justice Mosk believes that when the state supreme court is interpreting provisions that are identical in the U.S. Constitution and the California Constitution, the court may use the state constitution as grounds for a more expansive, but not a more restrictive, interpretation of constitutional rights. In areas such as search and seizure or the interrogation of criminal suspects by police officers, the California court has been more solicitous of individual rights than has its federal counterpart. The theory is that "when the U.S. Supreme Court sets forth a rule on a constitutional issue, it is establishing a minimum standard. An individual state always has been free to establish a stricter rule."[3] Critics argue that the independent state grounds doctrine will cause basic rights to vary from state to state and that lower-level courts can use the doctrine to circumvent rulings of a higher court. Ironically, California voters have used the initiative process to overturn state supreme court decisions made on independent state grounds in such areas as busing, police searches, criminal convictions, and the death penalty.

The California Supreme Court has discretionary authority to hear appeals from the courts of appeal and the superior courts. Because of the supreme court's extensive caseload, the vast majority of these petitions must be denied. However, appeals in death penalty cases automatically go directly from superior court to the state supreme court. The state's highest court (and also the courts of appeal) has original jurisdiction to issue the following *writs,* or orders: **prohibition,** which prohibits a lower court from having a case before it; **habeas corpus,** which requires that a detained or jailed person be brought before a judge so that the judge may determine whether the detention is legal; and

The three "equal" branches of government.
SOURCE: Wallmeyer Cartoons

mandamus, which commands a public official to perform one of his or her official duties.

Supreme court justices serve twelve-year terms. They are elected in the same manner as justices of the courts of appeal. The governor fills vacancies, generally selecting justices who share the governor's views on legal and political issues. Once a justice is appointed, he or she is outside the governor's control. As an example, Governor Reagan appointed Donald Wright as chief justice and soon came to regret it. Reagan believed Wright to be a conservative, but Wright turned out to be a liberal. In general, legal and political issues are very similar; for instance, consider capital punishment, busing, and obscenity. Obviously, a person does not give up lifelong political convictions when he or she dons the black robes. But a judge's decision also depends on the facts of the case at hand, on legal precedents, and on whether the judge believes a given issue should be decided by the courts, or by the governor and the legislature—the branches designed to resolve strictly political differences.

The process followed by the California Supreme Court in deciding a case is diagrammed in Figure 8.1. The court must first determine whether it wishes to review the lower court's decision. A conference memorandum is prepared by the court clerks, who research the case and recommend for or against granting review. At its weekly conference, the court must then decide whether to accept the case. Acceptance requires at least four affirmative votes. Provided that review has been granted, one of the justices voting for review prepares a

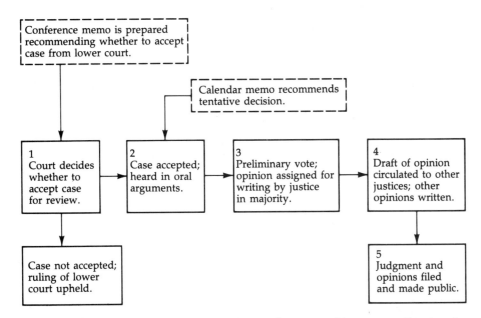

FIGURE 8.1 The California Supreme Court's decision-making process. Reprinted by permission from the *Los Angeles Times,* November 23, 1978, pt. I, p. 3.

calendar memorandum "stating the facts, applying the law, and recommending a ruling—a document that closely resembles a draft opinion."[4] Oral arguments by opposing counsel (the lawyers for each side) are then heard, and a preliminary vote is taken. One of the justices voting with the court majority is assigned the task of writing the majority opinion. This opinion is circulated among the justices, each of whom can sign it, suggest additions or deletions as a condition of signing, write a concurring opinion that agrees with the court's decision but bases the ruling on other grounds, or write a dissenting (minority) opinion. This process, which involves numerous editings, rewritings, and extensive negotiating, culminates in a final opinion (or opinions) that is made public and becomes the decision of the court.

Because of the extremely heavy workload of the court, Justice Mosk has suggested that the supreme court be increased to eleven justices and split into two five-member divisions, one to hear criminal matters, and the other to hear civil cases. The chief justice would retain administrative responsibility for supervising the court's total workload and could sit in either division to replace a justice who is disqualified or ill. The efficiency of the court was also improved by a 1984 constitutional amendment that allows the court to grant hearings on only specific parts of a lower court opinion, without having to decide every legal question raised by the case.

COMMISSION ON JUDICIAL APPOINTMENTS

The commission on judicial appointments must confirm the governor's appointments to the courts of appeal and the supreme court. Its members are the chief justice of the California Supreme Court, the senior justice of the court of appeal in the district of the appointment, and the attorney general. Two of the three members must vote to confirm the nominee. Only once has the commission rejected a governor's nomination. In 1982, owing to highly unusual circumstances, the commission rejected three of Governor Brown's courts of appeal nominees. The legislature had created a new appellate district in San Jose, and the governor nominated three people to fill the new posts. Since there was no incumbent senior justice for the district, the commission consisted only of the chief justice of the supreme court and the attorney general. Attorney General George Deukmejian, who would become governor in five days, blocked the three appointments. Opposition from the commission has occasionally forced the governor to withdraw the name of a controversial choice. The members of the commission are supposed to base their votes on whether they find the nominee to be "qualified" or "unqualified"; however, in practice the decision is sometimes based on the nominee's political philosophy.

COMMISSION ON JUDICIAL NOMINEES EVALUATION

The state bar association appoints a twenty-five–member commission on judicial nominees evaluation, which is supposed to make confidential recommendations to the governor on the fitness of lawyers he is considering for nomination or appointment as judges. The governor is required by law to submit the names of possible nominees for judgeships to the commission, which rates them "exceptionally well-qualified," "well-qualified," "qualified," or "not qualified." Although the governor may nominate or appoint whomever he chooses, the commission can embarrass the governor by making public its evaluation if he appoints someone they have judged to be unqualified.

The commission makes its evaluation after surveying at least seventy-five lawyers who know the candidate, and after interviewing the candidate. Since the commission meets in secret and does not disclose its sources of information, candidates (especially those rated unqualified) liken it to a star-chamber proceeding. Moreover, there have been instances of commission members leaking ratings of "unqualified" before the governor has received the evaluation.

COMMISSION ON JUDICIAL PERFORMANCE

The commission on judicial performance consists of nine members appointed by the supreme court, the state bar association, and the governor.[5] The purpose of the commission is to recommend that the supreme court retire, remove, or censure a judge whom the commission has found to be unfit. The constitutional ground for compulsory retirement is a "disability that seriously interferes with the performance of the judge's duties and is or is likely to become permanent." The grounds for removal or censure, as set forth in Article VI, Section 18c of the state constitution, are more complex: "willful misconduct in office, persistent failure or inability to perform the judge's duties, habitual intemperance in the use of intoxicants or drugs, or conduct prejudicial to the administration of justice that brings the judicial office into disrepute."

In the case of a supreme court justice, the commission on judicial performance makes its recommendation to a panel of seven courts of appeal justices selected by lot, and this panel then issues the order. In 1977, Supreme Court Justice Marshall McComb was retired because of senility. Usually, once an investigation has begun, the judge in question will retire quietly rather than face a public airing of the charges.

Soon after the 1978 elections, the commission on judicial performance began an investigation into charges that the supreme court had delayed issuing controversial rulings in order to assist Chief Justice Rose Bird in her 1978 election campaign. Chief Justice Bird, an outspoken liberal, had been targeted for ouster in that election by a campaign organized by conservatives, law-and-order forces, and agricultural interests. The commission had to investigate charges that the supreme court had decided to strike down the "use a gun, go to prison" law before the election but had delayed releasing this decision (and one other) in order to deprive Bird's opponents of an issue. Another charge was that one or more justices had improperly disclosed confidential information about the case (*People v. Tanner*, 151 Cal. Rptr. 299 [1979]) to the media.

As the public investigation dragged on, long-standing bitterness and mistrust among the justices came to light. Finally, Justice Mosk succeeded in closing the hearings, and the commission did not file any charges. The long-term reputation of the court probably has not suffered, but its prestige was momentarily tarnished.

JUDICIAL COUNCIL

The judicial council, headed by the chief justice, consists of twenty-one members; the twenty besides the chief justice are appointed by the chief justice, the state bar association, the assembly, and the senate.[6] The purpose of the council is to improve and make more efficient the California court system. Reassigning judges is one way to speed up the justice system. The chief justice may temporarily transfer a judge from a court with a light caseload to a court that is behind in its **docket,** or calendar. A judge from a lower court may be assigned to a higher court, but a judge from a higher court may not be assigned to a lower court without his or her permission. Retired judges may also be called into service. Many reassignments are made each year.

At each session of the state legislature, the judicial council reports to the legislature on the condition of the courts and suggests various court reforms. The council also sets rules of procedure for the state's courts and conducts seminars for new judges. The judicial council appoints as assistant an administrative director of the courts who conducts research on the court system.

ELECTORAL VULNERABILITY OF JUDGES

Until recently, California's judges had secure positions. No appellate justice had ever been defeated at the polls, and few trial judges were denied reelection or even challenged. However, the state's voters grew restless in the late 1970s, perhaps because of controversial court decisions in the areas of busing, abortion, and the rights of criminal suspects. Maybe even more important was the belief on the part of many voters that judges decide legal issues more on the basis of personal political values than upon long-established judicial principles, even though, as we mentioned earlier, these values are not easily separated.

In any event, more voters began to express dissatisfaction with incumbent judges. Table 8.1 shows the percentage of votes against supreme court justices elected from 1960 to 1986. The 1966 election marked a turning point because in that year many voters were angry at the court for striking down Proposition 14, passed in 1964, which had established the right to refuse for personal reasons to sell real estate to any individual; that is, to practice discrimination. Prior to 1966, from 9 to 12 percent of the voters usually voted against supreme court justices. Since 1966, the negative vote has stayed in the high 20- to 30-percent range and almost reached a majority against Rose Bird in 1978 and Cruz Reynoso in 1982. But then the unprecedented happened in 1986: Justices Bird, Reynoso, and Joseph Grodin were turned out of office by the voters. No court of appeal or supreme court justice had ever been defeated in the fifty-two years that California had used the judicial retention election system, but three justices were rejected in a single day. The depth of the voters' dissatisfaction is indicated by the fact that Bird lost by 32 points, Reynoso by 20 points, and Grodin by 14 points. A *Los Angeles Times* statewide poll of voters as they were exiting the polling place found that Cruz Reynoso, the first Latino ever appointed to the supreme court, even failed to receive a majority of votes from Latino voters.

The key issue in the defeat of Justices Bird, Reynoso, and Grodin was clearly the death penalty. According to a Field Poll taken before the election, 83 percent of all Californians favor the death penalty. Public opposition to the chief justice crystallized more than a year before the election, and then spilled over to the other two justices as election day approached. Opponents of the chief justice, led by the California District Attorney's Association, pointed out that Rose Bird voted to reverse all sixty-one death penalty conviction cases which came before the court during her tenure. As a result, a new trial was ordered on all or part of each of the sixty-one cases, or the convicted person's sentence was changed to life imprisonment. Hence, the opposition claimed that Bird was refusing to enforce California's death penalty law. Supporters of the chief justice argued in response that proper procedures were not followed by the trial courts in these death penalty cases, which led to a denial of the constitutional rights of the defendants. Furthermore, they said that it is the duty of the supreme court to protect procedural values such as due process of law, a necessary duty which may not be popular with the public. Moreover, Bird's supporters claimed that by protecting the constitutional rights of those accused of crime and providing justice for unpopular people, the court was protecting the rights of all persons.

Another important issue that arose in the 1986 campaign for and against Justices Bird, Reynoso, and Grodin concerned the nature of the California judicial retention election system itself. Defenders of the justices argued that in

TABLE 8.1 Percentage of Vote against State Supreme Court Justices, 1960 to 1986

1960	1962	1964	1966[a]	1970	1974	1978	1982	1986
Dooling 11.9	Gibson 9.2	Peek 11.8	Traynor 33.6	Wright 19.4	Wright 24.3	Bird 48.3	Reynoso 47.4	Bird 66.2
Peters 12.3	Tobriner 11.0		Burke 35.3	Burke 21.7	Clark 25.9	Manuel 37.2	Kaus 44.3	Reynoso 60.5
White 11.6	Traynor 10.3		McComb 20.8	Peters 27.6	Mosk 25.7	Newman 35.8	Broussard 43.5	Grodin 56.6
			Mosk 36.9	Sullivan 26.8	Tobriner 27.2	Richardson 27.5	Richardson 23.8	Mosk 26.5
			Peek 37.8					Panelli 21.4
								Lucas 20.6

[a]Since the constitutional revision of 1966, supreme court justices appear on the ballot only in gubernatorial election years.

order to maintain the independence of the courts, courts of appeal and supreme court justices should be retained in office unless they are "incompetent"
in the sense of being unethical or in the sense of being unable or unwilling to
perform their judicial responsibilities. Critics of the justices responded that
California already has the Commission on Judicial Performance for assessing
justices' competence, and that the voters may vote against a justice if they
dislike his or her decisions. These contentions raise some significant issues
concerning an *elected* judiciary (rather than one appointed for life). If voters can
deny reconfirmation to a justice based on dislike for his or her decisions, will
judges be continually looking over their shoulders as they make decisions? On
the other hand, electing judges is intended to keep judges responsive to the
needs of the governed and reflects a trust in the good sense of the public.
According to one observer: if the courts engage in the "business of reforming
and remaking society," they "lose their claim to protection from political ire of
those coming out on the short end of the judicial rulings. . . . People who
make policy ought to be accountable to someone in a democratic society."[7]

These significant issues may not be resolvable because they address the very
nature of an elective judiciary. However, much of the 1986 campaign was
waged on a considerably less enlightened level. Opponents of the justices
included the California District Attorney's Association, the California State
Sheriff's Association, the California Police Chief's Association, Republican
elected officials, farmers, and business and liability insurers who disliked
Justice Bird's decisions in personal injury cases. They accused the three liberal
justices of being "Jerry's judges" (a reference to the fact that the three had been
appointed by former Governor Jerry Brown, who was very unpopular at the
time) and they utilized relatives of murder victims in television commercials to
make emotional appeals for the death penalty. Governor Deukmejian called for
the defeat of the three sitting supreme court justices, which was a very unusual
act for an incumbent governor. On the other hand, retention of the justices was
favored by most Democratic elected officials, many law school professors,
lawyers who represent plaintiffs in personal injury cases (the California Trial
Lawyer's Association), and lawyers who defend persons accused of crimes.
They charged opponents of Rose Bird with being "bullies" and claimed that
Governor Deukmejian was trying to "pack" the court.

Effects of the defeat of the three justices are likely to be far reaching on the
California Supreme Court. Governor Deukmejian has appointed their replace-
ments, which has changed one of the nation's most liberal state supreme courts
into a conservative one. Since Deukmejian had already appointed two justices
to the court prior to the election, there is a court majority in favor of the death
penalty and many conservative legal doctrines. Moreover, the chief justice is
now Malcolm Lucas, a former state and federal trial judge and former law
partner of Governor Deukmejian.

If we turn to the trial court level, the high point for challenges to sitting
judges was 1978: twenty-eight superior court judges and forty municipal court
judges were challenged. The comparable figures for 1970 were six and five
challenged. In 1980, the number of challenged judges declined to fifty; two
years later the number was thirty-eight, and it has continued to decline. The

SOURCE: Scott Willis, *San Jose Mercury News*

challengers have usually been assistant district attorneys who stress law-and-order issues and fault incumbent judges for being soft on criminals. Other reasons for challenging trial judges are unpopular decisions rendered by that particular incumbent (for example, ordering busing of school children to improve racial balances in schools) or an embarrassing scandal involving the judge. This competition has raised the cost of judicial campaigns, as incumbent judges and challengers turn to campaign management firms. The fact that supposedly nonpolitical, impartial judges must rely on seasoned political professionals has profound implications for the California judicial system. Competition and campaign expertise mean that judicial candidates must raise large sums of money from business companies and businesspeople, court reporting firms, bail bondsmen, and especially other lawyers. The danger was expressed by one Fresno superior court judge: "What would you think if you were a litigant in my court and you knew the opposing counsel had contributed to my campaign? Wouldn't you wonder about the fairness of my decision if I ruled in his favor?"[8]

JURIES

Two different kinds of juries are found in California—trial juries and grand juries.

Trial Juries

Trial juries, or **petit juries,** determine the facts in civil or criminal cases and render verdicts in favor of one of the parties. Juries in felony cases must consist of twelve persons, and their decisions for conviction or acquittal must be unanimous. In misdemeanor cases and in civil cases, fewer than twelve jurors may be used if both parties consent. Both parties may also waive jury trial completely and have the case tried by a judge. Juries in civil cases may render a verdict on the basis of a three-fourths vote and a preponderance of the evidence. The state supreme court has ruled that counties may not rely solely on random selection of jurors from official lists of registered voters as the only method of selecting jurors. Such a selection procedure produces a disproportionately small number of black and Mexican-American jurors. Some counties also select potential jurors from lists of registered voters and motor vehicle license rolls.

Many authorities have found fault with the jury system and claim that jurors are influenced by emotional and nonrational factors (and that judges are not so influenced). One noted author has written, "To my mind a better instrument than the usual jury trial could scarcely be imagined for achieving uncertainty, capriciousness, lack of uniformity, . . . and unpredictability of decisions."[9] The alternative to a jury trial would be a judge trial, or bench trial, which some people believe produces wiser decisions. Jury trials in civil cases are also charged with being much more time-consuming than bench trials and thus contributing to court congestion. However, jury trials have their defenders, too. Juries of people with no legal training are thought to possess a commonsensical or natural feeling for justice that might be absent from a judge trial. Alexis de Tocqueville has written that jury service is "one of the most efficacious means for the education of people which society can employ."[10] Also, some people argue that trial by a jury of one's peers in a criminal case protects an individual from oppression by the state. A detailed study of the American jury system contradicts the charges of unpredictability and capriciousness: judges and juries agree on the verdict 78 percent of the time in criminal cases; in the minority of cases in which they disagree, the jury leans heavily toward leniency.[11] In civil cases, 78-percent agreement is also found, and in instances of disagreement, a jury is slightly more likely than a judge to decide in favor of the plaintiff in personal injury cases.

Whether one favors judge trials or jury trials, a key point to remember is that most cases never go to trial. Criminal cases are very likely to be resolved by plea bargaining (pleading guilty to a lesser offense), and civil cases are even more likely to be settled out of court.

Grand Juries

Grand juries consist of nineteen people (twenty-three in Los Angeles County) impaneled in each county for one year. Members are usually nominated by county judges; selection is by lottery. Grand juries have two primary functions: to return indictments and to investigate local (primarily county) government.

Grand juries return **indictments,** or charges, against suspected lawbreakers when requested to do so by the district attorney. Indictment by a grand jury means that sufficient evidence has been presented to justify a trial on criminal charges. Occasionally, though, when evidence is deemed insufficient, grand juries do not return indictments.

Grand jury proceedings in criminal cases are dominated by the district attorney. Proceedings are secret, and no judge is present. The possible suspect may not have an attorney present in the room, nor may he or she question any witness or object to the prosecutor's evidence. For these reasons, the California Supreme Court ruled in *James Hawkins v. Superior Court of San Francisco*, 22 Cal 3d 584 (1978), that suspects indicted by a grand jury are entitled to a prompt preliminary hearing in a municipal or justice court before they can be tried. Rather than go through a grand jury, district attorneys usually favor making the formal charges themselves by means of an **information,** a sworn statement of charges filed in superior court, or by a **complaint** filed in municipal court. It too must be followed by a preliminary hearing prior to trial.

Grand juries also review the operations of local government, watching especially for wrongdoing and illegal spending by public officials. The grand jury's investigation of local government is hampered by jurors' lack of expertise in this area, by lack of staff, and by jurors' terms of only one year. By the time the incumbents have penetrated the maze of local government, all but four of them must be replaced by new jurors. At the end of its term, a grand jury must file a report, which may suggest reforms, on the condition of local government.

The composition of grand juries has come under attack. Judges of the county usually nominate people they know and whose ability and character they can vouch for. Names are selected at random for the judges' lists. Not surprisingly, grand jurors resemble judges—they are older, more highly educated, wealthier, and Caucasian. In order to get a more representative grand jury, Los Angeles County mixes the names of volunteers with the judges' nominations.

EVALUATING CALIFORNIA'S COURT SYSTEM

Despite the various stresses and strains mentioned in the previous discussions, the state's court system does an excellent job. Specialists in state judicial systems rate California's court system as clearly the most professional in the nation. The state's citizens might respond, "It is also one of the slowest in the nation." Nonjury civil cases take more than thirty-eight months to come to trial in the rural area of San Joaquin County and twenty-two months in an urban area such as Los Angeles. Automobile accident cases have seriously crowded court **dockets.** Many observers have suggested that to speed things up, certain matters—such as uncontested divorces, auto accident cases, and some cases involving juveniles—should be turned over to arbitration by people other than lawyers. In 1978, the state legislature passed a law requiring that civil suits of less than $15,000 be sent to a lawyer–arbitrator. (The law applies only to counties with ten or more superior court judges and in some instances is increased to $50,000.) Eight-member juries in municipal or justice court civil cases are now allowed, and contending parties may also agree to a lesser number in open court.

SUMMARY

In this chapter, we have described the California court system, which consists of trial courts (municipal courts, justice courts, and superior courts) and appellate courts (the courts of appeal and the supreme court). There are two kinds of juries at the trial court level: grand juries and trial juries. Despite problems such as increased public dissatisfaction with many judges and crowded court calendars, the California judiciary is very highly rated by legal scholars and political scientists. The commission on judicial appointments, the commission on judicial performance, the judicial council, and the commission on judicial nominees evaluation promote high standards of service and efficiency in court operations.

DISCUSSION QUESTIONS

1. How do trial courts differ from appellate courts? Which California courts are trial courts, and which are appellate courts?
2. In what ways do the commission on judicial appointments, the commission on judicial performance, the judicial council, and the commission on judicial nominees evaluation serve to improve the California court system?
3. Describe the two kinds of juries found in trial cases.
4. If a judge's views on legal issues have much in common with his or her views on political issues, would it be better to have California judges run as candidates of a political party? Or should this state adopt the federal practice of executive appointment of judges for life, subject only to impeachment?
5. If the saying "Justice delayed is justice denied" is true, how do you rate the California court system? Would you like to try to sell the idea of swift justice to an indicted suspect whose attorney is trying to prepare an effective defense?

NOTES

1. Philip Dubois, "State Trial Court Appointment: Does the Governor Make a Difference?" *Judicature*, 69 (June–July 1985): 20–28.
2. At the first gubernatorial election after his or her appointment, the appellate justice is elected only for the remainder of the term to which he or she was appointed. After this remainder has been served, the justice may then run for a full twelve-year term.
3. Ronald Blubaugh, "The State Supreme Court's Declaration of Independence," *California Journal* (May 1976): 154.
4. Philip Hager, "How Secret Should State High Court Decisions Be?", *Los Angeles Times*, November 23, 1978, pt. I, p. 3.
5. The supreme court appoints five judges, the state bar association appoints two lawyers, and the governor appoints two citizens who are not lawyers.

6. The chief justice appoints the following members of the judicial council: another supreme court justice, three courts of appeal justices, five superior court judges, three municipal court judges, and two justice court judges. The state bar association appoints four lawyers. The assembly and the senate each appoint one of their members. All members serve two years except the chief justice.

7. Gideon Kanner, "Standard for Judging Judges: There Is No Such Thing as a Free Lunch," in California State Senate Office of Research, *The Chief Justice Donald R. Wright Memorial Symposium on the California Judiciary* (Sacramento: Senate Office of Research, 1986), pp. 12–13. See other articles in this volume, as well as Stephen R. Barnett, "Bird Lacks Qualities to Be Chief Justice," *Los Angeles Times*, October 29, 1986, pt. II, p. 7. Kanner is Professor of Law, Loyola of Los Angeles Law School, and Barnett is Professor of Law, University of California at Berkeley Law School.

8. Quoted in Dena Cochran, "Paying for Judicial Races," *California Journal* (June 1981): 220. Incumbents usually outspend challengers by a margin of at least two to one.

9. Jerome Frank, *Courts on Trial* (Princeton: Princeton University Press, 1950), p. 123.

10. Alexis de Tocqueville, *Democracy in America,* ed. Phillips Bradley (New York: Vintage Books, 1945), vol. 1, p. 296. See also John H. Jackson and Lee C. Bollinger, *Contract Law in Modern Society,* 2nd ed. (St. Paul, Minn.: West Publishing Co., 1980), pp. 572–575.

11. Harry Kalven, Jr., and Hans Zeisel, *The American Jury* (Boston: Little, Brown, 1966), pp. 58–64.

PART

4

Government in California encompasses not only the state but also counties, cities, special districts, and regional agencies. Cities and counties comprise the grass-roots government that has been celebrated since the time of Thomas Jefferson. In Part IV, we focus on local government and many of the quality-of-life issues we have discussed in this book. Consider some of the recent clashes in local government over such issues as land use and zoning, management of growth, and location of public housing for low-income people. One of the hottest issues in California in recent years—the property tax—was directly related to local government. Few issues incensed Californians more than rapidly increasing property tax bills.

Local government is important in the lives of Californians because at the local level the police power of government is exercised vigorously. By "police power" far more is meant than simply law enforcement. Police power is the authority of local (or state) government to pass laws regulating the health, safety, welfare, and morals of the people. Since this authority is so broad (very little is excluded from the definition), Californians concerned about the quality of life and about gaining control of the institutions that shape their lives should pay special heed to local government.

Local government in California encompasses 58 counties, more than 440 cities, more than 1,000 school districts, and about 4,200 other special districts. Local governments may exercise only the powers granted to them by state law or the state constitution. Each of the 50 state governments is thus a unitary system of government. The legal relationship between local government and the state government was stated long ago:

Local governments owe their origin to, and derive their powers from, the [state] legislature. It breathes into them the breath of life, without which they cannot

Local Government and State and Local Government Finance

exist. As it created, so it may destroy. . . . Unless there is some constitutional limitation on the right, the legislature might, by a single act, if we can suppose it capable of so great a folly and so great a wrong, sweep from existence all of the [cities] of the state, and the [cities] could not prevent it.[1]

Realistically, the state legislature is not going to abolish the city of San Francisco or even the city of Lodi. California has been one of the most permissive states in the amount of latitude granted to local governments. However, Proposition 13 of 1978 dramatically reduced local property tax revenues and caused local jurisdictions to depend financially much more on the state government. As a result, power has increasingly shifted to the state level, especially to the legislature, which must decide how much aid will be allotted to counties, cities, or special districts. The advisory commission on intergovernmental relations (ACIR) has ranked California eighteenth out of fifty states in the degree of discretion allowed counties and cities.[2]

In Chapter 9, we will describe the various local governments in California and discuss the financial issues these governments face. In Chapter 10, we will look at the state budget and state taxes, principally the income tax and the state sales tax.

NOTES

1. *City of Clinton v. Cedar Rapids and Missouri R. R. Co.*, 24 Iowa 455 (1868). These are words of the famous Judge John F. Dillon.
2. Advisory Commission on Intergovernmental Relations, *Measuring Local Discretionary Authority* (Washington, D.C.: ACIR, November 1981), Table 20.

9

Counties, Cities, Special Districts, and Regional Agencies

In June 1978, California voters passed Proposition 13 (the Jarvis–Gann amendment). Although the amendment dramatically reduced the property taxes on which counties, cities, and special districts so heavily depended, its effects were not felt immediately by local government. Unfortunately, that happy situation has changed. The huge state surplus which the state legislature used to help local governments is gone, and federal aid has been slashed significantly. How local governments have reacted to this fiscal stringency and how the "settling in" of Proposition 13 has altered intergovernmental relations are two of the main themes of this chapter. We will now consider the various types of local governments in California.

PERSPECTIVE ON CALIFORNIA'S COUNTIES

The first striking fact about California's fifty-eight counties is their diversity. In terms of area, San Bernardino County is the largest in the continental United States; covering 20,000 square miles, this county is 200 times larger than San Francisco County. In terms of population, Los Angeles County, with well over 8 million people, is the largest in the nation. By contrast, Alpine County has approximately 1,200 people.

Counties provide many services. They are the administering agents for various state programs, including welfare (although almost all the money and regulations for the welfare program are prescribed by the federal and state governments). Counties provide health care. They also provide police and fire protection in **unincorporated areas,** or noncity areas, and within cities that contract for these services; the county sheriff runs the county jail. Municipal, justice, and superior courts are funded in large part by the county. Counties conduct elections for cities, and they also attempt to meet recreational needs. Outside of cities (in unincorporated areas), county government serves as a general purpose local government, performing services usually rendered by city governments such as building streets and roads, regulating land use, and providing zoning and law enforcement. The importance of the role of county government in unincorporated areas is indicated by the fact that about 6 million Californians live in these areas. The county is an important keeper of records (wills, deeds, birth certificates, and so forth).

COUNTY BUDGET

Fourteen percent of the typical county budget is allotted to cover general government costs. Counties must provide for a legislative body (the board of supervisors), an assessor, and many other officials (either elected or appointed). Salaries must be paid, and retirement plans must be provided for all county employees.

The largest portion of a county's budget is for public assistance. The percentage spent on welfare varies somewhat from county to county, but 40 percent is an average figure. Although the county administers the welfare program, the bulk of the money is provided by the federal government and especially the state government.

Public protection of persons and property constitutes about 26 percent of budget costs. By public protection we mean the county's share of paying for the services of the courts (municipal, justice, and superior), the district attorney, the sheriff, the coroner, the county jail, and the probation department, as well as juvenile detention, fire protection, and activities such as building and safety inspection.

Counties spend 15 percent of their budgets on health and sanitation. In addition to operating the county hospital and mental health facilities, counties treat alcoholism, venereal disease, and other problems on an out-patient basis. Inspection of milk and control of pests and rodents are other important functions. To relieve financial pressures on counties because of the Jarvis amendment, the state government assumed all county costs of Medi-Cal.

Construction and maintenance of roads, bridges, and other facilities account for 5 percent of the budget. Supported by the state's gasoline tax, 42 percent of the state's road mileage is maintained by counties. As fuel supplies dwindle and as more and more counties come to be covered with an unhealthy, low-hanging layer of gray smog, alternate means of transporting people (such as mass transit) become a county concern.

The county allots 1.2 percent of its expenditures for education, primarily for libraries but also for the county superintendent of schools. Finally, county governments seek to meet recreation and cultural needs. About 1.3 percent of the money budgeted goes for parks, golf courses, and county beaches. Sources of county revenues are given in Table 9.1. Note that state and federal aid currently account for over 56 percent of county revenue. In the decade since the passage of the Jarvis–Gann amendment, county revenue collections and expenditures have grown significantly, but when these amounts are adjusted for the effects of inflation and population increase, both revenues and expenditures are lower than before the amendment. When cuts have been made, they have been for road and street construction and maintenance, and for jails, parks, and libraries.

TYPES OF COUNTIES

General law counties   Of California's fifty-eight counties, forty-six are general law counties. General law counties operate according to general laws, passed by the legislature and applicable statewide. Such laws might determine

TABLE 9.1 Sources of County Revenue before and after Proposition 13

Source	FY 1977 percentage	FY 1986 percentage
General property tax	35.36	23.90
Sales tax	2.18	1.87
Other taxes	.64	1.12
Licenses, permits, and franchises	.87	1.08
Fines, forfeits, and penalties	1.03	1.59
Use of money and property	1.56	3.19
From other governmental agencies:		
State	24.72	36.13
Federal	23.88	20.29
Other	.13	.19
Charges for current services	8.92	8.59
Other revenue	.71	2.15
	100.00	100.00

SOURCE: State Controller, *Annual Report of Financial Transactions Concerning Counties, Fiscal Year 1976–1977* (Sacramento, 1978), p. vii; State Controller, *Annual Report, 1985–1986,* p.vii.

the structure of county government, or require that certain public services be provided, or allow for the levying of various taxes. The state legislature classifies counties by population size and then passes laws covering particular classes of counties, regardless of where those counties are located. Since two counties of similar population may have widely different characteristics and needs, a desire for more flexibility paved the way for a second type of county, a charter county.

Charter counties   Although only twelve counties are charter (or home-rule) counties, about two-thirds of the state's population lives in these counties. The charter counties are San Bernardino, Los Angeles, Butte, Tehema, Alameda, San Francisco, Fresno, Sacramento, San Diego, San Mateo, Santa Clara, and Placer. Rather than general laws, a county's **charter**—a document similar to a constitution—determines how charter counties are governed.

General law counties must have a five-member board of supervisors, but charter counties can have more than five supervisors; more charter counties, especially very large ones, should use this opportunity. Charter counties can elect supervisors **at large,** rather than by district, as is the case in general law counties. This at-large provision can cause controversy, as we will see later in the chapter. In addition to choosing supervisors by district, voters in general law counties must elect the following long list of officers: treasurer, county clerk, auditor, sheriff, tax collector, controller, license collector, district attorney, recorder, assessor, public administrator, and coroner. In charter counties, as a service to tired voters, these officials (with the exception of the sheriff and district attorney) can be either appointed *or* elected. Those officers whose functions are basically technical and who do not establish basic policy for the county should be appointed by the supervisors. Many of the duties of these officials are combined, especially in charter counties.

To establish a charter, a board of freeholders must be elected. These citizens draw up a charter, which is then submitted to the voters for approval. Placer

County adopted a charter in 1980. One great asset of a charter is that a county can tailor its government to its needs and preferences. For example, a charter county can have a county manager rather than a chief administrative officer. (The difference will be explained later.)

City–county of San Francisco   Never known for being hidebound, San Francisco has a combined city and county. Unique in California, this arrangement was established in the city's charter. San Francisco is the only county to have more than five supervisors—it has eleven. The city–county has a mayor, who is elected separately from the supervisors; he or she has veto powers and substantial power over the budget and can appoint members of various powerful commissions (civil service commission, police commission, and planning commission). For a local executive in California, these are extensive powers.

COUNTY OFFICERS

Board of supervisors   The legislative body for each county is its board of supervisors (see Figure 9.1). County supervisors serve four-year terms; they are elected in nonpartisan elections that coincide with the party primaries in June of even-numbered years. If one candidate receives a majority of the total primary vote, a runoff election is not needed in November. Vacancies on the board of supervisors in general law counties are filled by the governor; vacancies in charter counties are filled by the supervisors themselves or by the governor. The board of supervisors adopts the county budget, about 90 percent of the expenditures of which are mandated by the state. The supervisors may sit as an appeals board to hear appeals regarding property **assessments** made by the assessor and also regarding land-use decisions made by the county planning commission. Prior to the passage of Proposition 13, the board of supervisors set each county's tax rate on real estate, but the Jarvis amendment set the maximum rate at 1 percent throughout the state. Finally, supervisors also oversee various county departments and decide the location of roads and bridges.

The small size of county boards of supervisors may be very unwise in large counties. Three counties have more than one million people, two have more than two million, and one has over eight million residents. Supervisorial decisions have immense impact in these counties, but five supervisors, even if all are present at meetings, may be too few to provide adequate representation and to be an effective decision-making body. Furthermore, to control policy with smaller boards, interest groups need to win over only three people rather than four, five, or six. Supervisors in urbanized, populous counties are heavily dependent on campaign contributions.

In recent years, turnover in the ranks of county supervisors has been high. Supervisors were once more likely to be older, Caucasian, Republican, conservative, and in favor of land development. Now supervisors are often minority-group members, Democrats, and environmentalists. Supervisors concerned about the environment are likely to give more thought to careful land-use planning and controls, especially in unincorporated areas of the county.

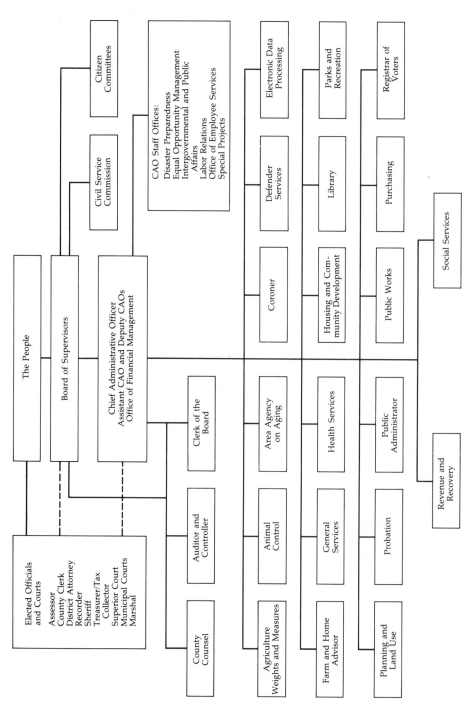

FIGURE 9.1 County organization

Chief administrative officer   California county government has no elected executive officer, but most counties do have an official appointed by the board of supervisors and usually called the chief administrative officer (CAO) or county manager (in charter counties). The CAO or county manager prepares the budget for board approval, administers the budget after it has been approved, provides the board of supervisors with information by which it can make better decisions, and implements those decisions. A county manager is normally given more authority than a CAO in budget matters and personnel decisions, but both officials are there primarily to integrate and coordinate county government. The following descriptions of other county officials will make the need for such coordination obvious.

District attorney   The district attorney prosecutes (brings to trial) those accused of crime. He or she must also investigate all shootings involving police officers. If the county has no county counsel, the district attorney will also represent the county in civil cases. The post of district attorney is an important stepping-stone to higher political office, such as a judgeship or the state legislature.

Sheriff and coroner   The sheriff and deputies enforce the law in unincorporated areas of the county and in any cities that contract for law enforcement services (under the Lakewood Plan described later). The sheriff's office provides bailiffs, or attendants, for the superior court and serves all processes and summonses. The sheriff also runs the county jail. In many counties, this office is combined with the office of coroner, which conducts inquests of all sudden, violent, or unusual deaths.

County clerk and recorder   The county clerk performs many significant duties. He or she is the clerk of the superior court and of the board of supervisors, and keeps minutes and maintains documents for both. The county clerk also keeps many other important records such as marriage licenses, articles of incorporation, and various filings (the clerk collects fees for these services). In addition, the county clerk registers voters and conducts elections. The office of county clerk is often combined with the office of recorder.

Public administrator, auditor, county superintendent of schools, and assessor   The public administrator administers the estates of people who die without clearly designating heirs. The auditor disburses checks (warrants) and reviews county books. The county superintendent of schools maintains statewide standards in local school districts, processes applications for teacher certification, and provides special programs for school districts such as migrant education and classes for handicapped children. Programs which cannot be economically provided by a small school district (for example, audiovisual services or data processing) are provided by the county superintendent of schools on a contract basis. The assessor determines the value of real estate in the county.

Local agency formation commission   Every county must have a **local agency formation commission (LAFCO)** composed of two members appointed by the board of supervisors, two appointed by mayors of cities in the county, and one appointed by the first four members of the agency itself. The purpose of the commissions is "to review and approve or disapprove all proposals to incorporate [form] cities, to form special districts, or to **annex** territory to cities or special districts. . . . The commissions' review powers . . . include consolidations, dissolutions, detachments, and mergers."[1] LAFCOs consider factors such as population density, land area, and land use. They also consider

- per capita assessed valuation
- natural boundaries
- proximity to other populated areas
- the likelihood of significant growth, locally and in adjacent areas
- the need for organized community services
- the adequacy of existing governmental services in the area
- probable future needs, and the ability of the proposed unit of government to meet them

In addition, LAFCOs study the impact a proposal is likely to have on nearby areas and on the entire county. Later in this chapter, we will discuss the role of LAFCOs in preventing the unnecessary creation of new cities and special districts.

One fact is readily apparent about California county governments: they are not each run by one elected executive (as at the national level) but by many elected executives. With authority so divided and dispersed, responsibility for county action or inaction is difficult to determine. Since the board of supervisors will ultimately be held responsible, it should be able to appoint officials—such as the auditor, tax collector, and coroner—who do not hold policymaking positions but rather technical, specialized, and ministerial positions. The supervisors should be given the power to appoint all these officers except the district attorney, who as public prosecutor should be responsible only to the electorate. However, were the state legislature to consider such action, the County Clerks Association, the County Treasurers Association, the County Recorders' Association, and other such organizations would lobby hard against the bill in Sacramento.

Perhaps the most serious problem for county government (and city government as well) is the need for a stable source of revenue. At the present time, counties are heavily dependent on state financial aid, which may vary from year to year depending upon the fiscal and political pressures to which the state government is subjected. But local governments need to plan over the long range; therefore the state constitution should be amended to guarantee a portion of the state income tax and a greater portion of the sales tax to counties and cities. A good start was made in 1984 when the legislature granted local governments all revenue collected from supplemental property tax assessments on purchases of new homes, and in 1986 when the voters amended the state constitution to guarantee motor vehicle license fees for local governments.

PERSPECTIVE ON CALIFORNIA'S CITIES

The vast majority of Californians live in one of the state's more than 440 cities. The term *cities* covers incorporated areas ranging from the city of Amador (in Amador County) with 160 people and Sand City (Monterey County) with 210 people to the state's metropolitan giants. Regardless of their sizes, cities influence the degree to which our lives are pleasant and improved by amenities, at least to the extent that government *can* make our lives pleasant. Cities supply police and fire protection; build and maintain streets and sewers; provide regulations such as building inspection, sanitation codes, and zoning; and furnish parks and libraries. Some cities operate public utilities.

The types of cities, following the same pattern as counties, include general law cities (numbering approximately 360), charter cities (numbering about 80), and the combined City and County of San Francisco. Although there are many more general law cities than charter cities, all of the state's large cities are charter cities. Because the state legislature has been giving general law cities more and more control over their own affairs, the difference between general law cities and charter cities is becoming unclear. However, what the legislature gives, it may also take away. The powers of charter cities are specified in their charters.

CITY BUDGET

The most important items in the city budget are police protection and the provision of electricity to the public. Other key budgetary items are fire protection, streets and storm drains, sewers, parks and recreation, libraries, and the provision of water. Table 9.2 shows sources of city revenue. Note that cities have a much more diversified revenue base than do counties. As the table shows, property taxes and state–federal aid have become less important and

TABLE 9.2   Sources of City Revenue before and after Proposition 13

Source	FY 1977 percentage	FY 1985 percentage
General property tax	23.78	7.84
Sales and use tax	15.47	12.19
Business license tax	2.77	2.51
Other nonproperty taxes	7.84	10.96
Licenses and permits	2.01	1.43
Fines and penalties	1.92	1.34
Use of money and property	2.93	6.20
Other governmental agencies	29.89	14.06
Charges for current services	8.64	37.67
Other revenue	4.75	5.80
	100.00	100.00

Note: The state controller has grouped together data from cities differing widely in population. The importance of each revenue source may vary considerably between very large and very small cities.
SOURCE: State Controller, *Annual Report of Financial Transaction Concerning Cities, Fiscal Year 1976–1977* (Sacramento, 1978), p. vii; and State Controller, *Annual Report, 1984–1985*, p. viii.

charges for current services much more important since the passage of Proposition 13. Examples of the latter are charges for sewer services, garbage collection, water, but especially electricity. In the decade since the passage of the amendment, city revenue collections and expenditures have grown significantly, but when these amounts are adjusted for the effects of inflation and population increase, both revenues and expenditures are lower than before the amendment. When cuts have been made, they have been for street construction and maintenance, parks, recreation, and libraries. When city taxes have been used, the following levies have been increased: the utility users tax, the business license tax, and the transient occupancy tax. The utility users tax is applied to a resident's electric, gas, or telephone bill, usually at a rate of 5 percent. City councils prefer this tax because it is collected by the utility companies as part of their monthly billings—any taxpayer anger is directed at the utilities and not at elected officials. Business license taxes are based on the total gross receipts of local businesses. Since cities apply the same percentage to businesses with a high net profit margin and those with a low net profit margin, the tax is burdensome for the latter. The transient occupancy tax, or hotel/motel tax, is a popular tax because it is paid by tourists or other nonresidents.

Cities have also greatly increased their use of **exactions**, which are the streets, sewers, sidewalks, parks, and police and fire stations that cities demand from developers in exchange for a building permit. According to a report issued by the state office of planning and research, these "are the legal, legitimate equivalent of extortion."[2] For example, in order to receive permission to build Rancho Carmel near San Diego, the developer had to provide $85 million in improvements, including a fire station complete with fire engines, a freeway overpass, traffic signals, and parks. Cities (and counties) have had to rely heavily on these fees as a result of Proposition 13, but these charges also add greatly to the cost of a new home because developers pass their cost on to purchasers. The increased cost of houses as a result of exactions makes many homes unaffordable to first-time buyers. Moreover, is it fair to make one part of the community (those buying homes today) pay for what benefits the whole community?

Another nontax source of income for cities is **user charges**. If a person visits a city museum or plays golf on a county course, he or she may pay a fee to help support that service. That those who receive a benefit should pay for it has long been urged by some scholars of taxation. (Other maxims of taxation in addition to the benefits-received principle will be discussed in Chapter 10.) Proponents of user charges argue that these charges are fair because no one is coerced into paying for a service that they do not receive and that user charges promote conservation: water and electricity are conserved because they must be paid for, and conservation increases when the unit price rises with consumption. Opponents of user charges argue that poor people may be denied some government services and that some benefits cannot be financed in this manner. Air pollution control programs or flood control programs are so-called collective goods that benefit all citizens. These services could not be financed by user charges.

INCORPORATION

Cities come into being (incorporate) for numerous reasons: to maintain local control of local services, especially police protection and the issuance of construction permits; to "secure the power of zoning [in order] to preserve existing land-use patterns or to prevent proposed changes"; to avoid being annexed by another city; to assimilate and tax a local industry or shopping center; and to keep taxes down by negotiating money-saving service contracts with the county.[3] Cities are sometimes formed not for people but for special interests. Industries may want to create a city containing little but industries so that the assessed valuation is high, since a low tax rate will still raise the small amount of money needed for services. Vernon is a city of this type.

The steps for incorporation are as follows:

1. Either at least 25 percent of the landowners representing at least 25 percent of the assessed value of the land, *or* 25 percent of the registered voters sign an incorporation petition; or the board of supervisors passes a resolution.
2. The local agency formation commission holds a hearing to review the matter and may approve or deny the application.
3. The county supervisors conduct a hearing at which written protests are reviewed. The supervisors can decide to terminate the process or can call for an incorporation election.
4. If a majority of voters favors the formation of the new city, the city is established. If the proposal is rejected, incorporation may not be attempted again for two years.

Cities not only may be born but also may die, as happens when the city stops electing officers. The city that once served as the county seat of Alpine County ceased to exist.

FORMS OF CITY GOVERNMENT

The first form of city government we will discuss is the mayor–council city. Here, the city council possesses the legislative power. Executive power is wielded by a mayor, who may be either strong or weak, depending upon the amount of power granted to the office. Strong mayors in mayor–council cities are directly elected by the people. They have veto powers and can appoint some department heads. Most large cities have strong mayors, but in these cities many powerful independent boards and commissions may dilute a strong mayor's power. All major cities (except Long Beach) elect the mayor directly. Weak mayors in mayor–council cities are elected by the city council and are members of those councils. Since a weak mayor's duties are largely ceremonial, the post is often rotated annually among council members.

The second form of city government, and the most prevalent type in California, is the council–manager city. Here, council members serve on a part-time basis, and there is no mayor, but the council appoints a full-time city manager.

Well-trained, highly paid, and usually very competent, city managers run most of California's cities, although ultimate power rests with the councils. Although they serve at the council's pleasure, most managers are given wide authority and discretion.

Since the city council may meet only once a week or once every two weeks, the manager is held accountable for the details of city operation and administration, and must run the city from day to day. He or she has the power to appoint and dismiss some department heads such as the police chief, prepares the agenda for council approval, and draws up the city budget for adoption by the council. The influence of a politically astute city manager can be immense, especially since council members are part-time elected officials, while the manager is a full-time trained professional. Some observers have noted that since the manager and his or her staff have a "near-monopoly of technical competence," the policymaking process may be one in which the manager proposes and the council disposes.[4] It is true that because the manager is responsible for running the city on a daily basis, he or she has far more information about city operations than does any council member, even those with long service on the council. A city manager with strong beliefs about policy may be in a position to "limit the range of possible policies that the council considers and to reduce the council essentially to the role of saying yes or no to his own policy recommendations."[5] However, this is not the case on very controversial issues or on matters regarding which the council has strong preferences. Critics of the council–manager form of city government fear that the manager may not apprise the council of alternatives to his or her recommendations or present the disadvantages to those proposals which the manager favors. Despite the fact that this form of city government vests great power in a person who has never stood for election, it is well to remember that the influence and tenure of managers varies from city to city, that the council hires and fires the manager, and that the ultimate power to pass ordinances and to appropriate money rests with an elected city council.[6]

City councils usually have five members (a few have seven) elected in nonpartisan elections for four-year terms. (The Los Angeles City Council has fifteen members, but it is a full-time legislative body.) Council members usually serve part-time and receive little or no salary. Most members are elected at large (the whole city votes for each member of the council), and elections are held separately from elections for partisan offices. Scheduling municipal elections separately from national and state elections and making local elections nonpartisan are intended to insulate these races from other contests so that local issues will be debated on their own merits.

Methods of selecting local legislators (both city and county) have been increasingly criticized. Both at-large elections and elections by districts have advantages and disadvantages.

At-large elections allow the most capable candidates to be selected, regardless of where they might live. Those selected will put the interests of the whole city (or county) above district interests. Gerrymandering is impossible, and district boundaries need not be frequently redrawn to keep up with population shifts. However, racial or ethnic minorities concentrated in a particular area may be consistently outvoted by the majority. Also, at-large elections make for long ballots and increase voter **information costs**—that is, voters must inform themselves about many candidates rather than just a few. For example, if a city has five districts, each with seven candidates, a voter must be informed only about the seven candidates in his or her district. If all council members are elected at large, voters must decide among thirty-five candidates. In addition, campaign costs rise because the whole city is the electoral arena, and people of modest means may not want to run for office. In any event, at-large elections may be feasible only in small or medium-sized cities.

Election from districts allows candidates to be more familiar with, and accessible to, the constituents. Minorities are more likely to place a member in the local legislature, and voters may be able to cast a more informed ballot. On the negative side, representatives are encouraged to care more about the interests of their districts than about those of the whole city. A five-member council uses the "rule of five" to apportion discretionary funds: divide the amount of money to be spent into five equal amounts, one-fifth for each district. Unfortunately, this procedure means that the areas for the city with the greatest needs may not get the largest amount of money.

A compromise method of selection would require a legislator to live in the district he or she represents but to be elected by the entire city. When there is a vacancy on a city council,

> the remainder of the council may fill the vacancy by appointment or leave the vacancy unfilled until the next regular election or until a special election can be called. . . . It is a practice in some communities for a councilman electing not to seek reelection to resign from the governing board about two months before the end of his term.[7]

The other council members may then select anyone they choose to fill out the last two months of the term, and the member chosen can run as an incumbent for a position on the council. Nearly a fourth of California's city council members may initially have reached office through appointment.[8]

CITY COUNCILS IN ACTION

American government is celebrated as government of the people and by the people. The level of government most accessible to average citizens is city government. We urge the reader to attend a meeting of his or her city council to see government in action. Here is the usual order of business:

- The council is called to order and the presence of a **quorum** of members is determined. A quorum is the minimum number of members who must be present for the council to conduct business officially.
- The minutes of the previous meeting are read, corrected or amended if necessary, and then approved.
- Petitions or memorials are called for. These may be presented by a group of local citizens who are present.
- Officers and committees present their reports.

- Unfinished business from the last meeting is taken up.
- New business is called for. Ordinances (described later) are presented and voted upon at this time.
- Announcements are called for.
- Adjournment.

Enactments, or laws, passed by the city councils are called **ordinances.** Except for emergency measures, they do not become effective for thirty days. This delay allows dissatisfied citizens the opportunity to circulate referendum petitions.

A study of voting behavior on city councils in the San Francisco Bay Area found three patterns: (1) unipolar, a unanimity often induced by social pressure, in which "no lineups ever occur [and] . . . all members vote together" with only an occasional dissenter; (2) nonpolar, in which no stable voting alignments persist over time; and (3) bipolar, in which long-standing factions, stemming from liberal or conservative points of view, from the backgrounds of members, or from personal differences, vote as blocs.[9]

Local legislative bodies are covered by the Ralph M. Brown Act of 1953, the open meeting law. Orders convening meetings "must be posted on or near the door where the meeting is to be held twenty-four hours before the session. The notice, in addition to specifying time and place, must indicate the business to be transacted, and no other business is to be considered."[10] All local government meetings are open to the public except those in which an employee or officer is to be appointed, hired, or fired; those in which an employee or officer brings charges against another; those in which the council meets with its attorney to consider legal action; or those in which the council meets with its labor negotiators or with its real estate agent to discuss the purchase of property. In 1986, the state legislature added a requirement that local legislative bodies must post a specific agenda before both regular and special meetings, that no new items may be added during the meeting, and that no action be taken on any item not on the agenda. This stipulation was prompted by newspaper accounts of the Los Angeles City Council raising its salary without having had the raise issue appear on its agenda or be posted in public, or even be discussed by the council. However, criminal penalties for violation of the Brown Act are extremely hard to enforce.

CONTRACTING AND COOPERATION

California pioneered a practice called the **Lakewood Plan.** When the citizens of Lakewood decided in 1954 to incorporate, they also decided that their city would provide them with no services directly but would instead contract with the County of Los Angeles for all desired services. The **contract cities** idea was born. Today, Los Angeles County has about 1,500 contracts to provide 50 different services to cities. Lakewood, which now provides some of its own services, received 41 separate services, ranging from helicopter service to road maintenance.[11] Contracting with the county is thought to keep taxes down by avoiding large capital expenditures and maintenance costs of equipment.

Cities can also pool their resources to provide better services at reduced rates. Joint agreements may be formal or informal. Joint sewage disposal, police radio facilities, or water supply, along with cooperative purchasing, can avoid duplication and increase efficiency. Under the Joint Exercise of Powers Act, two cities that can take an action individually can also act jointly. Gonzales is one of three cities that jointly hires a building inspector; Westminster is one of four cities sharing fire training and communications operations (at a cost reduction of approximately 30 percent); Upland provides police radio dispatching for three other cities. By acting jointly, small cities may be able to take advantage of economies of scale.

Cities also contract for services with private suppliers. For example, Imperial Beach receives paramedical services and bus service from private companies, San Jose uses private contractors to cite parking violators, Garden Grove contracts out management of its health insurance plan, and West Covina contracts out its recreation program. Service areas in which cost-conscious cities have been able to save the greatest amount of money are: janitorial service, asphalt paving, street cleaning, lawn and street tree maintenance, traffic signal maintenance, and residential refuse collection.

The provision of governmental services by private suppliers has both advocates and critics. In the opinion of some, advantages include the following:

1. If a service is needed only infrequently, it is more cheaply purchased as needed than provided by permanent personnel.
2. If the service requires expensive equipment, particularly equipment used only occasionally, a private supplier is more economical.
3. If the service is provided by personnel who must possess specialized knowledge, training, or skill and who therefore can command extraordinarily high salaries, local government should hire such people on contract.
4. If the persons providing the services must be unusually flexible or innovative, such people should be sought outside of the public sector. [12]
5. Private provision of a service can serve as a yardstick to evaluate public provision of the same service. (Ironically, however, in the 1930s the federal Tennessee Valley Authority set efficiency standards against which private power companies could be judged.)
6. A survey of procurement administrators in eighty-nine cities nationwide found that private contracting costs less than government delivery of services and results in better quality of service. [13]

It should be stressed that contracting is usually urged only in extraordinary circumstances or for fairly narrow purposes and is not normally advocated as the way to provide most mainline local government services.

Critics of private provision of governmental services stress the following arguments:

1. Any cost savings realized by contracting may be eliminated by the expense of monitoring the service contract. Furthermore, some contracts allow cost overruns.

2. Since the private supplier is a profit-making enterprise, it may scrimp on the quality of service in order to make more money.
3. Contracting may foster favoritism and corruption because the contractor that makes the most generous campaign contributions to mayors and city council members may be most likely to receive the service contract. By this means, an inefficient firm can prevail over superior competitors.
4. Representatives of public employee groups claim that the services of private suppliers cost less because those suppliers pay lower wages and offer fewer benefits than does the public sector.[14]

The debate over private provision of public services is likely to intensify as financially strapped cities adjust to receiving less financial assistance from both Sacramento and Washington.

HARD CHOICES AHEAD FOR CITIES

Life in California is for the most part urban life. The kind of environment that cities in California provide for their residents is therefore particularly important. Unfortunately, the types of problems that exist nationwide in the areas of crime, education, poverty, health, housing, and minority group relations are all greatly intensified, and decay is beginning to afflict California's older cities, too.

The state's newer cities may have been incorporated because residents wanted to protect a lifestyle. Recall our discussion in Chapter 1 of attempts to manage rapid growth in a way that preserves beauty and natural resources. Many local planning commissions have become centers of intense controversy because these bodies must decide how land will be used. Citizens who want to build contend that their private property rights are infringed on by restrictive zoning policies. Others retort that unless planners halt headlong development, many beautiful cities will be covered by asphalt parking lots, gas stations, and fast-food chains.

The attempts of some California cities to control or end growth have attracted considerable attention. Petaluma led the way by rationing building permits, Santa Cruz has set growth-rate limits, Belmont, Redlands, and Oceanside have restricted the number of new dwellings, and Riverside has established minimum lot sizes (a measure that cuts population density but also excludes low-income people). Those seeking to limit growth hope to avoid crowded schools, congestion, the loss of a city's small-town character, and tax increases. Moreover, any plan to limit the supply of housing increases the resale value of existing housing. These explosive issues came to a head in the November 1985 fight over Proposition A in the city of San Diego. The proposition was an initiative measure requiring a majority vote of the public to approve any city council decision that would remove land from the protection of the city's urban reserve (land set aside for development only after 1995). Local slow-growth forces were stirred to action after the council had removed over 5,000 acres from the reserve. The campaign was exceptionally bitter as proponents of the initiative claimed it was the only way to prevent the "Los Angelization" of San Diego and that the city council cannot be trusted because it is too dependent on the campaign contributions of local land developers. To the surprise of nearly all observers, the measure passed by a vote of 56 percent to 44 percent. Opponents of the measure, who were development interests, spent over $670,000 (93 percent of all money expended in the campaign) on an expensive media and direct mail campaign in an attempt to defeat the proposition. Moreover, Proposition A was opposed by all local newspapers, radio and television stations, and by almost all local political leaders. (The fact that the measure passed despite these unfavorable circumstances runs counter to much of the information presented in Chapter 5.) In the words of a pollster who worked for the "No on A" campaign, it was "a symbolic lashing out against growth. People are frustrated by it. People go to Mission Valley shopping center and they can't get a parking space. They see what they thought was a vacant lot now has a condominium being built on it. They wanted to do something—anything—against growth."[15] The proposition was clearly a way for the average citizen to register discontent, much as was Proposition 13 of 1978 (described in the next chapter). San Diego voters seemed to be saying, "I'm mad as hell and I'm not going to take it any more." In any event, San Diego is the largest city in the state, and possibly in the nation as well, to pass such a measure. Use of the initiative and referendum to decide issues of planning and zoning has been increasing in recent years, especially in northern California. Slow-growth activists see it as a way to achieve their goals without having to use the normal legislative process, which involves compromise. Members of city councils and boards of supervisors usually act as brokers between progrowth and slow-growth forces. Environmental groups, on the other hand, can get all of what they want by direct democracy processes. The danger is that slow-growth activists may not be trained for the technical and complex issues involved in community planning and may put ill-conceived measures on the ballot.

The strategy of providing for an urban reserve is closely related to another strategy called "infill," which has been used by San Jose, Sacramento, Stockton, and other cities to develop unused land within the city before allowing homes, stores, offices, and factories to be built on the outer edges of the city. In addition to reducing urban sprawl, infill has numerous advantages. People living on infill sites usually do not drive as far to work or shop and thus conserve gasoline and reduce air pollution. Streets and sewers, schools and libraries, police stations and fire stations have already been built near infill sites. Infill, therefore, preserves agricultural land or open space areas on the outskirts of the city.

Streets and sewers, police stations and fire stations, and bridges are part of California's local infrastructure, which has fallen into serious disrepair. For example, California cities lose 80 billion gallons of water each year because of unrepaired leaks in municipal water systems. As a result of fiscal limitations, and the necessity to fund operating budgets, local officials have neglected to maintain the immense public investment in these facilities, which are essential to preserve the state's economic health. Budget-conscious elected officials defer repair and maintenance as long as possible, especially past the end of their terms so that their successors can deal with the problem. The fact that some of these facilities are out of sight, such as sewers and water systems, makes it easier to postpone necessary repairs. However, these postponed repairs cost more in the long run.

Two policies that seek to improve the poorer areas of cities are community redevelopment (also known as tax-increment financing) and enterprise zones. About two-thirds of California's cities have redevelopment agencies (which are often the city council sitting in another capacity) that designate parts of the city as blighted. The existing property tax base in the blighted area is noted by the agency as the base year, and increases in property tax revenues from that base (called the tax increment) are used by the city agency to improve the area over a twenty-five to thirty-five year period. Other local governments serving the area continue to receive revenue from the base, but do not receive any of the tax increment unless the agency agrees to give them some of it. Using condemnation if necessary, the redevelopment agency purchases property in the blighted area, tears down old buildings, and signs agreements with developers for new construction in the area. New office buildings, hotels, shopping centers, housing projects, and warehouses have been built in this manner; examples include the Embarcadero Center in San Francisco, Bunker Hill in Los Angeles, and Horton Plaza in San Diego. In response to complaints that redevelopment has destroyed too many homes of poor people, the state legislature has required that 20 percent of the increment must be used to build low- and moderate-priced housing.

Community redevelopment has sparked numerous controversies in recent years. For example, areas determined by the redevelopment agency to be "blighted" in fact may lack only public improvements or be characterized by unproductive vacant land with weeds. Tax-increment financing has also been used to improve areas in which development would have occurred anyway without it. In this instance, the city acting through its redevelopment agency denies counties and other local governments the property tax revenues they would have gotten normally. Moreover, community growth that has been spurred by redevelopment places severe burdens on local school districts, which in turn want a cut of the tax increment. Redevelopment has also been used in growth areas to build projects that might have been financed through the normal city budget: to build streets, sewers, storm drains, parks, and other public facilities. It is often seen by city officials as a way to get around the limitations of Proposition 13. Finally, the urban redevelopment agency can force the owner of a parcel of private property to sell his or her land to the city, which later sells the land to a different private party. This process, which can infringe on basic rights, takes place without a vote of the public and without supervision by the state government.

On the other hand, proponents of community redevelopment point out that it is intended to do more than just renew blighted areas and build low- and moderate-priced housing. Other objectives are to encourage revitalization of the urban core; preserve buildings with architectural, cultural, or historic merit; provide shelters for the homeless; expand downtown job markets; and encourage sound planning and urban design. Furthermore, the redevelopment process allows many different small parcels of land currently under various ownerships to be assembled into usable land. [16]

SOURCE: Scott Willis, *San Jose Mercury News*

Tax increment financing has been available in California for almost forty years and has been used extensively in the last ten, but a newer strategy for encouraging investment in the depressed parts of inner cities is enterprise zones. Over twenty states designate areas with concentrations of poor people and high unemployment as enterprise zones into which businesses are urged to relocate and hire local people. Businesses moving into these zones receive tax credits on wages paid to disadvantaged employees, income tax exemptions on investment outlays, low-interest loans, relaxed or suspended building codes and zoning laws, and a streamlined environmental review process.

SPECIAL DISTRICTS

Special districts are units of government formed when citizens desire a service unavailable from the city or county. Excluding school districts, more than 4,200 special districts exist in California. They provide an amazing variety of services, including fire protection, water, street lighting, cemeteries, recreation and parks, and mosquito abatement. They range in size from a small cemetery district to the huge Municipal Water District (MWD) of Southern California.

Special districts are necessary when local governments do not have the power (or the willingness) to tax and to borrow in order to finance the service that citizens desire. Citizens in unincorporated areas may create a special district in lieu of annexing themselves to a city or incorporating. This would happen because they believe that annexation or incorporation will increase their taxes, or because they do not want the full range of services cities provide. Finally, since adding another special district is a small-scale, incremental change, it is politically acceptable to existing governments.

The state's nonschool special districts outnumber the combined total of all other local governments by about three to one. However, nearly half of the nonschool special districts are classified as dependent districts; that is, their governing boards are either city councils or county boards of supervisors. Although dependent districts are not really autonomous units of government, they are counted in the total number of special districts. Some special districts charge for their services (enterprise districts), and others rely on property taxes (nonenterprise districts) to finance those services. Enterprise districts include those that charge for waste disposal or sell water or power. Nonenterprise districts, hit hard by Proposition 13, have come to rely heavily on the state legislature for support.

Special districts have been called "the least understood, least cared about, and most used of any class of government in California." The problem is that

> special districts pile up . . . like an uneven stack of pancakes. Many a citizen . . . [is] located in eight or ten special districts, . . . the citizen is failing to receive the coordinated benefits of true municipal government . . . [and] his community's future is largely determined by the agglomeration of uncoordinated, single-interest special districts.

The boards of special districts do not consider themselves engaged in overall community planning, but willy-nilly, they are: "When a water main is laid by a utility district, the spread of housing developments is determined and assured—in an area that might best be reserved for a park."[17]

Special districts present a problem—they are nearly invisible. Californians do not know how many special districts serve them; many citizens don't even know that special districts exist. The levies of districts supported by property taxes appear on the *county* tax bill and are often not separately and specifically listed. Finally, turnout in special-district elections is very low, often below 5 percent. Who knows the issues? (Everyone is for abating mosquitoes.)

The most prevalent special district is the school district. The number of both school districts and nonschool special districts remains fairly constant. At the present time, there are approximately 660 elementary school districts, 115 high school districts, 265 unified school districts, and 70 community college districts. Although two-thirds of the state's elementary and secondary school students attend school in unified districts, a very large number of school districts consist of only a single school.

REGIONAL AGENCIES

Many problems on the local government agenda span cities and counties and have a regional dimension: "In metropolitan areas everything connects with everything else; . . . an action in one community affects another community."[18] Since problems such as pollution, transportation, or land use spill beyond city and county boundaries, regional agencies have been developed to deal with regional problems. Examples are the Municipal Water District of Southern California, the Bay Area Air Pollution Control District, the Bay Area Rapid Transit District, and **councils of governments (COGs)**. These units of government provide either a single service (such as water or transportation) or do regional planning. They are *not* "genuine multipurpose governments in the major metropolitan areas of the state, governmental bodies that . . . not only plan but also provide [a full range of] services directly to the citizens of the area."[19]

Of particular importance are two councils of governments, the Association of Bay Area Governments (ABAG) and the Southern California Association of Governments (SCAG). Each serves as a forum where the region's local governments can meet to discuss regional issues and use the councils' large staffs for research and planning. ABAG consists of representatives of nine counties and ninety-two cities in the Bay Area, and is especially important in developing regional plans to protect the quality of the air and water. SCAG (composed of one hundred thirty cities and six counties) was patterned after its northern counterpart. It has been particularly active in the field of regional transportation policy. An important function of both the ABAG and the SCAG is to review local governments' applications for federal grants-in-aid. These councils of governments draw up comprehensive areawide plans and then decide whether local requests for aid conform to these plans. A recent study argues that COGs have not been successful at land-use planning because they have been unable to stop urban sprawl, but that they provide valuable services such as credit pooling, technical support, and research reports to their member governments.[20]

THE MANDATES ISSUE

In order to alleviate its revenue problems, the state could require local governments to pay for public services mandated (imposed on them) by the state. This strategy has been illegal since 1972, when the legislature, in senate bill 90 (SB 90), required that the state reimburse local governments for any costs imposed on them by the state. However, the legislature excluded costs mandated by court decisions, the federal government, or the voters. In November 1979, Paul Gann's Proposition 4 placed these rules into the state constitution. (Additional aspects of Proposition 4 will be considered in Chapter 10.)

If the state does not fund a program it mandates, local governments can seek a court order excusing them from compliance or declaring the mandate unconstitutional. However, soon after the legislature passed SB 90, it began to insert into bills a disclaimer stating that no new costs were being required of local governments. The legislature most often asserts that only minor costs will result from a bill; the legislature also claims that a bill will effect savings that will offset any new costs. Because of the legislature's actions, the state constitution should be amended to make unfunded mandates optional for local governments. In any event, mandates are automatically repealed after six years unless they are reauthorized by the legislature.

SUMMARY

In this chapter we have studied counties, cities, special districts, and regional agencies. These units of government were once thought to deal with only noncontroversial matters, but some of the issues mentioned in this chapter indicate otherwise. Local government finance in the post-Jarvis era, the election of city council members by districts or at large, attempts by cities to manage growth, the creation of more special districts, and the changing roles of regional agencies—all of these matters, and many more, come before the thousands of citizen–legislators serving part-time on county boards of supervisors, city councils, special-district boards, and regional agencies. It is important that those who select these representatives understand the operation of California local government.

DISCUSSION QUESTIONS

1. Who is (are) your county supervisor(s)? Can you name your county treasurer? Since you probably cannot name the latter, do you think the supervisors should appoint this person?
2. Does your county or city have a charter? Does it need one?
3. Does your city have a city manager? What are the city manager's duties?
4. What are some of the arguments for and against municipal contracts for public services?
5. Suppose the streetlight in front of your house or apartment stopped working. What unit of government should you contact: city, county, or special district? Does uncertainty about whom to call indicate that responsibilities in local government are fragmented? On the other hand, does it matter who does the job as long as the job gets done?
6. Name some of the services provided by the 4,200 nonschool special districts in California.
7. What is the purpose of regional agencies? What functions do councils of government serve?
8. How have counties and cities responded to the passage of Proposition 13? Do you favor user charges? Why?
9. Why is community redevelopment so controversial?

NOTES

1. Jane Gladfelder, *California's Emergent Counties* (Sacramento: County Supervisors Association, 1968), p. 24. See also Leroy Clyde Hardy, *California Government*, 4th ed. (San Francisco: Canfield Press, 1973), p. 118. For those rural counties having no cities, LAFCO membership is different.
2. Quoted in Ron Soble, "Government's Search for Money," *Los Angeles Times*, June 9, 1983, pt. II, p. 5.
3. George S. Blair, *Government at the Grass-Roots*, 4th ed. (Pacific Palisades, Calif.: Palisades Publishers, 1986), p. 122. See also Samuel E. Wood and Alfred E. Heller, *The Phantom Cities of California* (Sacramento: California Tomorrow, 1963), pp. 47–48.

4. Ronald O. Loveridge, *City Managers in Legislative Politics* (Indianapolis: Bobbs-Merrill, 1971), p. 100.
5. Demetrios Caraley, *City Governments and Urban Problems* (Englewood Cliffs, N.J.: Prentice-Hall, 1977), pp. 233–234. See also Loveridge, *City Managers in Legislative Politics*, pp. 130–131.
6. Many California cities (including San Francisco and Los Angeles) have a mayor–council–chief administrative officer form of city government.
7. George S. Blair and Houston Flournoy, *Legislative Bodies in California* (Belmont, Calif.: Dickenson Publishing Co., 1967), p. 74.
8. Heinz Eulau and Kenneth Prewitt, *Labyrinths of Democracy* (Indianapolis: Bobbs-Merrill, 1973), p. 278.
9. Eulau and Prewitt, *Labyrinths of Democracy*, p. 174.
10. Blair and Flournoy, *Legislative Bodies in California*, pp. 87–88.
11. The service relationships are not a one-way street: the city of Hollister operates the San Benito County dump, and some city libraries serve as county libraries on a contract basis.
12. Rosaline Levenson, "Public Use of Private Service Contracts in Local Government: A Plea for Caution," in *Public-Private Collaboration in the Delivery of Local Public Services*, ed. Institute of Governmental Affairs (Davis, Calif.: University of California, 1980), p. 23. See also pp. 20–22.
13. Patricia Florestano and Stephen Gordon, "Public v. Private," *Public Administration Review*, 40 (January/February 1980): 33.
14. Supporters of contracting, such as E. S. Savas, acknowledge that private firms provide fewer fringe benefits, but they claim that wages are slightly higher and that lower costs result because fewer people are needed to do the job, absenteeism is lower, and more modern equipment is used by private companies. See "Should Private Firms Do Government Work?" *Sacramento Bee*, November 16, 1981, p. C3.
15. Quoted in Ralph Frammolino, "Proposition A: Voters Say Slower is Better," *Los Angeles Times*, November 7, 1985, pt. II, p. 1. See also Mark Stein, "Growth Policy: Voters Putting the Brakes On," *Los Angeles Times*, March 10, 1986, pt. I, p. 1.
16. For more information on redevelopment, see Leo Wolinsky, "Cities Fatten Budgets on Redevelopment Law," *Los Angeles Times*, September 23, 1984, pt. I, p. 1; Dena Cochran, "Cities and Counties Fight; Fatter Tax Revenues the Prize," *California Journal* (October 1984): 410; Bradley Inman, "Redevelopment Benefits Most Cities in State," *San Diego Union*, August 11, 1985, p. F21; *City of Los Angeles Community Redevelopment Agency*, "Central Business District Redevelopment Project Biennial Report," April 1986. A valuable source of data on local fiscal matters in general is California Tax Foundation, *California Local Government Finance: Part 2* (Sacramento: California Tax Foundation, 1984).
17. The three quoted passages in this paragraph are from Wood and Heller, *Phantom Cities*, pp. 44–45. For an opposing view, see Robert B. Hawkins, Jr., "Special Districts and Urban Services," in *The Delivery of Urban Services*, ed. Elinor Ostrom (Beverly Hills, Calif.: Sage Publications, 1976), p. 182.
18. Grover Starling, *Managing the Public Sector*, rev. ed. (Homewood, Ill.: Dorsey Press, 1982), p. 81.
19. Randall Shores, "Regional Government: Its Structure, Functions and Finance," *California Journal* (January 1973): 15.
20. J. S. Taub, "Failures as Regional Planners, COGs Search for a New Mission," *California Journal* (November 1986): 551–554.

10

Expenditures, Revenue, and Debt

Money is the focus of this chapter—how government raises it, borrows it, and spends it. A point to remember is that fiscal matters are not solely dollars-and-cents decisions but basic political questions: Who should pay for government services? Who should receive the benefits of government services? To what extent should future generations be obligated by today's fiscal decisions?

STATE BUDGET

The budget submitted by Governor George Deukmejian for fiscal year 1988 was the largest state budget in the nation at $39 billion. The expenditures may be classified according to function as follows (figures indicate percentage of budget):

- 31.6 elementary and secondary education
- 12.7 higher education
- 24.3 social welfare (aid to the elderly, blind, and disabled, and to needy children); public health; and mental hygiene
- 6.3 agencies in the business, transportation, and housing fields
- 7.5 shared revenue (the state government collects certain taxes—such as sales taxes, liquor license fees, and motor vehicle taxes—part of which must be returned to local governments)
- 4.9 prisons
- 2.2 property tax relief for homeowners and senior citizens
- 2.7 resources (conservation, reclamation, water)
- 1.2 state and consumer services
- 6.6 other expenses, such as costs of the legislative branch, executive branch, and most of the judicial branch

About three-fourths of the state budget is aid to local government (such as school aid or local aid to the aged and disabled). Only $1 out of every $4 in the state budget goes to finance state services. A small portion of the rest is for capital outlays such as highways.

We mentioned in an earlier chapter that a major portion of revenues are earmarked for specified purposes by statutes or by the state constitution. For example, motor vehicle license fees are designated by the state constitution for local governments. Similarly, many expenditures are channeled to programs that continue from year to year, such as highway funds and aid to local school districts. Therefore, very little of a governor's budget is discretionary—the governor must request certain money and the legislature must spend it whether either party likes the appropriation or not. Table 10.1 compares California's spending to that of other states.

TABLE 10.1   California Spending Rankings[a]

Elementary and secondary education	31st
Higher education	31st
Welfare	9th
Health and hospitals	25th
Total state and local spending	29th

[a]Data are for fiscal year 1984 and do not include lottery money; all rankings take into account state personal income.
SOURCE: Advisory Commission on Intergovernmental Relations, *Significant Features of Fiscal Federalism, 1985–86 Edition* (Washington, D.C.: ACIR, 1986), Tables 113–115.

REVENUE

The previous section of this chapter was entitled "State Budget," but it could just as accurately have been called "Where the Money Goes." In this section, we deal with where the money comes from. Not surprisingly, most of the money comes from you in the form of taxes.

Certain canons, or principles, of taxation are generally accepted:

1. Taxation should be based on ability to pay. The California income tax is **progressive**—that is, as a person's income increases, the tax rate as a percentage of income also increases. Sales taxes, on the other hand, are **regressive**—that is, as a person's income increases, the tax paid as a percentage of income tends to decrease. For this reason, a higher percentage of a poor person's income goes to sales tax.
2. The state or local governments should have a diversified tax structure. Neither should rely too much on a single tax. As we have seen, California city governments meet this criterion.
3. A person receiving a specific benefit should pay for that benefit. (The benefits-received principle was discussed in Chapter 9.)
4. Taxes should be economical to administer and collect.
5. "Taxes should be easy to understand and as convenient to pay as possible . . . taxes due from each taxpayer should be definite and sure of collection."[1] Taxes should be difficult to evade.
6. Taxes should produce sufficient revenue.

Estimated revenues for fiscal year 1988 are from the following sources (figures indicate percentages of revenues):

- 32.9 personal income tax
- 28.3 sales tax
- 11.7 bank and corporation tax
- 5.7 motor fuels tax
- 4.7 motor vehicle license tax

- 2.8 insurance tax
- 0.6 cigarette (stamp) tax
- 0.9 inheritance and gift taxes
- 0.3 alcoholic beverage tax
- 12.1 other (including the lottery and fees on amounts wagered at horse races)

Figure 10.1 shows the trend of recent revenue increases: in the 1970s, the sales tax was clearly a more important revenue producer than the personal income tax. But this is no longer the case.

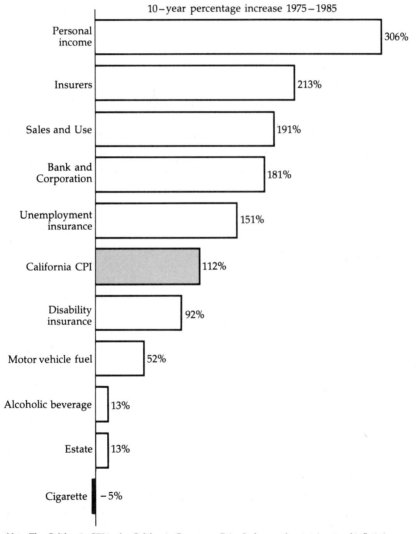

10–year percentage increase 1975–1985

Personal income	306%
Insurers	213%
Sales and Use	191%
Bank and Corporation	181%
Unemployment insurance	151%
California CPI	112%
Disability insurance	92%
Motor vehicle fuel	52%
Alcoholic beverage	13%
Estate	13%
Cigarette	–5%

Note: The California CPI is the California Consumer Price Index, or the state's rate of inflation.
SOURCE: California Tax Foundation, *California Tax Outline* (California Tax Foundation, 1985), p 15. Reprinted by permission.

FIGURE 10.1   Major state tax revenue

CALIFORNIA TAXES

Although the income tax is progressive, is it harsh? Before answering yes, consider the following data:

- At $15,000 annual income, California's personal income tax is 37th highest in the nation.
- At $25,000 annual income, California's personal income tax is 32nd in the nation.
- At $50,000 annual income, California's personal income tax is 24th in the nation.

In most states, inflation increases government revenues. People are pushed into higher tax brackets as salaries are raised to meet increased costs of goods and services. State government gets something of a tax windfall. In fact, state government can get more money *without having to raise the tax rate.* California voters adopted a 1982 initiative measure to deal with this situation. (See Proposition 7 in Figure 5.1) By establishing permanent and complete **indexing** of income taxes, California's income tax brackets are adjusted for the effects of inflation. Indexing income taxes makes elected officials more accountable because higher income rates result from overt state legislative action rather than as the silent consequence of inflation. It should also be noted that as inflation makes the price of taxable items go higher, sales tax revenues are also boosted.

The sales tax is a regressive tax, as we have noted. Low-income people pay a larger percentage of their income to sales taxes than do wealthy people. The sales tax violates the ability-to-pay principle. However, California mitigates the regressive effects of the sales tax by exempting medicine, food purchased in a store, and some other items. Because it is used in conjunction with other taxes, the sales tax diversifies the tax structure. It is a good revenue producer and is easily understood, convenient to pay, and somewhat difficult to evade. Table 10.2 compares California taxes to those of other states.

TABLE 10.2   California Tax Rankings[a]

Personal income tax	12th
Sales tax	17th
Bank and corporation tax	3rd
Property tax	30th
Total state and local tax collections	22nd

[a]Data are for fiscal year 1984 and do not include lottery money; all rankings take into account state personal income.
SOURCE: "State and Local Tax Collections," *Cal-Tax Research Bulletin* (January 1, 1986): 4–5.

Another important tax—and one less controversial than the others—is the motor fuels tax (the gas tax). It is included in the price of gasoline, and so out-of-state tourists pay this tax too. The sales tax is also applied to gasoline, and is computed not only on the cost of the gas itself, but also on state and federal gasoline taxes, which makes it a tax on a tax. The proceeds from the sales tax on gasoline may be spent on mass transit, but the gas tax itself may only be spent on mass transit guideways and on building and maintaining roads. When people register their cars, they must also pay a motor vehicle license fee based on the age and cost of the car. This is really a local personal property tax on cars that is collected by the state in lieu of a city and county personal property tax on cars. Since the money is returned to the cities and counties, it is called the "in lieu" tax.

California's taxes compared to its personal income are not markedly different from those in other states, but the contribution from each source varies significantly. Of particular importance are the so-called **sin taxes**: those on tobacco and alcoholic beverages, which are extraordinarily low. The California tax on wine has not changed since 1933 and is the lowest in the nation. The tax on beer has not been changed since 1959, and only one state has a lower beer tax. The distilled spirits tax has not been changed since 1967—just four states have lower liquor taxes. Finally, the cigarette tax, also unchanged since 1967, is half that of other industrial states. Although a precise definition of "sin" can never be universally agreed upon, these taxes clearly should be raised, especially if overall revenue shortfalls threaten vital public services. However, the wine tax has been kept low to protect an important state industry. Moreover, the wine and spirits wholesalers are represented in Sacramento by James Garibaldi (noted in Chapter 4), one of the state's premier lobbyists.

In times of fiscal retrenchment, one political group may want to reduce services, while another group wants to raise taxes. Both policies will probably be followed simultaneously. Which taxes are raised and by how much depend on state wealth, interest group strength, and the prevalent political philosophy. There are different ways of measuring state wealth, and the most common is per capita personal income, on which California is ranked fifth. Another measure is tax capacity, which includes not only income but also factors such as energy resources and real estate values. California stands seventh by this standard. But there is another, more politically relevant ranking—tax effort, the ratio of tax collections to tax capacity. California is now twenty-second in tax effort.[2]

Table 10.2 shows that California's bank and corporation tax is the third highest in the nation. It is frequently asserted in legislative debates in Sacramento that high corporate taxation hurts this state's economic development and employment prospects. One recent aspect of this long-standing dispute was the fight over modifying or replacing California's unitary method of taxation, or unitary tax. The procedure operates in this manner:

> The state calculates what percentage of a company's worldwide sales are in California, what percentage of its worldwide payroll is in California, and what percentage of its worldwide property is in California. The state then averages these three percentage figures. The result is the percentage of worldwide profits on which California levies its corporate income tax. . . .
>
> California and the other states argue that it is necessary to tax multinational companies in this way to prevent them from using accounting "shell games" to shift profits out of the United States to countries with lower tax rates. The corporations complain that it is unfair and misleading to take into account the earnings of

their foreign subsidiaries, because wage rates are generally lower and profits higher overseas.[3]

Those favoring repeal claimed that the unitary tax discourages foreign investment in California (especially from England and Japan) and that jobs are at stake. Proponents argued that repeal would give multinational corporations an unfair advantage over small businesses and would cost the state treasury too much revenue. Furthermore, they charged that the foreign corporations are really bluffing about not investing in California (Chapter 1 mentioned that taxes are not the most important factor in business location decisions) and that repeal benefits foreign governments at the expense of California's government. England and Japan give their multinational corporations credits for taxes paid to foreign governments; therefore, repeal would not benefit corporations but foreign treasuries—and Japan is hardly a down-and-out nation. Cynics claim that the unitary tax debate, which raged in the state legislature for years, was a classic example of a "juice bill" purposely kept alive so that some legislators could squeeze campaign contributions out of the affected interests. Finally, the legislature in 1986 allowed corporations to choose to get out of the unitary system by paying an annual fee of .03 percent of the value of their business receipts, property, and payroll in California. Receipts from this fee are earmarked for public works projects which foster economic development and for special programs which promote California trade. Corporations choosing to be free of the unitary tax are instead taxed solely on the California share of their business operations within the United States. Revenue losses to the state government because of unitary tax repeal are approximately $80 million per year, which is far less than earlier versions of repeal.

FEDERAL TAX REFORM

In 1986, Congress reformed the federal tax code, enacting sweeping changes by lowering rates, shifting tax burdens, and altering tax advantages of almost every description. Between 1986 and 1991, taxes paid by individuals will go down by $121.7 billion, tax as paid by corporations will rise by $120.4 billion, and miscellaneous taxes will increase $1.5 billion. Because of California's special characteristics, the law's effects will be felt differently here than in most other states.

The old tax code, with fifteen tax brackets ranging from 11 percent to 50 percent, will now have only two brackets: 15 percent and 28 percent. The breakpoint between brackets is $29,750 on joint returns. Liberals dislike the fact that federal taxes are no longer progressive, as defined earlier in this chapter. The two-bracket system does not redistribute income from those who have more to those who have less, as a progressive system is intended to do. However, other changes in the law increase progressivity; for example, capital gains (profits from the sale of assets held more than six months) are now taxed at the same rate as ordinary income. Because Californians have higher incomes than do other Americans and also formerly relied more heavily on a wide range of deductions and tax shelters now restricted by tax reform, the law may not benefit individual Californians as much as people in other states. Moreover, state and local sales taxes can no longer be deducted on federal tax returns, and residents of this state pay a significant amount in sales taxes.

The federal corporate tax rate has also been reduced from a top rate of 46 percent (on taxable income over $75,000) to 34 percent. The minimum tax has been revised to make it more difficult for corporations and individuals to combine tax benefits in order to avoid paying any taxes at all. We noted in Chapter 1 that California has a postindustrial economy, and this attribute benefits the state under provisions of the tax law. Other states that rely on capital-intensive manufacturing industries such as heavy metals, industrial machinery, or chemicals regret the tax law's repeal of the investment tax credit and its reduction in permissible deductions for depreciation. California's retail and service industries do not depend on the investment tax credit and depreciation allowance as heavily as do capital-intensive industries. Moreover, lower tax rates will assist California companies.

Federal tax law revision also has important effects on the interest earnings of bonds. Bonds are certificates similar to an IOU that a corporation or unit of government issues in order to borrow money. The interest earned by investors on newly issued Industrial Development Bonds intended for private purposes is now subject to the federal individual income tax. Since the construction of apartment buildings in California is heavily dependent on this type of financing, there may be fewer new apartments and thus higher rents. On the other hand, interest earned on bonds issued by California state and local governments for public purposes such as roads and prisons is still exempt from the income tax. These bonds are now one of the few remaining investments with favorable tax advantages for high-income Californians seeking to reduce their tax liability. Since lower federal tax rates mean that these bonds provide a smaller tax break, one unfortunate consequence is that California state and local governments may have to offer higher interest rates in order to attract buyers. Finally, California utilities claim to be hit with a "triple-whammy": they have lost the federal investment tax credit, their depreciation deduction is reduced, and interest on their bonds is now subject to tax. All of these factors are supposed to make it more difficult for utilities to finance their construction needs.

How the massive federal tax reform will affect California residents, corporations, and governments will only be known after many years of experience in both good and bad economic times. Clearly, this much is certain: the federal tax game will be played under dramatically different rules.

THE PROPERTY TAX AND PROPOSITION 13

Long before Proposition 13 burst upon the political scene, the property tax was a controversial method of raising revenues for counties, cities, and nonenterprise special districts. The following are typical objections to the property tax:

1. It does not measure ability to pay. Everyone pays the same rate, regardless of income or wealth. The property tax is very hard on retired people

living on a fixed income. (However, the state government has moved to relieve this burden: homeowners sixty-two and older whose yearly family income is less than $34,000 may postpone paying property taxes until their homes are sold. In the meantime, property taxes are paid by the state government, which recoups its money, plus 7 percent interest, when the home is sold. The program also applies to blind and disabled persons, regardless of age.)

2. The property tax taxes income-producing industrial and commercial property at the same rate as residential property. However, California might adopt the **split-roll** technique, by which income-producing property is taxed at a higher rate than residential property.

3. The property tax taxes real property—land and buildings—but not personal property. **Personal property** is either intangible (cash, stocks, bonds, patents) or tangible (furniture, appliances, cars, clothes, jewelry). Moreover, some **real property** is exempted from taxation by the state constitution. Property owned by nonprofit or charitable organizations (churches, colleges, libraries, museums, hospitals, retirement homes) is exempt. Land owned by the federal or state governments is not taxed. Whenever any property is exempted, nonexempt property must bear a heavier burden.

4. Assessed valuation varies from area to area. Those locations with the lowest assessed valuation may have the highest need for public services.

5. Property taxes, unless paid monthly with the mortgage, are paid twice a year in two lump sums, a very inconvenient way to pay taxes. (However, when taxes are withheld as are income taxes, or paid in small amounts, as are sales taxes, people may not realize how much they are being charged. This situation gave rise to the much-quoted statement by former Governor Reagan, "Taxes should hurt.")

The property tax, despite its drawbacks, is not a public menace. Proponents of the tax point out that it is a good revenue producer. Because real property appreciates in value, the base for the property tax constantly expands. Proponents also point out that real property cannot be hidden from the assessor and that people are used to the property tax, even if they don't like it. In addition, proponents ask how local government might otherwise raise money: the income tax is the preserve of the federal and state governments, and the sales tax already falls heavily on the poor.

In June 1978, California voters, furious at rapidly rising property taxes, passed a drastic initiative constitutional amendment know as the Jarvis amendment (Proposition 13). Howard Jarvis and Paul Gann, the sponsors of the amendment, needed about half a million valid signatures to put the measure on the ballot—they received 1.2 million signatures. Angry Californians passed the measure by a 65–35 margin, with support high in all areas of the state. A number of factors converged to spark this nationally publicized revolt: inflation, rising property assessments and waste in public services, and a huge state revenue surplus. These factors led the state's voters to demand lower taxes and more frugal government.

The provisions of the Jarvis amendment are as follows:

1. Property taxes shall not exceed 1 percent of the market value of the property. This provision reduced average property taxes by 57 percent and cut revenues to counties, cities, school districts, and special districts from $12 billion to only $5 billion.
2. The assessed value of all property shall be rolled back to the assessment of March 1, 1975. Assessments may rise from the 1975 figure by 2 percent *per year*. Property is to be reassessed only when sold.
3. Increasing state taxes requires a two-thirds vote, rather than a majority vote, of the state legislature. New state property taxes are forbidden.
4. An increase in local nonproperty taxes requires a two-thirds vote of the qualified local electors. However, local voters may not raise property taxes.

Before Proposition 13 went into effect on July 1, 1978, the state legislature passed a $5 billion local government rescue measure that included $4.1 billion of the state's surplus and a $900 million emergency loan fund. The bill guaranteed that local governments would receive all but $2.9 billion of their $12.4 billion revenue loss, an average reduction of 9.7 percent. In a significant move, the state also agreed to pay the counties' $4.5 billion share of welfare and Medi-Cal. Since 1978, the state legislature has continued assistance to local governments; in fact, this revenue transfer has become a regular part of the state budget process. One of the many effects of Proposition 13 has thus been to concentrate power in the state legislature.

Not long after Proposition 13 passed, the state supreme court, under the leadership of liberal Chief Justice Rose Bird, issued three rulings that significantly limited the scope of the amendment. In *Los Angeles County Transportation Commission v. Richmond*, 31 Cal. 3d 197, the court ruled that a majority of local voters, rather than two-thirds, can raise nonproperty taxes such as sales taxes. However, that unit of government seeking the increased taxes may *not* be one that previously had relied on a property tax. In *City and County of San Francisco v. Farrell*, 32 Cal. 3d 47, the court held that nonproperty taxes used for general governmental purposes and placed in the general fund may be raised by a majority vote (rather than two-thirds) of the city council or of the people. On the other hand, raising nonproperty taxes for a specific purpose requires a two-thirds vote of the people. As one of the dissenting justices in the case pointed out, the court's decision had strange consequences: the power of cities to levy their normal nonproperty taxes is not limited by Proposition 13, but their ability to use much more unusual and limited specific purpose taxes is perversely limited by a two-thirds vote requirement. In 1986, the voters adopted an initiative statute which reversed the *Farrell* decision and required that general purpose taxes may be raised by local governments (except charter cities) only by a two-thirds vote of the governing board followed by a majority vote of the people. Finally, the supreme court decided in *Carman v. Alvord*, 31 Cal. 3d 318, that cities and counties may increase by a majority vote property taxes above the 1 percent limit set by Proposition 13 in order to support an employee retirement fund. Furthermore, it ruled that this increase does not require a vote of the public. However, the state legislature has passed a bill permanently blocking cities and counties from levying the excess tax.

These important decisions of the California Supreme Court can be evaluated from different perspectives, depending upon one's point of view. On the one hand, they can be interpreted as an attempt to thwart the will of the people by creating loopholes in Proposition 13. The amendment passed with 65 percent of the vote and was clearly intended to reduce taxes. On the other hand, these decisions could be viewed as an effort by the court to assist revenue-starved local governments in their hour of greatest need. In any event, the court's decisions (especially *Farrell*) allowed local governments to raise important additional sources of revenue. Cities increased business license, utility users, and transient occupancy taxes. Counties also increased the latter.

An important and unresolved issue concerning Proposition 13 is the implications of the requirement that property be reassessed to current market value only when sold. If there are two identical houses on the same block, but one is sold and resold many times while the other is never sold, the owners of the two properties will pay widely different amounts of property taxes. Moreover, some state aid-to-local-government formulas use assessed valuation as a measure of local wealth. But property turns over four times as frequently in some counties as in others. High-turnover counties therefore show an artificially high assessed valuation, while those with extensive industrial or agricultural holdings that are sold less frequently may appear to be poorer than they actually are.

OTHER SOURCES OF INCOME

California state and local governments receive a substantial amount of federal aid: $10.6 billion in fiscal year 1985. In addition, the state receives money from leases for oil and gas production on the state's tidelands, from motor vehicle license fees and personalized license plates, from student fees at the University of California and the state universities, from charges at state hospitals and state parks, from fish and game licenses, from interest earned on state bank accounts, and from other sources.

In 1984 California voters overwhelmingly approved an initiative to establish a state lottery, which has subsequently become the most successful public lottery in the country. Fifty percent of the ticket price must go for prizes, 16 percent for administrative costs, and 34 percent for elementary, secondary, and higher education. Proponents of the lottery point to its strong support among the public and tout it as a painless way to raise money for education. Moreover, participation is voluntary, whereas revenue raised through taxation is procured by means of a coercive process. Hence, the lottery is said to yield the most feathers with the least squawk. Opponents of the lottery, on the other hand, cite a long list of particulars. If the lottery has been such a huge success, this must mean that an even larger number of Californians are losers. Is it proper for government to trick its citizens in this manner? The odds of winning the $2 million prize are 25 million to 1; the public should be told this fact. If the lottery produces compulsive gamblers, then participation is not voluntary for some people. Moreover, pathogenic gamblers will risk financial ruin for what one psychologist calls the "gambler's high" or the "momentary elation experienced while waiting for the roulette ball to settle, the Big Spin Wheel to stop turning, or the silver coating to be scratched off an instant game card."[4] Finally, the Field Poll reports that poorer people or those with less education are the ones most likely to play the lottery most intensively. "Big Spin" finalists appearing on television are often unemployed, or on welfare, or in poorly paying jobs. The lottery is not a tax, but it is regressive in effect. In conclusion, we noted in the first chapter that the gold-seeking 49ers, with their get-rich-quick mentality, were the Founding Fathers of California. The author is willing to bet that their legacy is still alive today.

DEBT

Governments, like individuals, sometimes live beyond their means and go into debt. However, state and local debt results from the need to finance expensive construction projects. When government borrows money, it issues **bonds**, which investors purchase. The bond indicates how much it is worth, what its rate of interest is, and when the bond is to be redeemed. The two most important bonds are **general obligation bonds** and **revenue bonds.** General obligation bonds are guaranteed, or backed, by the full taxing power and the good credit of the state of California. When Proposition 13 passed, it ended the ability of local governments to issue general obligation bonds. Because the amendment limited the property tax to 1 percent of assessed valuation, local governments did not have the ability to levy unlimited property taxes, that is, they could not make the "full faith and credit" commitment required to back these bonds. Local capital improvement projects suffered as a result. However, a ballot proposition on the June 1986 ballot was passed that authorized local governments to increase property taxes to repay general obligation bonds with a two-thirds vote of the electorate. General obligation bonds are cheaper for local governments because, since their security is high, their interest rates are low, and because local governments are not required to maintain the reserve funds necessary for revenue bonds. The latter are issued to finance a revenue-producing project, such as a toll bridge or a college dormitory. The income from the project pays off the bond. Since a revenue bond may be somewhat riskier, its interest rate is higher.[5]

All state bond issues require majority approval (local bond issues need two-thirds approval). A bond measure appears on the sample California ballot in Figure 5.1. California governments have generally been prudent in issuing bonds: per capita outstanding debt is far less in this state than in other states.

PROPOSITION 4 (THE GANN LIMIT)

Public finance in California is circumscribed by the limits of Proposition 4 of November 1979. This was an initiative constitutional amendment sponsored by Paul Gann and is sometimes known as the "Spirit of 13" amendment (after

Proposition 13). It limits increases in appropriations by state and local governments to the rise in the U.S. consumer price index or the rise in California per capita income (whichever is lower) and to increases in population. Furthermore, the state government is constitutionally required to reimburse local governments for any programs it requires of them. Proponents of the initiative argued that such a limitation was necessary because interest groups have successfully pressured the governor and the legislature to fund their pet programs, but nowhere in the legislative process is there a mechanism to protect the taxpayer.

The Gann Limit was initially not taken very seriously by observers of state government: appropriations subject to limitation represent less than half of all the state's general and special funds, the legislature has adroitly channeled funds into accounts exempt from the measure, and federally funded programs are not covered by the limit. However, the low inflation rate of the mid-1980s pushed the state and its local governments up to the spending limit. Proposition 4 has led to some unfortunate, albeit unintended, consequences. The state government is encouraged to evade the limit by creating tax credits or tax loopholes rather than using direct expenditures to achieve its objectives. In addition, governments are more likely to borrow money to pay for purposes that previously they would have paid for all at once. By borrowing money today, they stay within the Gann Limit now—but it will cost more over the long run in large interest payments. For example, the amount of bonds placed on the November 1986 ballot was the largest in the state's history, exceeding even the $1.75 billion needed to build the State Water Project. Revenue sources such as tidelands oil money, proceeds from the sale of land, and user fees are excluded from the limit. Since all revenues received by government over the limit must be refunded to the taxpayers, the state legislature will probably try to define various taxes as user fees to get around the limit. Moreover, they may tinker with the price index upon which the limit is based and change it to a more generous one. Some critics even claim that the limit retards economic growth because state and local governments may have difficulty paying for education or highways. In any event, Proposition 4 will surely enhance the governor's power vis-à-vis the legislature because he or she has an item veto. The governor can claim that since the spending limit has been reached, new programs can be created by the legislature only if they eliminate equivalent existing ones.[6] Another effect of the Gann Limit is that local governments that have reached their spending limits find mandates imposed on them by the state to be especially burdensome. A 1987 study showed that 58 out of 60 local elections secured voter approval to spend tax revenues above the Gann Limit.[7] The additional revenues were usually earmarked for police protection or street improvements.

SUMMARY

In this final chapter, we have studied the objects of state expenditures, the sources of state and local revenue, debt, and some principles of taxation. The Jarvis amendment of 1978 thrust issues of taxing and spending to the forefront

SOURCE: Wallmeyer Cartoons

of political discussion. As never before, Californians came to view public money as *their* money, and they wanted to know how it was being spent.

In concluding this chapter, we emphasize that budgeting is political—that is, a budget expresses values and preferences. It is far from simply being an economic or accounting document. A budget is a statement of priorities for both governors and legislators. Those programs commanding ideological or interest group support will usually be generously funded.

DISCUSSION QUESTIONS

1. When we classified the state budget according to function, we showed what percentage of the budget is spent on social welfare, education, property tax relief, business regulation, conservation, and other projects. If you were given complete financial direction over (made "dollar dictator" of) the state of California, which of these functions would you spend *more* money on? Which would you spend *less* money on?
2. Looking at the revenue side of the state ledger, which taxes would you alter? Sales tax? Income tax? Bank and corporation tax? How about the cigarette tax? (Warning: No state can print money, not even those with dollar dictators.)
3. What are some criteria against which different taxes may be judged? In terms of these principles, how would you rate the sales tax and the income tax?

4. State bonds are usually marketed only with large face values. If you had the amount of money necessary, what kind of bond would you buy?
5. Name the provisions of the Jarvis amendment, Proposition 13.

NOTES

1. Russell W. Maddox and Robert F. Fuquay, *State and Local Government*, 4th ed. (Monterey, Calif.: Brooks/Cole, 1981), p. 207. See also pp. 211–213.
2. Advisory Commission on Intergovernmental Relations, *Significant Features of Fiscal Federalism, 1985–86 Edition* (Washington, D.C.: ACIR, 1986), pp. 113, 130, 137.
3. Jim Mann, "States Can Tax Global Companies," *Los Angeles Times*, June 28, 1983, pt. I, p. 1.
4. Ellen Chapman, "A Pandora's Box of Social Change," *California Journal* (June 1986): 293. See also Field Poll, Release no. 1315, December 13, 1985.
5. In 1985, the state legislature gave cities and counties the authority to issue limited obligation bonds, which are repayable from a specific source of income such as the sales tax or even a nontax revenue. Yet another type of bond is the lease revenue bond, which is used by municipalities: "These bonds are sold, not by the municipality, but by a non-profit corporation or special authority set up by the municipality. The temporary entity constructs the needed facility and leases it to the municipality. The lease payments constitute the revenue to service the bonds and are in effect the purchase price of the facility. When the bonds are retired, the municipality takes title to the facility" ("Proposition 46 on the June Ballot," *Cal-Tax Research Bulletin* [May 1, 1986]: 7).
6. Richard Paddock, "The Awakening of Prop. 4—and Spending Curbs," *Los Angeles Times*, June 30, 1986, pt. I, p. 1.
7. "Article XIIB Spending Limit," *Cal-Tax News*, March 1, 1987, p. 1.

GLOSSARY

Absentee voter If a registered voter knows that it will be inconvenient to go to the polling place on election day, he or she may request an absentee ballot in advance and may vote by mail. (p. 75)

Advanced industrialism A society and economy that rely on high-technology industry that is itself based on scientific knowledge and research. Because such an economy is knowledge-intensive, a high percentage of the population works in service industries such as education, law, medicine, or communications, rather than in manufacturing. (p. 7)

Advisory opinion Legal opinion issued by the California attorney general regarding the legality or constitutionality of proposed or completed courses of action. These opinions are requested by state agencies or state officials and must be obeyed until the issue in question is ruled upon by a court. (p. 134)

Amendment An amendment is used to make a change in a law or constitution, for example, the proposed Equal Rights Amendment (ERA) to the U.S. Constitution. (p. 47)

Annexation A city attempts to acquire legal jurisdiction over a nearby unincorporated area or over another city. *See* unincorporated area. (p. 185)

Appellate court An appellate court hears appeals from trial courts. In California, the courts of appeal and the California Supreme Court are appellate courts. *See* trial court. (p. 160)

Assessment When real estate is assessed, its value is determined. The property tax rate will be applied to the property later. (p. 182)

At-large elections In this type of election, the entire city (or county) votes for each member of the city council (or board of supervisors). (p. 181)

Bicameral A legislature is bicameral when it has two houses, or chambers. A unicameral legislature is a one-house legislature. (p. 145)

Biomass conversion The burning of organic waste material from orchards, farms, logging operations, and packinghouses to generate heat or electricity. (p. 19)

Bond A borrowing device (IOU) issued by a unit of government to a lender. The unit of government promises to pay the lender the amount borrowed, plus interest, on a specified date. In California, bonds must be approved by the voters. *See* general obligation bonds, revenue bonds. (p. 211)

California Progressives *See* Progressives, California.

Capital There are four different meanings for this word: (*a*) It can refer to buildings, to construction projects, or to land on which to construct a building, as in "the budget for capital expenditures." (*b*) It can refer to the death penalty or crimes punishable by death, as in "capital punishment." (*c*) It can refer to the city that is the seat of state government, as in "Sacramento is the capital of California." (*d*) It can refer to the wealth or assets used in business by a person or corporation to produce profits or wealth. If all this is not enough to confuse you, there is also a "capitol" (spelled with an "o"). This is the *building* that houses the legislature and the governor. (p. 124)

Charter   The document (similar to a constitution) that provides for the powers of a city or county and also provides for their structure of government. (p. 181)

Civil law   Disputes between private persons or private organizations usually constitute civil law. Some examples are breach of contract, dissolution of marriage, defamation of character. *See* criminal law. (p. 160)

Clemency powers   The governor's power to grant pardons, commutations, and reprieves. *See* commutation, reprieve. (p. 124)

Cogeneration   The use of waste heat (steam) to generate electricty. (p. 19)

Commutation   The governor reduces the sentence of a convicted person. (p. 124)

Complaint   After a preliminary hearing in a municipal or justice court, a district attorney may file a complaint—a sworn affidavit of charges—in municipal court. This procedure is an alternative to seeking an indictment. *See* defendant, indictment, information. (p. 173)

Conference committee   When the assembly and the senate pass different versons of the same bill, a conference committee is called to reconcile differences. (p. 150)

Constituents   The people represented by an elected official. For example, this includes all Californians in the case of the governor, or the residents of a particular state senate district in the case of a state senator. (p. 98)

Constitutional convention   A group of citizens elected by the voters to make a wholesale alteration of the state constitution or to write an entirely new document. Their work must be submitted to the voters for approval. *See* amendment, revision commission. (p. 47)

Contract cities   Cities may contract with the county for the county to provide services desired by the city. Examples of such services are police protection, helicopter service, street maintenance, and library service. *See* Lakewood Plan. (p. 191)

Councils of government (COGs)   Regional planning agencies that cities and counties may join in order to deal with areawide problems. COGs draw up comprehensive areawide plans and then decide if local governments' applications for federal grants-in-aid conform to the plan. Examples include the Association of Bay Area Governments (ABAG) and the Southern California Association of Governments (SCAG). (p. 198)

Counsel   A lawyer. The legislative counsel is a lawyer employed by the legislature to aid it in bill drafting. (p. 155)

Criminal law   Criminal law deals with crimes, and determines what punishment (if any) is appropriate. *See* civil law. (p. 160)

Cross-filing   A California practice, now prohibited, in which a political candidate ran in the primaries of both the Democratic and Republican parties without revealing his or her real party affiliation. By this means, a candidate could be nominated by both major parties. Cross-filing was modified and later abolished in the 1950s. (p. 77)

Defendant   The person being sued (in a civil law case) or charged (in a criminal law case). *See* civil law, plaintiff, criminal law, indictment, information, complaint. (p. 160)

Deinstitutionalization   The policy of moving mentally ill people out of large state mental institutions and into smaller community facilities closer to their homes. (p. 36)

Direct democracy   Initiative, referendum, and recall constitute direct democracy. By means of these three processes, average citizens decide public issues directly, rather than through representatives. *See* initiative, referendum, recall. (p. 105)

Docket   A court's calendar of cases. (p. 173)

Earmarked funds   A large part of state revenue is earmarked (designated) by law or by the state constitution to be spent for specified purposes. *See* revenue. (p. 129)

Electorate   Can be used to indicate all persons qualified to vote, or to indicate only those people actually voting in a particular election. (p. 128)

Ex officio   If the law provides that whoever holds office A automatically gets to hold office B, that person serves in the second office ex officio. For example, the lieutenant governor is an ex officio member of the state lands commission. (p. 130)

Exactions   Improvements such as streets, sewers, sidewalks, parks, and police and fire stations that cities demand from real estate developers in exchange for a building permit. (p. 187)

Extradition   When requested to do so by the governor of another state, the governor of California is legally required to extradite (return) a fugitive to the state from which he or she has fled. The correct legal term for this process is *rendition*. (p. 50)

Fiscal   The word used as an adjective refers to budgets or to money matters, as in "the governor's chief fiscal advisor," or "the legislature's two fiscal committees." (p. 30)

Full faith and credit clause   This provision of the U.S. Constitution requires that civil obligations (e.g., mortgages, leases, contracts, and wills) that are enforceable in a civil proceeding in one state are enforceable in any other state. (p. 50)

General obligation bonds   Bonds guaranteed (backed) by the full taxing power and good credit of the unit of government issuing them. *See* bond, revenue bonds. (p. 211)

Geothermal power   Hot steam in the earth is tapped to drive turbines that generate electricity. Used at The Geysers plant in the Napa–Sonoma area. (p. 20)

Gerrymander   State legislatures draw the boundary lines for their own districts and for their state's U.S. representatives. When the political party that has a majority in the state legislature draws district lines that will enable the party to win even more seats, a gerrymander occurs. *See* redistricting. (p. 71)

Grand jury   A grand jury exists in each county. It returns indictments and investigates county government. *See* indictment. (p. 172)

Grants-in-aid   Through grants-in-aid, the federal government gives money to state and local governments. However, the money always comes with restrictions on how it may be spent. *See* revenue sharing. (p. 52)

Gross National Product (GNP)   The total annual output of goods and services in the economy. (p. 8)

Gubernatorial   An adjective derived from the noun "governor." We can say "the governor's powers" or "gubernatorial powers." (p. 121)

Habeas corpus, writ of   An order from a court that requires that a detained or jailed person be brought before a judge so that the judge may determine if the detention is legal. (p. 163)

Ideology   A consistent point of view on many topics. Liberalism, conservatism, feminism, and socialism are ideologies. An ideological person is known as an ideologue. (p. 73)

Incumbent   The person who now holds a particular office. For example, "the incumbent state senator in this district is A. Grizzly Bear." (p. 72)

Indexing   When income taxes are indexed, income tax brackets are automatically adjusted for inflation. (p. 204)

Indictment   If a grand jury (at the urging of a district attorney) believes that there is sufficient evidence of a crime, the grand jury will vote an indictment (charges) against an accused person. *See* defendant, information, grand jury. (p. 172)

Information   After a preliminary hearing in a municipal or justice court, a district attorney may file an information—a sworn affidavit of charges—in superior court. This procedure is an alternative to seeking an indictment. *See* defendant, indictment, complaint. (p. 173)

Information costs   These are the costs in time and effort required for a citizen and voter to be informed about political affairs, candidates for office, and so forth. (p. 190)

Initiative   A process voters can use to enact laws, amendments to the state constitution and local charters. *See* direct democracy. (p. 46)

Item veto   The governor may reduce or eliminate (but not raise) any item in an appropriations bill, including the budget. (p. 122)

Judicial review   The power of a court to review and to declare unconstitutional (strike down) a law passed by the legislature or an action taken by the executive branch that violates the California Constitution or the U.S. Constitution. (p. 101)

Judiciary   The court system. (p. 160)

"Juice" committee   A committee of the state legislature that reviews legislation affecting important economic interests such as insurance, horse racing, or alcoholic beverages. Members eagerly seek appointment to these committees (such as the finance, insurance, and commerce committee or the governmental organization committee) because they want to squeeze money out of these interests. (p. 147)

Lakewood Plan   Cities may contract with the county for the county to provide services desired by the city. Lakewood, a city in Los Angeles County, was the first city to contract for services such as police protection, helicopter service, road maintenance, and library service. *See* contract cities. (p. 191)

Legislative advocate   The formal term used for a lobbyist. *See* lobbyist. (p. 94)

Lobbyist   A person who represents an interest group in Sacramento or in local government. *See also* legislative advocate. (p. 94)

Local agency formation commission (LAFCO)   A unit of county government that approves or disapproves proposals for the formation of new cities or special districts, and proposals for the annexation of territory by cities. (p. 185)

Majority vote   When a candidate or ballot issue receives at least half of the votes in an election, a majority vote has been obtained. *See* plurality vote. (p. 47)

Mandamus, writ of   An order from a court that commands a public official to perform one of his or her official duties. (p. 164)

Negative purge   The names of nonvoters are removed from the voter registration rolls by notifying these people by postcard, and if the post office returns the cards as undeliverable or if the cards are returned by the person now living at the address, the voter's name is removed. *See* positive purge. (p. 75)

Nonpartisan election   An election in which no party labels appear on the ballot. (p. 68)

Office-block ballot   An election ballot that groups candidates together under the title of the office sought. This ballot, which is used in California, facilitates ticket-splitting. *See* party-column ballot, ticket-splitting. (p. 77)

Open-seat race   An election in which there is no incumbent running for reelection. *See* incumbent. (p. 97)

Ordinances   The enactments (laws) passed by local governments are called ordinances. (p. 191)

Party-column ballot   An election ballot that lists party candidates for various offices in columns. The voter is initially given an opportunity to vote for all of the party's candidates by marking a circle at the head of the column. *See* office-block ballot. (p. 78)

Patronage   The awarding of a government job to a recipient because that person has worked for or supported a political candidate or political party. (p. 69)

Personal property   Property *other than* land and buildings. Examples are cash, stocks, bonds, patents, furniture, appliances, cars, clothes, jewelry. *See* real property. (p. 208)

Petit jury   *See* trial jury. (p. 172)

Plaintiff   The person bringing suit in a civil law case. *See* defendant, civil law. (p. 160)

Plea bargaining   The practice of pleading guilty to a reduced charge or sentence rather than standing trial on a more serious charge. (p. 39)

Plurality vote   When a candidate in an election gets more votes than anyone else but the candidate does *not* get at least half of the votes, the candidate has received a plurality vote. *See* majority vote. (p. 74)

Police power   The power of state governments and local governments to pass laws promoting the health, safety, welfare, and morals of the people (a power much broader than simply providing for law enforcement officers). (p. 176)

Positive purge   The names of nonvoters are removed from the voter registration rolls by notifying these people by mail, and if they do not respond, their names are removed. No longer used in California. *See* negative purge. (p. 75)

Primary election   Partisan primary: an election held in June in which each party selects its candidates to run in November's general election. Nonpartisan primary: an election held for mayors, members of city councils, and school board members. If no one receives a majority vote, a runoff must be held later between the two top vote-getters in the nonpartisan primary. No party labels are on the ballot. (p. 76)

Progressive tax   A tax (such as the income tax) that provides that as a person's income increases, the tax rate (expressed as a percentage) also increases. Its opposite is a regressive tax. (p. 202)

Progressives, California   Part of an early-twentieth-century national political movement seeking to control special interests and return government to the people. The California Progressives gave California direct democracy, weak political parties, nonpartisan local elections, and other reforms. *See* direct democracy, nonpartisan election. (p. 68)

Prohibition, writ of   An order from a higher court to a lower court that prohibits the lower court from exercising jurisdiction over a case before it. (p. 163)

Quorum   The minimum number of members of a legislative body that must be present for the legislative body to conduct business officially. (p. 190)

Real property   Real estate is real property, hence land and improvements (buildings) are real property. *See* personal property. (p. 208)

Recall   Voters may remove from office before the end of his or her regular term any elected state or local official by using the recall. *See* direct democracy. (p. 105)

Redistricting   After each U.S. Census, all federal, state, and local legislative district lines must be redrawn to provide for equal-population districts. *See* gerrymander. (p. 71)

Referendum   A procedure that allows the electorate to vote down or sustain laws passed by the legislature. *See* direct democracy. (p. 105)

Regressive tax   A tax (such as the sales tax) that falls most heavily on those least able to pay. Its opposite is a progressive tax. (p. 202)

Rendition   *See* extradition. (p. 125)

Reprieve   The governor postpones the carrying out of a convicted person's sentence. (p. 124)

Revenue   Money received by government, usually in the form of taxes. Charges, fees, and intergovernmental aid are also regarded as revenue. *See* earmarked funds. (p. 129)

Revenue bonds   Bonds issued to finance a revenue-producing project (e.g., a toll bridge or a college dormitory). The income from the project guarantees the bond. *See* bond, general obligation bonds. (p. 211)

Revenue sharing   A former program in which the federal government gave substantial amounts of money to local governments with few strings attached. (p. 55)

Revision commission, constitutional   A group of leading citizens and legislators meets to change (revise) substantial amounts of the constitution. The commission's recommendations must be forwarded to the legislature for approval before being submitted to the voters. *See* amendment, constitutional convention. (p. 47)

Select committee   Policy committees of the state legislature that have a narrow or limited jurisdiction and that do not consider a large amount of legislation. An example is the committee on child abuse. *See* standing committee.

Severance tax   A tax on the extraction of a depletable natural resource such as oil, gas, coal, timber, or metals.

"Sin" tax   Taxes on tobacco, alcoholic beverages, and horse racing bets. These taxes were originally established not only to discourage the use of these objects, but also to raise revenue. They now serve primarily the latter purpose. (p. 205)

Small claims court   A division of the municipal court in which individuals or corporations disputing less than $1,500 represent themselves before a judge. (p. 161)

Special election   An election called to fill a vacancy in public office (resulting from death, resignation, or another cause). Another kind of special election occurs when a school district asks the voters to approve a bond issue or a tax-rate increase. (p. 78)

Split-roll property tax rate   Under the split-roll technique, income-producing, or business, property is taxed at a higher property tax rate than residential property. (p. 208)

Standing committee   Committees of the state legislature that have a broad jurisdiction. Examples include the finance or natural resources committees. *See* select committee. (p. 151)

Ticket-splitting   This occurs when a voter selects some Democrats, some Republicans, and so forth. Hence, the voter splits the ticket, or ballot. (p. 63)

Trial court   A court in which the trial of a case takes place. Such courts are often called courts of original jurisdiction, because cases almost always originate there. California's trial courts are the municipal courts, justice courts, and superior courts. *See* appellate court. (p. 160)

Trial jury   The purpose of a trial jury is to determine the party at fault (in a civil case) or to determine guilt or innocence (in a criminal case). *See* grand jury, civil law, criminal law. (p. 172)

Turnout   The percentage of people who vote in a particular election. (p. 76)

Unincorporated area   A part of a county that is not part of a city. (p. 179)

Unitary system of government   When a lower level of government may exercise only those powers granted to it by a higher level of government, the system of government is unitary. This is the legal relationship between California local government and California state government, but it is *not* the relationship between (any) state government and the national government, which is a federal relationship. (p. 176)

Urgency law   A law to protect immediately the public peace, health, or safety. These laws must pass the state legislature by a two-thirds vote, and they take effect immediately. (p. 107)

User charge   A charge levied on the beneficiaries of a public service that is used to pay for that service. For example, a person visiting a city museum or playing golf on a county golf course may pay a fee to help support that service. (p. 187)

Author Index

Subject Index